MOBILIZING RESENTMENT

JEAN HARDISTY

MOBILIZING RESENTMENT

Conservative Resurgence

from the John Birch Society

to the Promise Keepers

FOREWORD BY WILMA MANKILLER

BEACON PRESS   BOSTON

BEACON PRESS
25 BEACON STREET
BOSTON, MASSACHUSETTS 02108-2892
WWW.BEACON.ORG

BEACON PRESS BOOKS
ARE PUBLISHED UNDER THE AUSPICES OF
THE UNITARIAN UNIVERSALIST ASSOCIATION OF CONGREGATIONS.

05 04 03 02 01 00 99   8 7 6 5 4 3 2 1

EARLIER VERSIONS OF A NUMBER OF THESE CHAPTERS HAVE APPEARED IN *THE PUBLIC EYE*,
THE NEWSLETTER OF POLITICAL RESEARCH ASSOCIATES: "CONSTRUCTING HOMOPHOBIA"
APPEARED IN VOL. VII, NO. 1 (MARCH 1993); "THE RESURGENT RIGHT: WHY NOW?" APPEARED IN
VOL. IX, NO. 3/4 (FALL/WINTER 1995); "KITCHEN TABLE BACKLASH" APPEARED IN VOL. X,
NO. 2 (SUMMER 1996); "WHAT NOW?" APPEARED IN VOL. XI, NO. 1 (SPRING 1997);
"LIBERTARIANISM AND CIVIL SOCIETY" APPEARED IN VOL. XII, NO. 1 (SPRING 1998).

EARLIER VERSIONS OF "KITCHEN TABLE BACKLASH" APPEARED IN *EYES RIGHT: CHALLENGING THE
RIGHT WING BACKLASH*, EDITED BY CHIP BERLET, SOUTH END PRESS, 1995; AND IN *UNRAVELLING
THE RIGHT*, EDITED BY AMY ANSELL, WESTVIEW PRESS, 1998.

EXCERPTS FROM "CONSTRUCTING HOMOPHOBIA" APPEARED IN JEAN HARDISTY AND AMY
GLUCKMAN, "THE HOAX OF 'SPECIAL RIGHTS': THE RIGHT WING'S ATTACK ON GAY MEN AND
LESBIANS" IN *HOMO ECONOMICS: CAPITALISM, COMMUNITY, AND LESBIAN AND GAY LIFE*,
EDITED BY AMY GLUCKMAN AND BETSY REED, ROUTLEDGE, 1997.

THIS BOOK IS PRINTED ON RECYCLED ACID-FREE PAPER THAT CONTAINS AT LEAST 20 PERCENT
POSTCONSUMER WASTE AND MEETS THE UNCOATED PAPER ANSI/NISO SPECIFICATIONS FOR
PERMANENCE AS REVISED IN 1992.

TEXT DESIGN BY DANIEL OCHSNER
COMPOSITION BY WILSTED & TAYLOR PUBLISHING SERVICES

LIBRARY OF CONGRESS CATALOGING-IN-PUBLICATION DATA

HARDISTY, JEAN V.
    MOBILIZING RESENTMENT : CONSERVATIVE RESURGENCE FROM THE JOHN
BIRCH SOCIETY TO THE PROMISE KEEPERS / JEAN HARDISTY.
      P. CM.
    INCLUDES BIBLIOGRAPHICAL REFERENCES AND INDEX.
    ISBN 0-8070-4316-8 (CLOTH)
    1. CONSERVATISM—UNITED STATES. I. TITLE.
JC573.2.U6H35 1999
320.52'0973'09049—DC21   99-28147

For Antoinette E. Hardisty
1894–1970

CONTENTS

FOREWORD

Many people of my generation came of age during both the relative consonance of the 1950s and the extraordinary social upheaval of the 1960s. Whether we were conservative, liberal, or progressive, we were profoundly affected by the anti-apartheid, civil rights, women's rights, anti-war, and free speech movements in the late 1960s and 1970s. On college campuses throughout the world, students questioned the values of a society that could wage war in Southeast Asia, denigrate women and minorities, and even allow the shooting of students at Kent State. In a search for an alternative way of living, many young middle-class men and women streamed into San Francisco's Haight-Ashbury District. Even the music was changing. The possibilities seemed endless.

Decades later, many of us remain committed to the ideals of a just and equitable society and would describe ourselves as progressives or liberal-leaning. How then did it come to pass that we find ourselves standing in the dawn of the twenty-first century with no place to go? Why do we not have a coherent faith-based response to the extremism of the religious right? Where is our collective reaction to those who define any attempt to eliminate racist or sexist stereotypes as "political correctness"?

This important book helps answer these questions, and many more, as Jean Hardisty takes the reader on a fascinating journey through the political right's construction of powerful grassroots coalitions and its eventual control of the U.S. Congress. She movingly describes her own often-conflicted feelings about some of the decent people she has met while attending meetings of the right's most important organizations. Her careful analysis of the right's manipulative use of a campaign of exaggeration and misinformation to address issues important to working- and middle-class families is well researched and balanced.

Mobilizing Resentment also clearly documents the left's staggering underestimation of the right's ability to organize families around issues they care about. Hardisty illustrates how the key players in the progressive movements of the 1960s and 1970s failed to build the kind of broad grassroots movement that could have sustained a progressive agenda over the long haul. In the absence of that broad movement, and aided by historical conditions, the right was able to capture the debate about feminism, civil rights, and other issues important to liberal-leaning people. For example, Hardisty argues that progressives were unable to mount a collective battle against the right's redefinition of affirmative action as a plan for minorities to take jobs away from more qualified people. The right correctly perceived a certain uneasiness among some white working-class families about the dramatic increase in minority populations and their own place in a more racially diverse society. The right used manipulative propaganda to raise an alarm about affirmative action and then offered simplistic solutions like the elimination of "quotas."

There are a few scattered signals that the right is becoming splintered as more and more Americans reject its extremism. Moderate Republicans are regaining the voice they lost when the Republican Party was taken over by its right wing. Progressives are rebuilding the social justice movement and are engaging in a soul-searching dialogue about what went wrong and how to shape a new progressive vision. This ever-so-slight shift in national politics opens an opportunity for progressive people to regain control of the debate about the major issues of our time.

Mobilizing Resentment provides a wealth of information for anyone interested in how to refocus the energy and idealism of the progressive movement on the building of institutions that are relevant to the lives of most Americans. In this step-by-step description of the growth of the right, Jean Hardisty's gift to us is to remind us that there is no easy way to revitalize a progressive movement in this country. It has to be done person by person, family by family, and community by community. But it can be done. The possibilities really are limitless.

Wilma Mankiller
Stilwell, Oklahoma

High in the bleachers of the Worcester Centrum Centre I am one of a handful of women in a stadium of 5,000 men. I watch as the men drop to their knees at the rousing, deafening command of the preacher who controls the stage. As they do, they shout, moan, wave their arms, and occasionally speak in unintelligible language, celebrating their faith. I know the men on their knees are joyous. But they sound and look like a suffering sea of humanity. These Promise Keepers, Christian evangelical believers who call themselves "men of integrity," are at the end of a five-hour day of singing, shouting, hugging, and praying. They are 5,000 men who have become a mass movement—an army for Jesus.

I am struggling to control my feelings of anxiety, and even some fear. But, above all, I am profoundly depressed. I've been suckered again. For the first four hours of this Promise Keepers rally, I had seen only the revivalism I had expected. I know that people have a right to be fundamentalist Christians, and that men have a right to meet together and practice their religious beliefs. I adamantly respect these rights, sometimes to the point of feeling protective of those who want to exercise them. My guard is down, because I think that the Promise Keepers have become so "boxed in" by criticism that they dare not speak a homophobic, sexist, or racist word from the podium. And they don't. During those first four hours, I think maybe we've been too hard on them. It's not my brand of religion, but what if it really does make them better husbands to their conservative, antifeminist wives?

Then comes the final act of the revival, when an inspiring African American preacher from North Carolina takes the stage and leads a rousing exhortation about what these excited, transfixed, enraptured men now must *do*. The volume becomes ear-splitting. The preacher begins to organize the men into a "force" that will leave the stadium and go into battle. The veneer of respectability is dropped. Now it becomes clear what the real agenda is. Again and again the men are told they must go home and *prophesy*. They must teach the uncompromising message of fundamentalist Christianity in every corner of their lives—to their wives, their children, their friends, others in their churches, even their colleagues at work. If they meet resistance, they must insist, and insist again. This evangelism is not kindly. It is self-righteous, intolerant, impassioned, and *angry*. When the men rise from the kneeling position, they begin swaying, arms raised in prayer.

It takes me two full days to recover from the experience. The first night I have bad dreams—not vivid nightmares, just hours of dread and swimming images of the day. I tell the story to one friend after another, attempting to speed my recovery so I can get back to work. I'm short-tempered and depressed, and I find men—even strangers—irritating. I feel like I've been had again. After all these years.

My reaction to the Promise Keepers' rally reflects many of the contradictions of my everyday experience of studying, analyzing, teaching, and organizing about the right. For twenty years, I have immersed myself in a political movement that exists to roll back everything I believe in, that teaches people to hate me because I am a progressive feminist whose secular humanist values are not those sanctioned as "American," and that constructs ideologies that justify my exclusion from society. Yet I continue to believe that, within that movement, there are people who are decent and capable of great caring, who are creating community and finding coping strategies that are enabling them to lead functional lives in a cruel and uncaring late capitalist environment. Far from hating them, I sometimes feel defensive on their behalf.

When I speak to audiences about the right, telling them about its leaders, its organizations, and the complex map of internal contradictions among its sectors, my goal is to help each audience gain an accurate understanding of this frightening force. Most often, the audiences are made up of those targeted by the right—feminists, lesbians and gay men, immigrants, welfare recipients, abortion rights activists, progressive educators, and other demonized social justice activists. When these audiences listen to a sustained discussion of the movement that targets them, it is inevitably slightly stressful and can be frightening. But they know they will walk away when the talk is over. They wonder how I can stay in this world, not for a morning, but year after year.

So, after my talk, there may be several questions about its content and there may be some points of agreement or disagreement with my analysis, but the questions most reliably asked are, How do you do this work and not get depressed? What do you wear to right-wing conferences? How do you act? Do you use your own name? Who do you say you are? *What is it like?*

In some ways I welcome those questions, because they allow me to demystify the process of studying those who are "other." I talk about the extreme normalcy of most of the right-wing conferences I attend: the dreary workshops; the overwrought young speakers trying to break into the leadership by being more extreme and alarming than the previous speakers; the predictable methods of manipulation; the trite, overused metaphors; the inevitable delivery of "proof" in a pie chart or bar graph. I talk about my research techniques—always write out notes as you hear the information (not later when you'll remember it less accurately); always have your meals with participants and engage in genuine, honest conversation; always use your own name; always dress comfortably; always pick up material that you can read later; always build in time for a walk or some other form of break; and *never* drink caffeine.

The questions also allow me to talk about the unexpected fun in this work—the moments of hilarity, the flashes of insight, the sense of hearing something important for the first time, the glimpse of a leader's charisma that explains the followers' devotion. In the early 1980s, when

Phyllis Schlafly was leading the crusade to defeat the ERA, I attended a conference in Washington, D.C., where she spoke about homeschooling her six children. I sat in the audience, fighting off boredom and doodling in my notebook. Schlafly was telling a relevant aside about her home life. It seems that Schlafly's housekeeper had told her that she wished she too could homeschool her own children, but asserted that of course she was not skillful enough to do any such thing. Oh no, Schlafly protested, any well-intentioned woman who was willing to make the commitment could homeschool her own children.

My first reaction was to grimace at the obliviousness of the remark. Indeed, every woman except those who work all day taking care of someone else's house! This sort of careless arrogance and insensitivity is *de rigueur* for right-wing speakers. But suddenly I bolted awake. *A housekeeper? Phyllis Schlafly had a housekeeper?* All those years of modeling the perfect wife and mother, upholding the model of the traditional woman, helping women to get in touch with their conservative values of hearth and home—and all the time she had a housekeeper?

A moment like that is worth several hours of William Bennett and his *Book of Virtues.*

But, still, a part of me always dreads those questions about my work. If I were to be completely honest, I would have to admit that it's a constant challenge, it intrudes on my personal life, and it imprisons me in two male-dominated worlds—the sexist world of the right and the male-dominated world of progressives who study the right. When asked what I "do" by strangers, I often fudge the answer because I don't want to have to deal with how they might react. I know that some of the people I meet casually find what I do slightly unsavory. For others, it arouses suspicion. Common questions, such as: Who funds you? Who uses that research? How do you define the right? often have a hostile edge.

In the early 1990s, whiling away a layover of several hours in the Miami airport, I struck up a conversation with an older, retired couple who lived in the suburbs of Washington, D.C., my childhood hometown. They too were laying over, waiting to depart for an elderhostel trip to Chile. I've always thought well of the elderhostel trips. They seem designed for intellectually engaged tourists who want to learn about another culture as well as be in the sun. I'm also drawn to people older than

I, who so often have an interesting perspective or unusual stories from their past. Because I was on my way home from vacation, I was relaxed and unguarded.

Before I knew what had happened, I was on the defensive, under blunt-edged attack for my ignorance and wrongheaded views. I hadn't even been paying attention to what I was saying—just describing my work. I quickly realized that the avuncular gentleman and his kindly wife were card-carrying right-wingers, who had found in me a source of entertainment during their airport waiting period. They were settling in for a good run of "get-the-liberal" when I realized that I had unwittingly switched from vacation to work.

When I decided I wasn't willing to return to work prematurely and extricated myself, they were disappointed and miffed. I'm sure my retreat was further proof to them that, when push comes to shove, those liberals just can't justify their insane ideas. For the rest of the trip home I had a familiar, sinking feeling that I had again been trapped by my naive belief that an appearance of kindliness cannot coexist with brutal intolerance.

Why then stay in this work? Surely it's possible to do research without constant face-to-face encounters with your political enemies. I am a baby boomer who grew up in a genteel, white, upper-middle-class southern family. In that setting, racism was woven into my everyday life. As my parents' daughter, I went to the right boarding school and attended the right cotillions. I was seldom exposed to the ugly realities of poverty and violence. Only one member of my family, the aunt to whom this book is dedicated, tried to prepare me for the real world. Even with her help, I knew I was never really supposed to enter it.

But in the late 1960s, I was a college graduate, struggling to come to grips with the water cannons and napalm that shaped the consciousness of many people of my generation, when I first found a compatible home for my growing interest in social justice. Though I had tried to pursue it within the Episcopalianism of my parents, I had been thwarted at every turn. Aided by the idealism of the civil rights movement, the protests against the Vietnam War, and the women's movement, I finally had the opportunity to see how my own life might become part of larger issues and a more noble vision. I then received further invaluable help from an accident of life. Understanding that in the long run I would need more than the idealism and good intentions I had to offer, I found a way to further my education that would also feed my growing political engagement. I stumbled into graduate school in political science.

There I was drawn not to a career, but to the larger, almost spiritual questions of what makes a good society. I don't know why these questions captivated me, but I have lived ever since with the result of choosing the field of political philosophy. Today I no longer consider political philosophy to be my work, but still the questions of what makes a good society motivate my thinking, research, and writing. I now address those questions as a political analyst who exposes and opposes the agenda of injustice promoted by the right.

I am not entirely suited to this assignment. As demonstrated by my visit to the Promise Keepers, I have a persistent streak of idealism that often blinds me to the right's astounding cynicism and will to power. I'm inclined to defend religious conservatives from the arrogant dismissal and even disdain they have received from liberals, progressives, and the political mainstream because of their religious faith and lack of sophistication. That defense, however, can make me slow to see the full extent of intolerance, hate, and reactionary backlash that the right, especially its leaders, represents.

But a strong commitment to individual rights and freedoms for everyone, even my political enemies, has helped me in my study of the right. It helps to block my urge to demonize the rightists who demonize feminists and lesbians. Still, I know it is important to balance a commitment to civil liberties with an objective understanding of the right. The best analysis captures the complexity of the right's ideology, agenda, and methods. Holdng fast to that complexity is the most challenging aspect of the work I do, because when I give rightists the benefit of the doubt, out of respect for their right to their own worldview, they reward me every time with a kick in the teeth.

I have found the best inoculation against giving my political opponents too much benefit of the doubt is a firsthand encounter with them. In trying to understand the right, there is no substitute for being there. For instance, I might underestimate Dan Quayle unless I am lucky enough to catch him as he works an audience, using his good looks and boyish charm to whip a crowd to increasing peaks of hostility and intolerance. I might think that Jim Woodall, former Vice President of Concerned Women for America, who ran the organization for nearly ten years and traveled everywhere with CWA's charismatic leader Beverly LaHaye, was the brains of CWA until I hear him speak, and see that he is breathless, disorganized, halting, and poorly prepared. I might characterize the typical Klansman as a coward or a dupe unless I see the fire of hatred in his sneer and the conviction in his eyes. I might think that women in politics are mediators and nurturers unless I hear an "equality feminist" attacking her "victim feminist" sisters before an approving audience.

Firsthand encounters such as these have confirmed the intuitions that led me to found Political Research Associates in 1981. That was the year of Ronald Reagan's inauguration, the release of the hostages in Iran, and the triumphant Republican pronouncement that "America is Back!" Mainstream liberal organizations such as the American Civil Liberties Union, Planned Parenthood, and Norman Lear's People for the American Way were responding to the election of Reagan and the rise of the New Right with sloganeering and an oversimplified analysis of this sudden appearance of right-wing political muscle.

My colleague Chip Berlet and I had modest goals for Political Research Associates. We hoped it would serve as a vehicle to correct the most severe of several misconceptions being promoted about the New Right. The first was that the New Right was a *new* political phenomenon. Second, that it was a movement made up of uneducated, Bible-thumping rednecks whose frightening right-wing populism was being unleashed by a conspiracy of religious fundamentalists and right-wing Republicans. The image of a band of the unwashed coming to get the good, cultured, urban liberals of the east coast and upper midwest was an excellent analysis for fund-raising, but it was viciously anti–working class, and wrong.

The contemporary right is not new; it is a direct descendant of earlier right-wing movements, especially its immediate predecessor, the Old Right. It is primarily a white, middle-class movement; the policies it advocates benefit the white middle and upper classes. It manipulates working-class people by providing scapegoats for their frustrations and appealing to their fears. It is much more complex than a simple conspiracy, though much of its success can be traced to the fact that the leaders of its many sectors make a point of conspiring together. It is not a populist movement, though it promotes an anti-elite message, which has the effect of masking its anti–working class agenda.

I encountered the fallout of that early, mistaken analysis throughout the 1980s as I heard time and again from audiences that right-wingers weren't "smart enough" to win, that they were "dupes" of this or that force, and worst of all, that although they were "scary," "creepy," and "frightening," they should not be taken too seriously. My work at Political Research Associates might be summarized as trying to get people to take the right seriously. That means understanding that it is a mass movement, that it is internally complex, that its leaders are distinct from its followers, that it changes its agenda and its strategies over time, and that it is hip, modern, plugged in—the very personification of late capitalism.

Taken together, the chapters of this book represent my understanding of the right. I have not addressed every aspect of the movement, but just those aspects that I feel are less understood or have unrecognized importance. I have not, for the most part, addressed the far right, the sector of the right that is explicitly white supremacist and/or anti-Semitic, often armed, and that specializes in violence, intimidation, and apocalyptic predictions. My research has focused on the right as it operates within the electoral sphere and as a social and cultural force within popular culture.

I paint a picture of a well-financed, well-coordinated, savvy movement that has developed brilliant techniques of manipulation and has captured and molded a hospitable moment in history. The right's quest for political power has become a frightening reality. We can be paralyzed by this analysis, or we can learn from it. We can be energized by a fresh understanding of the importance of resistance. We can recognize the right's assault on social tolerance and human dignity and mount a strong, principled, and effective progressive response. We can and we must.

Chapter 1

THE RESURGENT RIGHT:
WHY NOW?

rotest is an almost sacred word among activists in this country who work toward progressive goals. Protest movements, such as the civil rights movement and the women's movement, have fought to expand rights, correct injustices, and expose corruption. The sectors of a successful protest movement converge and unite and, by capturing widespread support, grow into a social movement.[1] Eventually, a social movement develops sufficient political clout to effect change. As a young woman in the 1960s and 1970s, I worked doggedly in support of the New Left, which grew out of (and in reaction to) the Old Left—the socialist, labor-oriented movement that provided much of the political demand for the liberal reforms of Franklin Delano Roosevelt's New Deal and Lyndon Johnson's Great Society. It was a social movement with an idealistic vision of a more egalitarian society. We thought it was a widely shared vision.

But protest movements can also be reactionary. The protest can be a backlash against the changes that most recently occurred. A reactionary protest movement seeks to restore a previous period, one that is usually seen as a better, more peaceful, and more secure time. When conditions are hospitable, a protest movement can bring about a dramatic shift in the country's view of itself. It can cause one vision that dominates social, political, cultural, and economic life to be replaced with another. We have experienced just such a dramatic shift. The protest movement mounted by the right found fertile ground in the conditions of the last quarter of the twentieth century, became a social movement, challenged liberalism, and captured political power. The right's movement is fractured and constantly under challenge from centrist, liberal, and progressive sectors, but, as the century ends, it is the most powerful movement in the political arena.

Periodically throughout U.S. history, right-wing forces have dominated—promoting such themes as white supremacism, scapegoating of Jews, violent opposition to unions, and rabid anticommunism. During Reconstruction in the South after the Civil War, many whites mobilized racial hatred to destroy gains made by Blacks, and then in the 1920s used racial scapegoating to create a period of unchecked lynchings. During the first several decades of this century, right-wing forces scapegoated immigrants, Jews, and Catholics as "carriers of socialism" and "Papal loyalists," and violently attacked union members during the 1920s and 1930s. The communist witch-hunts of the 1950s are a recent example of rightist resurgence.[2]

But the right's current resurgence is *not* business as usual. Nor is it simply a political departure. It is, more accurately, a new paradigm, one that will be with us for many years to come. Since the 1970s, the right has created a juggernaut, an overwhelming force that has now gained state power. For progressives and liberals, the specter of a powerful right is alarming. That alarm is justified. The contemporary right combines reactionary social policies with ideological fervor grounded in fundamentalist religious beliefs and long-standing racial bigotry. The negative effect of economic restructuring has caused large numbers of working- and middle-class people to feel resentful and insecure. Such feelings are fertile ground for right-wing populism. As Howard Phillips, a New Right ideological purist, said in 1995, "The French Revolution was, to some degree, fueled by economic concerns. So I think what will trigger [a right-wing Christian revolution] is the economic problems."[3]

Just thirty years ago it looked as if the country were poised to address our dismal historical record. Policy reforms, such as expanded access to the vote, legal services for the poor, or food and shelter for the elderly, people with disabilities, and those who could not provide for themselves, seemed to reflect a growing support within American political culture for equality and justice. Many of the objections to liberal reforms came from progressives who argued that the reforms were not adequate to bring about real equality and justice.*

At the end of the 1990s, the political swing to the right is so complete that liberalism has become a political orphan: not primarily because it is a compromised ideology of reform, but because the right has painted it as socialism in disguise. Secular humanism—one ideological source of enlightened liberal reformism—is now under attack from religious fundamentalists. The left, weakened and on the defensive, is unable to exploit the widespread disillusionment with liberalism to promote its own analysis. Altogether, these political conditions have resulted in a period in which the right has dominated the politics of the country.[4] Not sur-

---

* In the past, important political distinctions between liberals and leftists, the Old Left and the New Left, reformers and social change radicals were more precise and widely understood. For instance, journalists, activists, and academics once could agree that liberals were those who favored reform of the economic and political system to make it more egalitarian and inclusive. Leftists of the Old and New Left, on the other hand, saw capitalism as an evil system that ultimately could not deliver social justice on anything more than the margins. When the right captured the presidency in 1980, much of its ride to power was achieved by demonizing liberals and liberalism. Sensing the mood of the country, liberals ran for cover, abandoning the term "liberal" for the less tainted term "progressive." Leftists of the Old and New Left often did the same, finding that to describe themselves as leftist automatically placed them outside the dominant political debate. For leftists of the New Left, the Progressive Movement of the late nineteenth century provided a historically noble label they could live with. Leftists of the Old Left, however, have never been comfortable with the fuzziness of the label "progressive."

In the post-Reagan era, I draw a distinction between liberals and progressives (formerly called leftists). Quite often, left-leaning liberals will collaborate with progressives. In those instances, they become part of the "progressive movement." I do not include in the term "progressive" the many liberals of the 1960s and 1970s who have moved substantially to the right in the past twenty years, are now centrists, and are aligned with the "new Democrats" of the Democratic Leadership Council. They are substantially more conservative than left-leaning liberals, who support affirmative

prisingly, those least able to protect themselves suffer most from the right's power grab.

During my years of working to oppose the right, I have seen innumerable dedicated liberals and progressives, enraged by the right's resurgence, make the mistake of oversimplifying both the right and the times in which the right has thrived. Though it is painful to watch the vision and social programs of a more liberal and tolerant era dismantled, disrespected, and defeated, I try to avoid the temptation to see the rise of the right as a struggle between "us" and "them," because that formulation inevitably leads to grouping both the leaders and followers of the right as "them." Whenever I am in a setting with "them," at a right-wing conference, rally, or meeting, I see skillful leaders recruiting discontented followers by offering simple explanations, complete with scapegoats, for their resentments. Most of the followers seem grateful to be led. They are hearing someone speak their truth.

A full explanation for these times is, above all, complex. Such a major historical shift is never executed by a few individuals, or even one group or sector of society. Although it may spring from skillful political leadership, it will succeed only if the leadership accurately reads the historical profile of the times—the complex interaction of economic conditions, social changes, technological developments, and mass psychology.

The right's leadership has simultaneously caught the spirit of the times and influenced it. In order to oppose the right effectively, we must know, as precisely as we can, how the leadership has been able to do this. We must understand the nature of the protest movement that serves as the engine of the shift to the right, and we must understand the environment in which it has thrived. We must take into account the widespread public sentiment that is finding expression in the right, and also the way the right has captured, manipulated, and mobilized that sentiment. Such an understanding will provide us with a clear map to guide our response to the right and to chart our course for the next decade.[5]

---

action and social welfare programs. Therefore, when I use the term "progressive," I am referring to left/liberals and leftists. Because "new Democrat" liberals and progressives often work together, and both are often under attack from the right, I often refer to "liberals and progressives" to include all three groups—"new Democrats," left/liberals, and progressives. The distinctions among the three groups, however, are often imprecise.

RIGHT-WING MOVEMENT-BUILDING

Social, political, and economic discontent, no matter how strongly powered by mutually reinforcing conditions, results in revolutionary change only when an effective political movement exists to capture political anger and to direct it. The contemporary right is a well-financed and well-run movement that combines shrewd strategic planning for political success with a rigid set of ideological principles, backed by certitude and based in implicit and explicit religious beliefs. It has an exceptionally strong "movement infrastructure," made up of membership organizations, networks, think tanks, media outlets, campus publications, coalitions, interest groups, PACs, and funders. Most important, the movement's leadership is in constant discussion: working to coordinate political campaigns, recruit and mobilize followers, and plan long-term strategy. The right's ability to capitalize on the economic insecurity, racial tensions, and social discontent of the current historical moment reflects, in large part, its leadership's ability to work collaboratively to build a coordinated political movement.

While a movement cannot succeed without substantial mass sentiment to support it, the strength and effectiveness of its infrastructure shape its precise level of success.[6] Public education, which is key to any change in political direction, depends on movement-oriented think tanks, research centers, publishing houses, TV and radio outlets, and schools and universities. Capturing electoral power requires political consultants, PACs, media expertise, and grassroots training programs for potential candidates. Legislative initiatives to press movement goals require political institutes, legal firms, and active membership organizations to pressure legislators. The right's strategists, funders, organizers, and activists have modeled the creation of an effective movement infrastructure. By carefully attending to the many aspects of movement-building, they have created a juggernaut—an overwhelming force that swept the right to power and swept away liberal reformism in fifteen short years.

As a result, when the right's leadership identifies a particular target, such as bilingual education or gay marriage, it has in place every component it needs to launch a full-scale campaign to press its attack.[7] Local, single-issue organizations can call on the resources of national, right-wing legal firms, research centers, publishing houses, funders, and membership organizations. This strong movement infrastructure has allowed the right to train the firepower of the entire movement on the political work of the smallest grassroots right-wing effort.

The right's movement infrastructure has been especially effective in knitting together secular and religious conservative activists. These two groups might have existed side by side had there not been a conscious effort by the movement's leadership to coordinate and integrate their work.[8] By combining forces through its networks and coalitions, each sector of the right has dramatically increased its impact. United, the secular and religious right has seized power. Separately, that would have been unlikely.

The right also has excelled in strategic planning, a crucial aspect of movement-building. Without clear analysis, defined goals, and developed strategies, even the strongest movement will spin its wheels, failing to capture power. One of the major strategies for the movement, which represents the right wing of the Republican Party, has been to take control of the Party. The right has done so by paying constant attention to electoral politics, running more and more of its followers for office, recruiting more and more disciplined right-wing voters, and exercising control of the Republican Party's platforms by any means necessary.[9] Another strategy has been to search for new electoral cleavages to exploit within the Democratic Party. The leadership correctly saw the potential of the "social issues," such as abortion, homosexuality, single parenthood, juvenile crime, and teenage pregnancy, as sources of division among Democratic voters. A strategy of luring white, socially conservative Democrats away from the Democratic Party, which dates to the 1970s and was dubbed by journalists "the southern strategy," has increased the power of the Republican Party, and weakened the power of the Democrats and left-leaning independent voters.[10]

Strategies pursued by the right are largely, but not exclusively, intended to capture power for the Republican Party. When the right wing of the Republican Party came to power with the election of Ronald Reagan in 1980, its New Right leadership was pursuing a vision of a reactionary revolution. Its most logical and practical vehicle for that revolution was, and remains, the Republican Party. In the 1990s, when the Christian

Right and the "new" Republicans are dominant within the right, the movement's attitude toward the Republican Party has changed very little. Practical considerations, rather than loyalty to the Party per se, still keep the ideologues of the right within the fold of the Republican Party.[11]

One reason for such independence from the Republican Party is that many of the men and women of the right's leadership are not politicians or government officeholders. Many are "movement activists"—right-wing activists whose organizational base is outside the Party. Their political goals include control of the Party, but they are pursuing a right-wing vision that goes beyond Party loyalty.[12] This commitment to a vision allows the movement to retain the freedom to oppose the very Party in which it resides. Because the movement is not led by Republican officeholders, its leaders often ignore or defy Republicans they deem insufficiently loyal to the movement, and even occasionally threaten to bolt from the Party altogether.[13]

The right is, for the most part, hostile to the federal government, seeing it as an agent of liberal social change. But the role of the federal government in promoting or squelching a growing social movement, such as the contemporary right, is fluid and opportunistic. The government can be either a passive judge of competing movements and interests, or an active participant that promotes or inhibits them. The government can channel resources, confer legitimacy, and provide leadership for a social movement.[14] Government also has its own independent interests, primarily those of self-preservation and preservation of the status quo. In some cases, these needs may call for strengthening of one or another disadvantaged group, expanding the rights of a group, or promoting greater tolerance. In most cases, however, the government supports those holders of power whose interests it most strongly represents. When far right activists advocate the overthrow of the government or the massive disruption of the status quo, as in the case of some neo-Nazi or white supremacist groups, the government represses them.[15]

For the most part, elites outside government have financed the right's movement-building. In the early 1990s I was struck by the insights of Beth Schulman, then associate publisher of *In These Times* magazine, in an article that discussed the difference in funding patterns of progressive funders and right-wing funders. She pointed out that the right-wing funders invested in the building blocks or skeletal structure of their movement, such as publications, research centers, think tanks, and academic fellowships and chairs designated for rightist scholars, campus organizations, and youth groups.[16]

Instead of underwriting movement-building, liberal and progressive foundations funded social service programs and advocacy programs that promised to ensure better living conditions and promote equality and tolerance. Much of this funding could be classified as humanitarian aid, which was desperately needed to counteract the social service cuts of the Reagan-Bush years. Unable to ignore need and suffering, liberal and progressive funders lacked the ideological single-mindedness of the right's funders. The right's funders got greater political mileage for each dollar invested, because the organizations and individuals funded focused on a strategic plan for seizing power.[17]

The right has built a well-crafted and well-run political machine, capable of holding its various sectors together and punishing its political enemies. Its infrastructure of organizations has proved strong enough to weather setbacks, such as the loss of Ronald Reagan as titular head of the movement, the scandals of televangelists Jimmy Swaggart and Jim and Tammy Bakker in the late 1980s, and the public embarrassment of some of its leaders, such as Dan Quayle and Newt Gingrich. It is the key that has turned a compatible historical moment into a political triumph for the right.

RELIGIOUS REVITALIZATION

In the 1970s New Right strategists took the lead within the right by identifying white conservative Christians as potential recruits for the movement. Conservative Christians, especially fundamentalists and conservative evangelicals, are an enormous pool of people who support a traditionalist view of society and, until the 1970s, had most often been only marginally involved in politics and political activism.[18] In the first half of this century they had mobilized against the teaching of evolution, played a prominent role in promoting Prohibition, and rallied behind Father Charles Coughlin, the reactionary and anti-Semitic "radio priest" of the 1930s, but white conservative fundamentalists and evangelical Christians had, for the most part, stayed out of power struggles in the secular political sphere.[19] Black Christians, who had been excluded from politics by the white power structure, played a dominant role in the civil rights movement. Black churches, many of them evangelical and fundamentalist, were invaluable participants, serving as meeting places, networking mechanisms, and sources of spiritual and economic support.

Understanding that churches can play a powerful role in politics, the New Right's leadership recognized the importance to the movement of capturing conservative white Christian churches.[20] New Right leaders recruited Rev. Jerry Falwell as the point man to reach out to them. Falwell created a mass-based organization known as the Moral Majority, which worked in tandem with his Christian college, now called Liberty College. He also created a television show titled *The Old Time Gospel Hour*, for which, in a moment of hyperbole, he claimed to have 25 million viewers.[21] Falwell's brand of Christianity, Christian fundamentalism, was compatible with the New Right's vision. Fundamentalists adhere to many different and subtle religious beliefs, but in general are Christians who are "born-again," read the Bible literally, and fervently oppose secular modernity. Most, though not all, Christian fundamentalists are both socially and politically conservative.

By the early 1990s, Jerry Falwell had gained a reputation for extremism, was rejected by the general public, and lost much of his power within the right. Because his profile is now lowered, it is easy to underestimate the importance of his work during the 1970s and 1980s. Not only was Falwell giving voice to the discontents and resentments of many conservative Christians, but he was pointing them to a place where they could (and, he argued, *should*) act on that discontent. Falwell and others, especially Robert Billings of the National Christian Action Council, Ed McAteer of the Religious Roundtable, Paul Weyrich of the Free Congress Foundation, and more recently, Pat Robertson of The Christian Coalition, were largely responsible for recruiting Protestant fundamentalists and evangelicals and conservative Catholics into right-wing politics. They, and many others, provided the early organizing that ultimately has resulted in the powerful political movement known as the Christian Right.

But the skillful organizing of the New Right's Christian leaders does not entirely explain the growth of the Christian Right. Changes occurring in the religious life of many Americans enormously aided that growth. They organized at a time when the number of Christians identifying as born-again was skyrocketing. By the 1980s, conservative Christian churches—most outside mainstream Protestant denominations, but many affiliated with them—had become a locus of righteous fervor, individual meaning, and political organizing. As early as 1981, a Gallup Poll found that 38 percent of the U.S. population self-identified as born-again.[22] While not all born-again Christians are politically conservative, most are socially conservative.

Large numbers of people whose religious practice had "fallen away" have, within the last two decades, sought out various forms of spiritual practice. The growth in conservative Christianity is quite visible because the Christian Right exercises so much political clout. There is also corresponding, though less visible, growth in New Age practices and in the practice of more observant Judaism. Islam too is expanding at an impressive rate.[23] What drove so many people to adopt religious practices, and why are so many of them choosing the most conservative religious practices?

Part of the answer may lie in what anthropologists have identified as a "revitalization movement"—a conscious, organized effort by members of a society to deal with their social discontent by seeking to bring about change in the whole, or at least in substantial parts of, the existing cultural system. Sometimes a revitalization movement will seek to construct an entirely new, more satisfying culture.[24] When such movements are religious, they can be visionary, seeking to create a "new" society, or nostalgic, promoting religious values and practices revered in the past (such as the importance of adhering to a literal reading of the Bible). In either case, they inspire people's interest in religion as a source of healing and restoration. The movement's message may either reflect or create a sense of longing for real or imagined qualities now lost amidst rapid social and technological change.

The New Right launched its effort to mobilize conservative Christians at the outset of such a religious revitalization. The thrust of this revitalization is nostalgic rather than visionary. It appeals to large numbers of recruits because it emphasizes the customs, values, and even the natural world thought by its adherents to have been characteristic of previous, more satisfactory times. The revitalization's appeal lies in its promise to restore those characteristics that have been lost due to the "corruption" of the contemporary world. Its Christian manifestation is based in evangelical, fundamentalist, Pentecostal, charismatic and Reconstructionist Protestant, and conservative Catholic religious practices and values. It often receives support from conservatives within mainstream Protestant denominations, and sometimes from conservative Jews and conservative Muslims.

The right's leaders caught the spirit of a historical moment—one that provided a hospitable context for their efforts to mobilize conservative Christians politically. At a time when the number of conservative Christians was growing, so too was their interest in political power.[25] The result is the Christian Right, a political mobilization of conservative Christians that now dominates the right. What began as an outreach effort by the New Right leadership has become the force that now controls the entire movement. Meanwhile, mainstream Protestant and Catholic churches have suffered from low growth, dwindling finances, and a declining number of people entering the priesthood or ministry.

The Christian Right struck a chord with its negative message that rampant "moral decay" is traceable to the increasing influence of secular values. The message spoke to the discontent of many conservative Christians who feel that their lifestyle and morals had become devalued and, in many cases, nearly invisible, at least in popular culture. Such feelings of loss of status and of conflict with the dominant values are powerful in promoting a sense of alienation.

The Christian Right addresses that alienation with a compelling appeal—an offer to champion conservative Christians. Further, membership in a movement, in this case one with a profound spiritual dimension, offers an antidote to discontent and alienation. In confusing and frightening times, Christian Right groups provide clear rules of conduct and theologically ordained answers to life's problems. The more flexible principles of secular humanist thought, which emphasize open-mindedness and tolerance, are anathema to most conservative Christians.

Thus, it is no surprise that Christian Right activists score exceptionally high on tests of intolerance. In a 1990–1991 study that sampled members of two large Christian Right organizations, Rev. James Dobson's Focus on the Family and Beverly LaHaye's Concerned Women for America, researchers associated with the Bliss Institute at the University of Akron found that only 2 percent of Concerned Women for America activists and 6 percent of Focus on the Family members agree with the statement, "A diversity of moral views is healthy."[26] This is a frightening statistic to those who rely on, or simply support, social tolerance and open-mindedness.

CHRISTIAN MILLENNIALISM AND Y2K

Conservative evangelical Christians face a challenging test as they enter the turn of the century in the Christian calendar's year 2000. Many Christians associate a new millennium with the cataclysmic events of the end times and the Second Coming of Christ, as prophesied in the New Testament's Book of Revelation—the appearance of widespread decadence and immorality, followed by a period of confusion known as "the Tribulations," when the Antichrist attempts to seduce Christians and impose "one-world government," culminating in an enormous battle between the forces of good and evil (the Apocalypse), followed by salvation, the return of Christ, and a thousand years of peace. Because they read the Bible literally, many evangelical Christians, especially fundamentalists, stand poised for these events. The year 2000 need not signal the end times, but the date itself has aroused widespread expectation. The Christian Right's leadership must explain the meaning of the millennium to those followers who look to them for clarification. The leaders do not necessarily agree on that meaning.

Most of the Christian Right's leaders have not tied their credibility to the date itself, unlike a small number of cult leaders and self-proclaimed "prophets." But, predictably, the leadership is using the millennium as an opportunity for recruitment. Borrowing heavily from apocalyptic visions, the leaders dwell on the struggle of the Christian Right against the secular, even Satanic, forces of liberalism. The biblical characterization of the end times as a period of sinfulness, moral depravity, and crass materialism adds luster to the Christian Right's political campaigns against homosexuality, abortion, and school prayer. Crusading against sin (liberalism) thereby becomes a response to the biblical imperative to cleanse society of evil and is infused with special meaning when placed in the context of preparing for the return of Christ. Because the evil associated with those who oppose the right's agenda also carries extra weight, both the secular right and the Christian Right have used that greater significance to justify scapegoating and demonization.[27]

Adding anxiety to millennial expectations is the predicted Y2K crisis, the specter of entire computer systems crashing on January 1, 2000, when computers read the date as January 1, 1900. The millennial significance of these predictions stems from their association with the chaos of the Tribulations of the Book of Revelation. Most of the Christian Right's leaders have quite reasonably resisted the temptation to associate Y2K with apocalyptic predictions. Concerned Women for America's magazine, *Family Voice*, for example, advises readers to prepare themselves and take Y2K seriously, but to "keep your cool" by taking a middle ground between alarmism and indifference. The magazine does not attach millennial significance to the Y2K bug.[28] Nor does *World*, a mainstream conservative evangelical Christian magazine not affiliated with an activist Christian Right organization. Its 1998 article "Backward Christian Soldiers?" explicitly opposes a connection between the Y2K bug and the "End of the Age."[29]

Rev. Jerry Falwell, founder of the now-defunct Moral Majority, has marketed a videotape titled *Y2K: A Christian's Guide to the Millennium*. The hour-long sermon is a garble of contradictory messages. Falwell advises that Y2K "has the potential to be a very big problem, worldwide in scope and without historical precedent, unless you take the Tower of Babel as an example," and suggests that his listeners might want to buy ammunition. He also warns that "many sources are saying that January 1, 2000, will be a fateful day," yet he advises strongly that people not withdraw their money from the banks, which might cause a run on them. "It is very important that we be responsible, cautious, and practical."

Predictably, the bottom line of Falwell's message is recruitment. He paints Y2K as an opportunity for a spiritual awakening in which more people come to know Christ. He asks his followers to pray for that awakening, because "We are in the last days," "We are close to the edge," and "Y2K may be God's instrument . . . to start a revival that spreads the face of the earth before the rapture of the church."

Some leaders in both the Christian Right and the secular right warn that Y2K computer chaos will be an opportunity for government forces to create an "emergency," increase the abridgment of individual freedoms, and further their agenda of one-world government. This fearful prediction holds different meanings for different sectors. The major organizations of the Christian Right alert their followers to the threat of one-world government on an ongoing basis. It is a political theme that also resonates with Christian apocalypticism. For the John Birch Society, an unreconstructed Old Right organization, one-world government is also an ongoing political theme, but is based in the fervent anticommunism and grand conspiracy theories of Old Right ideology.[30] Rather than "reading" Y2K through a Christian lens of end-times anxieties, the secular right sees it as just another opportunity for a power grab by collectivist-minded elites.

A THREAT TO JEWS?

What does a growing and politically powerful Christian revivalist movement mean for Jews in the United States? Surely many conservative Jews, especially those whose religious practices are orthodox, feel a similar sense of alienation from secular society. Traditional Jewish religious practices are as threatened by modern tastes and practices as are those of conservative Christians. But it is unlikely that the Christian Right can provide answers that are satisfactory for substantial numbers of Jews, since the Christian Right so avidly believes in the singular validity of conservative evangelical Christianity that it inevitably sees all religious beliefs and practices other than its own as either erroneous or illegitimate.[31]

There are a very small number of Jews who publicly align themselves with the Christian Right. The conservative Jewish group Toward Tradition is one such group. Its head, Rabbi Daniel Lapin, argues that the proper practice of Jewish faith dictates a belief in moral values that are more closely aligned with those of conservative Christians than with those of liberals, whose "secular humanism" runs against the grain of all religious practice.[32] Some Jews support the Christian Right because of its consistent support for Israel. Prior to the breakup of the Soviet Union, Israel's role as a buffer against communism in the Middle East earned it the support of rightists for whom anticommunism was a central focus. Today, much of Israel's significance for conservative Christians stems from Christian biblical teachings asserting that the Jews must return to Israel in order for the Second Coming to occur. The Christian Right firmly supports the state of Israel and U.S. aid to it. For Jews who equate support for Israel with support for Jews, the Christian Right is a valuable and dependable ally.

Nevertheless, the relationship between Jews and the Christian Right is a source of considerable debate within the Jewish community. The Christian Right's political platform promotes the return of America to its "Christian roots." Most Jews find that platform, as well as the slogan, "America is a Christian country," alarming. Most conservative Christians advocate prayer in schools and the erosion of a separation between church and state, policies that inevitably result in discrimination against Jews. Many Jews are offended by the Christian Right's use of the term "Judeo-Christian" to describe its theology. To describe U.S. religious heritage as Judeo-Christian implies that Christianity has superseded Judaism. Worse still is the Christian Right's belief that those who are not born-again are not in an "appropriate" relationship with God.

The Christian Right's advocacy of these beliefs and policies causes a substantial part of the Jewish community to regard the Christian Right as anti-Semitic. Even while supporting Israel, some Christian Right organizations have simultaneously promoted a greater Christian presence in Israel and have proselytized for Jews to convert to Christianity.[33] The writings of Rev. Pat Robertson, whose Christian Coalition is one of the Christian Right's largest and most powerful organizations, are especially revealing. In his 1994 book, *The New World Order*, Robertson presents his own variation on a long-standing anti-Semitic conspiracy theory that features a sinister plot by secret elites to rule the world, financed by Jewish bankers.[34] In its 1994 publication, *The Religious Right: The Assault on Tolerance and Pluralism in America*, the Anti-Defamation League of B'nai B'rith provides clear evidence of the latent and active anti-Semitism that runs throughout the Christian Right.[35]

The current conservative Christian religious revitalization, while threatening to most Jews and to many others who fall outside its narrow definition of religious correctness, has contributed significantly to the growing size and power of the right as a political movement, and has boosted its increasingly dominant arm, the Christian Right. In the early 1980s, the New Right nurtured the fledgling Christian Right. At the turn of the twentieth century, the Christian Right dominates the right and holds the balance of power within the right wing of the Republican Party.

ECONOMIC CONTRACTION, REDISTRIBUTION, AND RESTRUCTURING

History and common sense tell us that hard economic times present opportunities for the right. Observing the farm crisis in the Midwest in the early 1980s, I saw a dramatic increase in the success of right-wing rural populist, neo-Nazi, and white supremacist groups. Faced with the unthinkable loss of their family farms, some farmers who had never credited the far right's explanation that (Jewish) bankers routinely conspire to steal and defraud found that theory far more appealing than they had when economic times were good.

The frequency of scapegoating of people of color, Jews, immigrants, liberals, welfare recipients, government employees, and lesbian/gay/bisexual and transgender people has risen in tandem with the resurgence of the right. Scapegoating is fixing blame for perceived loss of social status, economic loss, or loss of political power on a target group whose constructed guilt provides a simplistic explanation. Of course, scapegoating, white supremacism, and right-wing politics in general do not stem exclusively from economic and social stress. Individual ideological profiles have many roots, including the beliefs of the community in which a person is raised, life experiences, and individual psychological proclivities. But given the elimination of many industrial-sector jobs, the growth of lower-wage service jobs, the redistribution of wealth upward, an accompanying increase in the gap between the rich and poor, and the restructuring of the national economy to be more interdependent with the global economy, the economic hardship experienced by many working- and middle-class people clearly affects their political thinking.

Sweeping economic changes have occurred since the late 1970s, the period when the right began to experience political success. The transformation of the U.S. economy from one based in industrial capital to one dominated by the service and information sectors and finance capital has resulted in the loss of many blue-collar industrial jobs. Because maximum profits are now found in global capitalism, even small corporations locate many of their production facilities in Third World countries. This change, combined with the "downsizing" of lower- and middle-management corporate jobs, has left a large part of the U.S. workforce dislocated and disillusioned.[36] Much of the motivation for this restructuring comes from greater international competition, which necessitated not only globalization, but also increasingly speculative business behavior, in order to maintain a high level of profits. Industrialists, financiers, and business professionals must now chase profits by using increasingly complex schemes, including the takeovers, mergers, and buyouts of the 1980s and 1990s.

To understand how the right relates to the changing U.S. economic scene, we need to identify the economic interests it represents. Clearly the right's economic agenda (corporate tax cuts, changes in the tax rates to benefit wealthy individuals, deregulation, privatization, anti-union activism, and "defunding the left," among others) benefits business interests and high-income individuals. Yet there is conflict within the economic elite, with some corporate interests aligning with the right, others aligning with the moderate wing of the Republican Party, and still others with the Democrats. We must distinguish the differing interests of various sectors of business for this conflict to make sense.

In the late 1970s, when the New Right became the focus of media attention, its leadership openly declared the movement's allegiance to venture capitalism. Based largely in the West, especially the Southwest and California and to a lesser extent in the South, venture capitalism represents a sector of corporate business, such as oil, electronics, software, and some pharmaceutical companies, that is young, often small and independent, and characterized by high risk. In contrast, larger, older, multinational corporate entities, such as the "blue chip" companies often located in the Midwest and North Atlantic regions, have a different identity and different political needs. The two sectors are sometimes called the "Cowboys" and the "Yankees."[37]

The Yankees learned to tolerate liberalism's agenda of regulation, corporate taxation, and unionization when President Roosevelt's New

Deal programs pulled the country through the Great Depression and saved business from economic collapse and from the wrath of a desperate public. During post–World War II prosperity, they needed the stable workforce that unions provided, and could afford to "buy" that stability with benefits and relatively high wages. During much of the period between 1945 and 1975, liberalism and corporate America coexisted in an uneasy alliance. Their shared opposition to communism and even mild forms of socialism helped promote this coexistence. However, with the emergence of robust national economies, such as those in Western Europe (especially Germany), Japan, and the emerging Pacific rim countries, that threatened U.S. economic hegemony, the larger, multinational corporate sector was less able to compete effectively and became less tolerant of liberalism's programs. In the late 1970s, this sector began its own assault on regulatory laws and labor's pay rates and benefits packages. Though many factors played a role in the declining membership of unions, the relentless pressure on unions from big business was a major one. Professional union-busting firms perfected vicious techniques to discourage new unionization or to bust existing unions, and sold their services to businesses and corporations that wanted to become "union free."[38]

Simultaneously, for venture capitalists, the sector of capital for whom the New Right spoke, stability was less important than an economic and political environment that was hospitable to fast growth. Therefore, deregulation, deunionization, and lower corporate taxes were high on the New Right's agenda. As the 1980s progressed and the needs of the Yankee and Cowboy sectors converged, no strong voices were left to defend liberalism's economic policies of government regulation, strong unions, and corporate taxation.[39] The attack on those policies, aggressively mounted by the New Right, continues to be central to the agenda of the "new Republicans," while also supported more quietly by big business.

The result has been the preservation (even inflation) of profits, but at a high social cost. The right's economic agenda has been the equivalent of a "shock" treatment for the U.S. economy. In order to maintain slipping profits, the corporate sector has adopted a formula of increased economic speculation, a downsized labor force, and the concentration of profits in the hands of upper management and stockholders. The result has been a redistribution of wealth that allows big business to maintain profits, but at a punishing cost to the average wage earner.[40] Thus, even when economic times are good on paper, with low unemployment and high rates of economic growth, some people are getting richer, many are getting poorer, and the "American dream," the belief that hard work will equal success and a better standard of living for the next generation, has been shattered.[41] In this climate of economic upheaval, many white people are experiencing the tragic reality that has long plagued African American communities: hard work does not lead to success.[42]

When people have to work harder just to stay in place, the ground is fertile for political rabble-rousing. Beginning with the right's antitax message, promoted expertly by both the late Howard Jarvis, architect of California's groundbreaking 1978 antitax Proposition 13, and carried forward by Grover Norquist, now president of Americans for Tax Reform, the New Right mounted a campaign to blame liberalism and its constituencies for robbing the average person of prosperity and advancement.[43] With the collaboration of the Reagan Administration, the New Right created the scapegoats of welfare mothers, immigrants, poor Blacks, and other people of color, all demonized and declared by the right to be unworthy of "our tax dollars." The New Right built on existing political resentments, carefully laying the ground for its agenda of nationalism, tax protests, opposition to government "interference," nostalgia for a more "moral" time, and scapegoating.

RACE RESENTMENT AND BIGOTRY

White supremacism and racial bigotry are embedded in the economy and culture of U.S. society and take different forms at different times. Yet, when discussing the right, many white journalists seldom refer to race and racism.[44] Others, predominantly journalists of color, see racism as the principal social, psychological, and economic motivation for right-wing politics.[45] Certainly the right's political agenda and its rhetoric about "welfare queens," "reverse discrimination," and "illegal aliens" appeal to white people who resent an increase they perceive in the power of racial/ethnic "minority" groups. The decreased sense of economic security of many working- and middle-class white people that has resulted from economic restructuring fans and augments this resentment. Playing a subtle race card has been a winning political strategy in the right's recruitment of white followers.[46]

The intersection of race and class in the United States also obscures the right's racism. The leadership of the New Right, the Christian Right, and the "new" Republicans is almost exclusively white and middle-class. Because a Black, Latino, and Asian middle class (though as yet only a tiny Native American middle class) now exists, groups of people of color share the right's class status. That shared class status makes middle-class people of color less threatening and alien to both the leaders and followers of the right. In an effort to broaden the tent of Republican voters, the right has courted and promoted these middle-class communities of color, often by showcasing the members of those communities who will unite with the right's values and policies.[47]

There has been little discussion of racism in the commentary about the right written by white journalists, in part because, late in the 1970s, the New Right explicitly renounced racism, claiming to turn its back on the Old Right's association with the Ku Klux Klan and the George Wallace presidential campaign. Whenever someone from the right makes a racist slur or tells an indiscreet racist joke that becomes public, the right's leaders apologize and chastise the culprit. Faced with this response, most white journalists and many journalists of color, hamstrung by the institutional racism of their own newspapers or television stations, find it difficult to challenge right-wing politicians' and movement leaders' self-portrayal as non-racists.

Because they get most of their information about the right from journalists, Americans, especially white people who are not the right's target, do not properly understand the racial motivation of much of the right's program. An accurate assessment of the racial politics of the right requires an examination of the *consequences* of the right's political agenda for people of color.

Three public policy initiatives sponsored by the right exemplify the important role of racial bigotry and resentment in its political agenda: the attack on affirmative action, welfare "reform," and the anti-immigrant campaign. Here, the right barely conceals its racist language. In the case of welfare "reform" and anti-immigrant policies, the right has created negative stereotypes—the "welfare queen" and the "illegal alien"—then has encouraged its followers to associate people of color with these stereotypes.[48] Because the right is attacking the stereotype, rather than a specific racial group, it creates a "cover" for its racism. In the case of welfare, for instance, the right's leaders have stereotyped and scapegoated welfare recipients, whom they often portray as African American. Welfare recipients are, in fact, majority white. But when the white public "sees" welfare recipients as Black, it can simultaneously hold recipients and Blacks in contempt, without seeing this position as racism against African Americans.

In addition to stereotyping individuals, the right has used racially encoded concepts to make its case. Three of the most powerful are "individual responsibility," "dependency," and "states' rights." All three carry racist implications. The right promotes "individual responsibility" and "dependency" as challenges to the liberal concepts of social responsibility and the rights of the poor, both closely associated with the civil rights movement. "States' rights" has a long and ignoble history as the political tactic whites in the South used to justify preserving segregation, poll taxes, and separate facilities.

When the New Right came to power with the Reagan Administration in 1981, it was politically unwise for white politicians to explicitly advocate the rollback of civil rights gains. A muscular civil rights movement had demanded and achieved a number of liberal programs to address the conditions of Black life, from Jim Crow segregation to voting rights and unequal access to employment, housing, and education. Civil rights for all people of color had become widely accepted.

But, as we have seen, decoding the New Right's hidden racial agenda is not difficult. The inability of civil rights advocates to effectively unmask and counteract that agenda reflects, in part, their own weakness and fragmentation at a time when the right was exercising new and growing influence. For decades the civil rights movement had been under attack from the FBI, suffered from weak-willed executive branch civil rights enforcement, and weathered racist policing and brutal economic repression. Black leaders had been assassinated and activists of color had been attacked, harassed, and threatened by local authorities and independent racist groups.[49] In addition, Black nationalist groups such as the Nation of Islam, as well as opportunistic sectarian factions such as the New Alliance Party (a group that is controlled by a white man but claims to be "Black-led"), had created splits within the civil rights movement. Communities of color had been bribed and courted by right-wing dema-gogues such as Lyndon LaRouche and Rev. Sun Myung Moon.[50] As the right gained power, Latinos, Asian Americans, Native Americans, and African Americans found themselves divided by economic competition and cultural differences and had difficulty mounting a movement across race and ethnicity against the right.

Meanwhile, for many whites of all classes, the advances made by peo-ple of color seem to hold particular symbolic significance. In a climate in which many white people feel anxious and vulnerable, some resent those who appear "favored" by affirmative action and other liberal social pro-grams, and hold a false perception that Blacks have made gains faster than whites. Many white people focus their resentment on bilingualism, multiculturalism, and other hard-fought gains of the civil rights move-ment. White rightists have fanned this backlash by arguing that Blacks no longer suffer discrimination and therefore do not "deserve" a helping hand, and have promoted writers of color who take that position. In this context, the right has encouraged white people to scapegoat African Americans and other people of color, and blame them for what some white people feel is their own loss of status and opportunity.[51]

Would the right have had such success with its racial stereotyping and scapegoating if economic opportunity were expanding for "average" Americans of all races? Perhaps not, simply because without economic pain, there would be less need for scapegoats as targets for anger and blame. But much of U.S. racism is based in white culture and its rac-ist ideology of an "American heritage"—a long-standing vision of the United States as a country settled and built by Protestant European Americans. This nationalistic ideology has a life of its own. The right's leadership has found a way to promote "white rights" without publicly acknowledging the racism of its agenda. Once again, the right has caught the spirit of the times and packaged racial resentment as a recruiting tool.

SOCIAL STRESS AND BACKLASH

The right's success stems in large part from a shift in the voting public's values, as reflected in the growth of the Republican Party. More and more local, state, and national officeholders are ideologically aligned with the right. It is difficult to separate cause and effect: Has the right done well because values held by the majority of people shifted to the right, or did the right cause the shift by developing and marketing an appealing message? Both are true. The right captured a latent public sentiment, and organized its expression.

I have often wondered how, as a political scientist who taught political theory in the 1970s and often surveyed conservative political thought in my classes, I could have been so unaware of that conservative public sentiment. Perhaps I was too immersed in promoting the social changes of the 1960s and 1970s to see the backlash that was fomenting against them. Perhaps, too, I saw very little evidence of a vital conservative movement. The McCarthy era and the candidacies of Barry Goldwater and George Wallace seemed blips on the historical screen, rather than evidence of a serious mass-based political movement. When teaching about conservatism, I was forced to assign dated and simplistic primary texts, such as Friedrich Hayek's *Road to Serfdom* and Barry Goldwater's *Conscience of a Conservative*, because they were the best available.[52] Books about the far right, such as Daniel Bell's anthology, *The Radical Right*, or Richard Hofstadter's *The Paranoid Style in American Politics and Other Essays*, portrayed the far right as a dangerous and psychologically unstable fringe group. These authors failed to imagine that some of the far right's ideas might ever become mainstream.[53]

The social change movements of the 1960s and 1970s appeared to dominate public consciousness. Support for a liberal agenda of expanded rights, public assistance for the poor, and a growing sense of the United States as carrying the responsibility to address such international crises as famine, though not universal, seemed widespread. Conservative or traditionalist opinions, such as support for the Vietnam War or white opposition to busing, were often interpreted by liberal and progressive academics as the last gasps of reactionary politics. Most of us who were caught up in the liberal/progressive agenda considered much of conservatives' anticommunism fanatical and unrealistic. We viewed whites' fear of drugs and crime as motivated by racism, and religious reaction to liberalized divorce and abortion laws as anti-women.

But the New Right's pro-family, pro-market, nationalistic message, emphasizing traditional values, tapped the confusion, resentments, and fears that bubbled beneath the surface of public life. New Right strategists, especially Paul Weyrich and Howard Phillips, identified areas of liberalism's vulnerability, and with great skill, targeted "social issues" as the theme that would reinvigorate the Old Right and inspire its new identity as the New Right.[54] These issues, such as abortion rights, sexual freedom, the rights of children, and the legitimacy of lesbian and gay sexual orientation, had been identified by liberal reformers and progressives as areas in which individual freedom should and must be increased. The New Right appealed to age-old American cultural norms—the work ethic, sexual restraint, self-reliance, patriarchy, Christian worship, and patriotism—to strengthen an already existing backlash against those increases in personal freedom.

The New Right's message created a romanticized image of the 1950s, before the rise of Great Society liberalism, as a period of social harmony. By encouraging cynicism about the goals of "tax and spend" liberal government, the New Right identified the restoration of smaller government and traditional social norms as the answer to the widespread, if relatively unarticulated, anxieties and frustrations of a socially stressed public. The New Right organized muted protest into a protest movement.

The rightward tilt of public attitudes is a testimony to the right's brilliant message-delivery, as well as to the failure of liberalism to counter with an emotionally compelling vision. The result is a shift in "political culture," the core values held by people within the public sphere and in private life. Of course, there is enormous variation in the culture of any society, by class, race, gender, religion, ethnicity, and by idiosyncratic preferences. But a society's political culture is the body of values and attitudes held by the bulk of people, measured in the voting booth and in randomized opinion polls and focus group research.

The notion of a shift in political culture captures the breadth and depth of the social transformation that has occurred since the election of Ronald Reagan. A shift in political culture is never a smooth transition. The potential winners and losers are inevitably locked in struggle, as those who had been dominant try to hold onto power and the challengers strive to consolidate power. The power struggle is easiest to track in the political and economic spheres. It is harder to track in the social and cultural spheres, although that is a crucial location of struggle. For this reason, it is a mistake to watch only the right's success in public policy. It is equally important to pay attention to the "values questions." For without capturing the social and cultural spheres, no political or economic shift will hold.[55]

A rightward shift usually means a shoring up of the "establishment." But the contemporary U.S. right's conservatism is not system-supporting. Classical conservatism favors respect for the authority of limited government, reverence for the church as an institution, support for the nuclear family, and strict adherence to free-market economic principles. It views the individual as the most important unit in society. In major respects, the shift now occurring does not conform to classical conservatism. The contemporary right—both religious and secular—is more ideologically extreme. It fosters suspicion, if not hatred, of government, dismissal of the mainstream Protestant churches, and, contradiction of contradictions, an increased government role in policing individual sexual practices.[56]

Rather than a familiar *Father Knows Best* brand of Republicanism, the right has organized the expression of explicitly antisocial sentiments. It has reached out to those who feel a loss of status and those who feel they have not benefited from the changes that have occurred during the past thirty years. It has encouraged and organized feelings of anger, resentment, spite, vengeance, envy, loss, and bitterness.[57] Although the right is not the only originator of these feelings, it has fanned them and directed them toward now-familiar targets: liberals, feminists, people of color, and lesbians and gay men—all represented as the beneficiaries of liberal social change at the expense of the "average" white male.

A number of specific grievances underlie the right's successful organizing. An important one is anxiety on the part of white, suburban middle-class Protestants who were dominant for generations, but who in the 1970s began to see themselves as losing status and therefore became willing to join a protest movement. They had expected that a secure and predictable place in society, while not guaranteed, was likely, as part of the heritage associated with white skin, education, and middle-class family of origin. For many white, heterosexual, middle-class Protestants and Catholics, especially males, liberal policies designed to increase tolerance, pluralism, and equality threatened their standing. In the heat of disillusionment and right-wing propaganda, many of these white voters have abandoned the Democratic Party.[58]

But the right's resurgence is not based exclusively in the middle class. Working-class white people also suffer social stress and feel both loss of status and loss of opportunity. Many male, white, working-class voters especially resent their perceived competitors: African American men, women of all races, and immigrants. They also resent the New Class, the small but visible young urban professional nouveaux riches of the 1980s and 1990s. These "yuppies" are stockbrokers, professional couples without children, single women corporate executives, MBAs who mastermind mergers and buyouts, and lawyers who specialize in large real estate transactions. In short, they do not work with their hands, have excess income that they spend on luxury items and travel, and they are unattached, or only loosely attached, to church or neighborhood.

The right has reached out to working-class voters by offering an explanation for their anxieties and resentments that blames liberalism for making society more violent, more "sexually permissive," less orderly, and less predictable. The right has focused especially on the anxieties of parents raising children, because it knows that it is in the process of raising children that fears and anxieties become most concrete. For that reason, education, day care, and parenting have been important targets of the right's critique of liberal policies.

The right's caricature of liberalism as all-powerful and evil has proved elastic enough to encompass any grievance. Further, the demonization of liberals deflects anger away from upper-class Republicans, the only group that has remained relatively untouched by the economic contraction, social changes, and shift in political culture of the last three decades. Whether or not the right's social movement prevails, this group will remain stable. Helped by deregulation, globalization, and changes in the tax code, it is actually expanding. Although upper-class Republicans may be culturally uncomfortable with the right's middle- and working-class constituency, they benefit from the right's agenda, because it doesn't challenge their economic status and it obscures moral questions about their accumulation of wealth. As a result, few upper-class Republicans, except the weakened Republican "moderates" who support a more traditional brand of conservatism, have seriously opposed the takeover of the Republican Party by its right wing.

The grievances captured and exploited by the right could have served as the basis for a resurgence of liberal or progressive thought. Social stress can provide a hospitable environment for a leftward shift, and may yet if progressives can develop an effective and compelling way of addressing widespread social anxiety. But, in the 1980s and 1990s, a strong right-wing movement has succeeded in muting the political impact of progressive activism and analysis, in part through its effective and well-funded infrastructure. Still, we make a mistake if we think that the right simply outsmarted and out-organized the left. It did a masterful job of strategic planning and movement-building, but it also benefited from the economic and social conditions of its times.

Though I focus in this book on the shift to the right in the U.S. setting, that shift is occurring throughout Western Europe and Latin America. In Great Britain, Margaret Thatcher's Conservative Party policies paralleled those of the Reagan Administration's. Even with the 1997 overthrow of the Conservative Party, Thatcher's legacy of defunded social services and a reduced government role will persist for decades. In Russia and the Eastern European countries formerly allied with the USSR, free-market capitalism is the "new" economic system that has succeeded communism.[59] In Chile, and increasingly in other Latin American nations, neoliberalism—the "Reaganism" of the United States—is the dominant political ideology. In France, Jean-Marie Le Pen and his right-wing populist National Front have attracted at least 10 percent of the vote in every national election since the late 1980s.[60] Ethnic nationalism and religious fundamentalism are increasingly the basis for civil and military conflict, especially in Africa and Eastern Europe. Tax reduction, a shredded social safety net, and a hostile climate for labor are not confined to the United States.

A comprehensive explanation for the remarkable success of the right must, at the very least, take into account the five factors I have reviewed here: a well-funded and well-organized network of right-wing organizations working in collaboration; a conservative religious revitalization; economic changes that create widespread hardship and insecurity; specific racial resentments in the context of ongoing racism; and social stress as the result of rapid social change. I have not found another time in U.S. history when all five factors occurred at the same time.[61] Even more important, these factors reinforced each other, creating both a push and a pull to the right.

It would be helpful to determine the relative importance of each of the different factors in the right's resurgence. My guess is that the work of the right's movement infrastructure—the strategic funding of individuals and institutions, the skillful message-development work, the careful planning for the long term, and the constant attention to the recruitment of new followers—has been most influential. But I am confident that no single-factor explanation adequately explains the right's success. It has not been simply the result of the hard work of a group of white, male rightists; nor has it been entirely a product of runaway free market capitalism, with its tendency to create a cruel level of inequality; nor has it been merely a swing of the political pendulum, a backlash against women, a result of the breakup of the extended family, a spiritual crisis, or any other of the partial explanations that have been popularized since the political debut of the New Right in the 1970s.

We must piece together an understanding of the right's resurgence by looking very closely at what it has accomplished, how it has accomplished it, and where its accomplishments have occurred. Finally, we must ask what lessons liberals and progressives should draw from the right's successes. In the following chapters, I address various aspects of these questions, often by using case studies of the right's campaigns, to demystify what can sometimes seem—and be—a fearsome and dangerously intolerant juggernaut.

Chapter 2

MOBILIZING RESENTMENT: HOW THE RIGHT ORGANIZED AT THE GRASSROOTS

Whenever I talk about the right, I leave dozens of assumptions unstated. My greatest challenge is to make clear from the outset how I *see* the right: As a social movement? A vast conspiracy? A loose-knit group of single-issue organizations? A band of extremists who have executed a power grab? The credibility of my analysis rests on how well I answer that question, even if the question is not explicitly part of the conversation.

Having watched the right gain political dominance in a relatively brief period of time and with little compromise of its "rollback" agenda, most people have their own views. Conspiracists explain the right's impressive success as the political machinations of a small group of extremists who plot to overthrow liberalism and institute their own regime. That view imbues the right with a sort of Green Beret mystique; it becomes a political strike force made up of sophisticated and highly effective conspirators. Many feminists view the right as primarily reasserting patriarchy, as signaled by the right's early and consistent attack on reproductive rights, especially abortion rights. Many Republicans see the "danger" posed by the right as a fabrication by liberals who refuse to accept the rightward political swing of the country, a swing that expresses itself in the proliferation of conservative organizations and the election of large numbers of conservatives.

Although none of these analyses is fully accurate, each makes a valid point. Conspiracists focus on the right's methods and internal coordination and emphasize its brilliantly executed strategies, often accomplished by unethical and exploitative tactics. Feminists focus on the right's relentless drumbeat of antifeminist rhetoric, its emphasis on the "social issues," and organizations such as the Promise Keepers as evidence that the restoration of male privilege is its core agenda. Moderate Republicans focus on what they see as a fully justified social backlash and economic revolt against liberalism as the explanation for conservatives' success.

I see the right as a protest movement, in which organizations representing various right-wing ideological tendencies work in tandem, in a remarkably disciplined collaboration that has proved beneficial to all of them. In three decades of growth—the 1970s, 1980s, and 1990s—it has constantly expanded in three ways: by recruiting activists into the movement leadership; by increasing the base of movement members and followers; and by courting public opinion within the larger electorate with a marketable message—a vision of social and political change that captures broadly held aspirations, as well as deep-felt anger.

After the landslide defeat of Barry Goldwater in the 1964 presidential election, the right wing of the Republican Party recognized that its existing message was not popular. A core of right-wing leaders (Paul Weyrich, Howard Phillips, and Richard Viguerie, among others) saw the need for the Republican Party's right wing to reposition and rebuild itself. This process centered on mainstreaming the ideological positions of the Old Right and developing winnable policies. In developing the more "modern" message, these leaders dropped the explicit racism associated with the Old Right and its very public support for segregation, and highlighted a protest theme against a range of "social issues." They left other aspects of the Old Right's ideology unchanged, especially the anticommunism and patriotism that had been central to the ideology of Old Right supporters. But they modernized even that theme, by focusing almost exclusively on expansion of the defense budget. They retained, though in slightly altered form, the Old Right's opposition to government programs, which dated to the New Deal, and updated their opposition by caricaturing social welfare programs as "tax-and-spend" elite self-dealing. Though they painted liberalism as a step on the road to communism, theirs was a kinder, gentler McCarthyism, with a contemporary look and contemporary issues. The leadership made the ideological transformation official when, at the end of the 1970s, it renamed the Old Right the New Right.[1]

The New Right leadership developed a protest message that gained steadily in popularity. While that message resonated with adherents of the Old Right (such as Barry Goldwater's supporters, the followers of George Wallace, or members of the John Birch Society), it also appealed to those who had not been part of the Old Right, especially conservative evangelical Christians, conservative southern Democrats, some white ethnic working-class Democrats, and many conservatives within the Republican Party who had not seen themselves as part of the Old Right. Thus, the message was able to reach existing adherents, and also appeal to new adherents because it had shed the uncompromising "take it or leave it" quality of the Old Right's message, and appeared to explain the source of widespread discontent.

During the 1970s, the right's "new" message began to bear fruit, as New Right organizations identified large donors and developed policies reflecting New Right ideology. Simultaneously, conservative Christian evangelicals, especially Christian fundamentalists, began to protest certain aspects of liberal reformism. At the end of the decade, followers of the Old Right, the New Right, and Christian evangelicals—all inspired by the candidacy of Ronald Reagan—were influential in his 1980 election.

Three themes proved particularly effective in mobilizing these constituencies in the late 1970s: Social ills are the fault of liberalism; free-market capitalism delivers greater prosperity than that delivered by liberal economic programs; and the national defense is weak in the face of the communist threat. The Old Right had conjoined these themes in the 1950s and 1960s under the umbrella of "fusionism." Fusionism represented an agreement by conservative intellectuals to emphasize their commonalities rather than their differences. It had been crafted within the right most notably by William F. Buckley, Jr., founding editor in 1955 of the influential conservative magazine, *National Review*.[2] Once

Buckley led conservatives to cooperate and meld their ideological themes, those themes could become established in the public mind as the center of the New Right message. The New Right could then market conservative policies as the best means of restoring a romanticized past of economic security, traditional values, and national pride. In a post-Vietnam, socially anxious, and inflation-troubled United States, the image of a beaming, optimistic Ronald Reagan declaring that "America is back!" was a national intoxicant. Reagan himself became the Great Communicator of the New Right's message.

Certain social issues, especially abortion, school prayer, and the threat of crime, proved particularly effective as mobilizers. The New Right heavily used these issues, along with national defense, in the attack ads it developed during the 1980 elections. The result was a devastating defeat for liberals in Congress, as well as the removal of Jimmy Carter from the presidency. New Right influence soared as the Reagan Administration turned to the movement's showcase think tank, the Heritage Foundation, for its public policy blueprint. The New Right quickly gained virtual control of the Republican Party, helped sweep it along to success, and effectively silenced its moderate wing. It now faced the last challenges—to institutionalize its movement by building a permanent political infrastructure of stable organizations and to "grow" its leadership and its base. Although the Right used many strategies in its ascent to power, I will focus on one crucial aspect of its mobilization of movement resources—the recruitment of individuals to become activists, followers, sympathizers, and movement leaders.

PATHOLOGY OR GRIEVANCE?

The most important asset in mounting a successful social protest movement is a body of committed activists and followers. There must be a climate of substantial discontent—a critical mass within the public that believes that social and political problems exist. An effective leadership must then deliberately organize that critical mass for the benefit of the movement.[3] The work of "harnessing" this critical mass is largely determined by the values and ideology of the leaders, and by the leaders' place within the larger society (class, race, religion, and gender). These factors help to decide what groups the leaders target and what methods they use to mobilize those targeted groups.[4]

In the early 1980s, liberals and progressives greeted the New Right's success with alarm and a certain amount of disgust, in part because the New Right's leadership used underhanded tactics to attack them and unsavory methods of recruitment. Liberals and progressives saw the right's stereotyping, scapegoating, and use of manipulative propaganda as consistent with the dangerous nature of its leaders' values and ideology. It was hard for the right's opponents to "hear" the grievances represented by the New Right because they found the movement's tactics so repellent.

Many liberals and progressives also questioned the legitimacy of the right's followers, sometimes implying that they were dangerous "rednecks" and "Bible thumpers." Organizations such as People for the American Way and the American Civil Liberties Union, feeling particularly threatened by the right's success, characterized both leaders and followers as pathological. Though the New Right did promote militarism, dogmatic religious beliefs, and social intolerance, a focus on these deficiencies (often associated in white, middle-class American consciousness with a stereotype of uneducated, white, working-class people) caused liberals and progressives to delay a serious examination of the source of the New Right's popularity. It also prevented the realization that most New Right and Christian Right activists were not working-class but middle-class.

A number of New Right actions and statements do warrant the label "pathological." In the early 1980s, a leader of a California Moral Majority chapter called for the death penalty for homosexuality. More recently, William Lind of National Empowerment Television (NET was launched by the Free Congress Foundation, Paul Weyrich's think tank, which is heavily funded by Coors' family money) posted on the Internet a page titled "Exercising the Right Kind of Hatred." It begins by equating "political correctness" with "cultural Marxism" and goes on to state that "hatred of certain things is a family value, and a very important one. In fact if we are going to rescue our culture, we need a lot more hate." The villainous things that must be hated are "loose sexual mores, Feminism and bad behavior by certain racial and ethnic groups."[5]

Is the New Right an expression of pathology, or more accurately, a representation of grievances and concerns motivating believers to become involved in politics? I have seen actions and statements that could be considered expressions of political pathology during the New Right's history. But if we focus exclusively on such vitriol, we will miss the issues raised by the New Right that we need to examine and address with as much attention as we give to grievances of other groups in society.[6] The fears, anxieties, and prejudices expressed by "average" New Right followers often seem to stem from a sense of loss of control and impending chaos. For conservative Christian evangelicals, for instance, the sudden visibility of groups they consider threatening or immoral can cause anxiety that makes them prime candidates for recruitment by the right. When New Right and Christian Right leaders point to the presence of "threatening" groups—such as sexually active teenagers, lesbians and gay men (not to mention transgender people), and drug addicts—and tell potential recruits that the right supports the restoration of a moral order as determined by religious norms, it is not hard to understand the attraction that such a message would hold for anxious parents of adolescents, conservative Christians, and crime-weary urbanites.[7]

After capturing the allegiance of a critical mass of followers, the New Right's leadership was positioned to mobilize intolerance toward a wide variety of "outgroups" or "cultural minorities." They could then cast immigrants as the cause of social unrest and environmental degradation. Other such "outgroups" and cultural minorities include abortion rights supporters, self-confessed atheists, feminists who question traditional sex roles, and people of color who benefit from affirmative action programs.

But why was the New Right so successful in its quest for support? Progressives and liberals were using similar strategies to identify social problems and mobilize discontent, but their answers were not simple, did not promise quick solutions, and relied on government, however flawed, as the best agent of change. The right, by nurturing a backlash that had not been recognized by liberals and progressives, eclipsed this vision. The New Right captured and mobilized widespread social stress caused by rapid social and economic change. It did not create backlash sentiments out of whole cloth. They had already existed, at least latently. New Right leaders listened to them, took them seriously, and then mobilized and manipulated them.

Many liberals and progressives only slowly learned to listen to people's fears and anxieties. In 1989, I spent six months in Omaha, Nebraska, far from my Boston home. I could see that many white, working- and middle-class people in Omaha were anxious about drugs and gangs. I interpreted their fears simply as an expression of racism. What they really fear, I thought, is the "threat" of Omaha's growing racial diversity. While I was there, Omaha had its first drive-by shooting. I later learned that gangs in Los Angeles had targeted the city as primed for drug suppliers. Just as many people in Omaha had feared, drugs and gangs were increasingly threatening their neighborhoods and communities. Failing to listen to local residents' fears, I had not formulated a realistic response to them. Too often I saw the explanation for all social problems as poverty and the answer as more government programs. I have learned that the formation of any answer must start with careful listening.

The challenge for a social protest movement such as the New Right has been to synthesize various fears and anxieties into a coherent movement that can impact the larger political sphere. To understand that process, we need to study exactly what methods the leadership has used to motivate and recruit movement activists, followers, and fellow-travelers. We need also to focus on the informal networks and personal contacts within the movement, as well as the influence of such key mediating vehicles as TV, direct mail, talk radio, or film and video.

USING TECHNOLOGY TO TEST AND REFINE THE MESSAGE

In the wake of the Watergate scandal of the early 1970s, legislators enacted campaign finance reforms intended to limit the influence and power of large political donors—the "fat cats" of politics. As a result, it became desirable for campaigns or causes to find large numbers of smaller donors to make up for the money lost as a result of the reforms. Television and radio were natural mediums for reaching large numbers of people. Except for Christian television and radio, which had a track record of fund-raising on its programs, radio and TV had been used far more often to garner public support for a cause or candidate than to garner contributions.

The most effective small-donation, mass fund-raising strategy is to target sympathetic individuals and reach them directly through the mail or by phone. This approach requires both accurate lists of those individuals and the technology to reach them. The rapidly declining cost of computer technology in the 1970s made it possible for more groups to target specific voters around specific issues. The weakening of party alle-giances strengthened this strategy by causing the breakdown of party-line voting and opening the option of appealing to voters on the basis of issues rather than party affiliation.

Richard Viguerie, more than any other political professional, pop-ularized direct mail, the breakthrough message-delivery system that united available technology with shrewd political strategy. By computer-izing the lists of donors to the presidential campaigns of George Wallace and Barry Goldwater, Viguerie created the ultimate right-wing mailing list. He made his invention available exclusively to right-wing organiza-tions and conservative candidates supported by the New Right.

But Viguerie didn't just raise money for the New Right. His direct mail "drops" were also recruitment, public education, and movement-building tools. An example is a direct mail piece developed late in the 1970s for Americans Against Union Control of Government. In typi-cal Viguerie style, it followed a pattern. First, it raised alarm. Second, it identified the perpetrator of the problem. Third, it presented the action that would defeat the perpetrator. In this case, after a salutation of "Dear Friend," the letter creates the image of a burning house; it is the home of the letter recipient. The homeowner calls the fire department as "flames rage through your home, destroying valued possessions, perhaps even taking the life of a loved one." But there is no answer. Why? Because an illegal strike has been called by the "big union bosses" of the firefighters' union, as it has in "city after city in America." The letter goes on to de-scribe "how you can help prevent such a disaster."[8] Here, an extremely frightening event attached to the anti-union message personalizes the message and mobilizes the reader to become involved, by joining the or-ganization, sending a donation to support its work, or both.

Former Senator Tom McIntyre (D-NH) described the effectiveness of Viguerie's direct mail campaigns on specific Congressional legislation as early as the late 1970s. McIntyre recalled a Viguerie direct-mail cam-paign that promoted a 1977 federal right-to-work bill introduced in Congress by New Rightist Phil Crane (R-IL). A year later, Viguerie again cranked up his direct-mail operation to pump out a torrent of anti-labor propaganda aimed at turning people against the centerpiece of or-ganized labor's 1978 legislative program—labor law reform.[9]

Viguerie's direct-mail campaigns developed and refined much of the

New Right's message. Mass mailings are now no longer a novelty, so they are somewhat less effective, but in the 1970s, direct mail was a new technique and the public was not yet jaded. I cannot overstate the importance of Richard Viguerie's direct-mail business to the early success of the New Right. Perhaps his greatest contribution was that he made his direct-mail services available to a *movement*, choosing his clients on the basis of ideology and with movement-building as a goal. In the process, he became an influential shaper of the New Right, the author of its self-defining early mission statement, *The New Right: We're Ready to Lead!*, and owner of a business that had grossed $15 million a year by 1980.[10]

The development of relatively low-cost computer technology occurred at the same time as the development of mass media's negative campaigning, raised to an art form by Terry Dolan of the National Conservative Political Action Committee (NCPAC). Dolan's attack ads proved so effective against liberals running for the House and Senate in 1980 that he took (and deserved) much of the credit for the defeat of liberal Democratic Senators Frank Church, George McGovern, Birch Bayh, and John Culver.

It is no accident that Dolan's attack ads worked so well. The most vicious were those sponsored by political action committees, or PACs, rather than by a candidate's campaign organization. A PAC, the federally sanctioned campaign finance organization that allows individuals to pool their donations in support of a candidate, is free to use snide put-downs, name-calling, verbal assaults, innuendo, and red-baiting, while the candidate maintains political distance. Dolan and NCPAC developed and refined the attack ad style with such bravado that it caught the liberal opposition off guard. It proved so effective as a tactic that it transformed the style and tone of American political campaigns.

Another arena effectively exploited by the right was the media. Throughout the 1980s, the right vilified the mainstream media as liberal and biased against conservative and Christian views. By creating new media outlets, such as Pat Robertson's Christian Broadcasting Network, and by pressuring mainstream media through boycotts of advertisers' products and letter-writing campaigns, the right has gained remarkable media access. As early as 1993, the liberal watchdog group Fairness and Accuracy in Reporting demonstrated that even the opinions expressed on the television outlet most attacked by the right, PBS, ranged from centrist to right-wing.[11] At the end of the 1990s, except for the occasional cable TV talk show guest or independent film with a progressive theme, there is no progressive voice on television. Pacifica Radio is one of only a handful of radio outlets that airs a progressive perspective. As the political "center" moves to the right, debate increasingly occurs between centrist Democrats and rightists.

The New Right also quickly understood the potential of videotapes as propaganda tools. Inexpensive to make and duplicate, videos can be given away at little cost, and can often expose a potential recruit to a message that he or she might not bother to read. An especially striking use of video involved the production and distribution in the mid-1990s of *The Gay Agenda* and *Gay Rights, Special Rights*, two anti-gay videos distributed as part of the right's attack on lesbians and gay men through state-wide referenda and initiatives intended to deny them protection from discrimination. The two videos appeared at the time of the passage of—and subsequent successful legal challenge to—the best-known anti-gay initiative, Colorado's Amendment 2. The raw emotion of their homophobic, demonizing message, which, in part, pits African Americans (all allegedly heterosexual) against gay people (all apparently white) had far greater impact in visual form than could have been achieved through printed propaganda.[12]

The right also has used the Internet and the World Wide Web to spread its message and recruit new followers. Understanding that young people are heavy users of the Internet, many right-wing organizations have sophisticated Web sites that feature material with youth appeal or that contain material about youth.

Finally, the right has exploited an old and proven technique to harness discontent and organize it against scapegoats—the radio. A proven outlet for anger and extremism, radio has been an outlet for the right since its use in the 1930s by Father Charles Coughlin, who railed against the New Deal and, ultimately, became virulently anti-Semitic. Perhaps because the radio encounter is not visual, call-in programs seem to allow the host and callers to express their most antisocial opinions with complete freedom. In the hands of skillful demagogues like Rush Limbaugh, Bob Grant, and G. Gordon Liddy, talk radio has become effective not simply in building the careers of its hosts, but in encouraging, and even recruiting, faceless, angry, and disaffected voters to right-wing positions.

The "bad-boys club," as it was dubbed by media critic Laura Flanders, is both a money-making enterprise and a significant political force. Except for Beverly LaHaye of Concerned Women for America and Phyllis Schlafly of Eagle Forum, whose shows feature their own commentary and air only in limited markets, the hosts are nearly always men. The combative style of the male hosts emphasizes name-calling, scatological humor designed to shock, and explicit hate-mongering against liberals, feminists, people of color, and lesbians and gay men. Many women as well as men are, however, devoted fans of Rush Limbaugh and proudly call themselves "dittoheads."[13] Talk radio has proved to be one of the most effective organizing mechanisms in the right's arsenal.

The New Right has demonstrated a finely tuned ear for the fears and insecurities of the U.S. public. These fears were fodder for organizing. The right's strategists skillfully and effectively captured and directed them, using the latest technology, *before others had mastered it*, for political gain.

MOVEMENT BUILDING

The New Right, understanding that the boost it received from Ronald Reagan would not necessarily be sustained after he left office, consciously built an infrastructure of organizations intended to extend the life of its policies beyond the Reagan Administration. The infrastructure included think tanks, media outlets, law firms, publications, and campus organizations. Examples range from the Heritage Foundation and Concerned Women for America to Focus on the Family, a Christian Right organization based in Colorado Springs, Colorado, with an annual budget of $110 million and its own zip code. The result was a dramatic increase in the right's capacity for political mobilization. The New Right leadership gave equal attention to internal coordination within the movement, holding weekly meetings of the Religious Roundtable in Washington, D.C., and developing the Council on National Policy (CNP) to act as a coordinating body for the movement.

In the early 1980s, national organizations were at the center of the right's movement-building. Their focus was on Congress and the presidency. The leadership paid less attention to local, state, and regional work, though, of course, many of the national organizations were recruiting local-level memberships. With the 1988 ascendance of George

Bush, a man disliked and distrusted by the New Right, the leadership realized that even when the Republican Party held the White House, if the president was a more moderate Republican and movement Republicans did not control the Congress, its policies would not necessarily be implemented. When Reagan left office, the right recognized that it had lost an enormous asset.[14] In a pragmatic decision, the leadership turned its attention full force to its backup resource—local, state, and regional level offices and organizations. The American Legislative Exchange Council (ALEC), a network of state legislators and members of Congress whose goal was to "strengthen grassroots government as the alternative to centralized government in Washington" is an example of an organization that received increased attention. By 1989, ALEC claimed to have two hundred members who were officeholders.[15]

The fruit of that strategic decision was visible in the 1994 and 1996 local, state, and national elections. The right's increased attention to organizing at the grassroots level for state and local, as well as national, candidates and issues proved an enormous boon to its staying power. To this day, the right understands the importance of mobilizing the grassroots, coordinating internally, and collaborating within the movement across political differences. Elizabeth Drew, in her examination of the 1996 Presidential election, focuses on an example of this strategic orientation. She describes the weekly meetings of a loose coalition of primarily grassroots groups (seventy in all) convened by Grover Norquist, a right-wing professional who specializes in antitax activism and legislation. Norquist called the coalition the "Leave Us Alone" coalition, in deference to its members' shared agenda of lower taxes and fewer government programs. The coalition contained such powerhouse organizations as the Christian Coalition, the National Rifle Association, the U.S. Chamber of Commerce, the American Farm Bureau, and the National Right to Life Committee, as well as groups from the homeschooling movement, the "wise use" anti-environmental movement, and senior citizens groups supporting a free-market approach to Medicare. Each of the large organizations and groups had effective local operations that could turn out the vote for Republican candidates.[16] The Christian Coalition was especially well known for its ability to use its 45 million voter guides, usually distributed at churches the Sunday before an election, to mobilize voters at the local level. This get-out-the-vote effort culminated a longer-term effort by the Christian Coalition and other right-wing groups to identify, train, and support local- and state-level candidates for electoral office.

The right's movement-building had several advantages. First, conservative voters and activists tend to be willing to accept leadership from the top down, especially from a charismatic leader—an organizing style that makes for extremely efficient political work. Second, the "fusionism" of the 1960s combined the elaborate and competing factions within the right under the umbrella of opposition to its enemies—liberalism and communism. And third, there was both vertical and horizontal coordination among New Right organizations. Though the movement was not without its internal turf battles, it was, for the most part, willing and able to share resources for the greater good of its "moral" victories.[17] For example, in the right's promotion of Colorado's anti-gay Amendment 2 initiative in the early 1990s, a wide range of right-wing groups—including grassroots activist groups, Christian Right groups, right-wing law firms, anti-feminist women's organizations, and think tanks—worked in seamless collaboration to support Colorado for Family Values, the local group that sponsored the Amendment.

One successful movement-building strategy has been for the right to venture into what might appear hostile political territory, such as racial/ethnic/religious minority communities or communities known to be liberal strongholds. The right cultivated Black and Jewish conservatives, and held Republican Party rallies of "Latinos" (at which nearly the entire group was made up of anti-Castro Cubans). Movement rightists have frequently mounted challenges in a geographical area that is solidly Democratic. Both the Christian Coalition and Concerned Women for America have been active in Massachusetts, known for its liberal voting record and as the home state of two well-known liberals, Senator Ted Kennedy and the late Speaker of the House of Representatives Tip O'Neill. Right-wing activity in Massachusetts has been typically aggressive, with activists using intimidation, false information, and name-calling in attacks on local school committees. Aided by the resources of national organizations, including materials and training, local right-wing activists have claimed to represent large groups of people, such as "parents," though they are nearly always just a few activists following a well-tested game plan.

The right's politically brazen ventures into unfriendly constituencies included courting blue-collar trade unionists, whose voting patterns have been solidly Democratic, but who often dislike taxes, environmentalism, changing sexual mores, legalized abortion, affirmative action, or gun control, and tend to be religious.[18] Such a courtship helped the New Right disassociate itself from the Republican Party's reputation as the party of the wealthy. By highlighting the concerns of working-class people, the New Right camouflaged the way it simultaneously promoted an economic program that lowered the tax rates of the wealthy and attacked unions and workers in general. Not until the 1990s did unions mobilize to oppose Republican political candidates and strengthen their ties to the Democratic Party.

The Christian Coalition, Pat Robertson's large, mass-based national organization of conservative evangelicals and fundamentalists, has used this strategy of crossing into hostile territory. Its former director, Ralph Reed, developed and encouraged the strategy of a "stealth campaign," in which a candidate conceals his or her religious beliefs and right-wing political agenda until after the election in order to increase the chance of victory. A similarly duplicitous strategy was the Christian Coalition's call for "racial reconciliation" between its predominantly white members and African American and Latino Christians. Launched in 1997 and dubbed by Ralph Reed the "Samaritan Project," it would put the Christian Coalition's influence behind a package of Republican legislative initiatives that claimed to benefit the two communities. In this case, Reed's attempt to shed the image of Republicans as wealthy, white, and hostile to people of color by promoting racial harmony was an obvious publicity stunt. Nevertheless, communities of color in need of financial assistance could understandably be grateful for such an offer, and might be unaware that the Christian Coalition opposes affirmative action and other policies that would lead to greater racial equality.[19]

FROM ANGER TO INTOLERANCE

Anger and resentment drive protest movements. When this anger is so great that a nonviolent movement cannot contain it, acts of domestic terrorism become common. In the United States, we have seen domestic terrorism advocated and practiced by some sectors of the far right, ranging from bombings at abortion clinics to the 1995 bombing of the

Alfred P. Murrah Building in Oklahoma City. But a social movement benefits far more from successfully *organizing* individual anger and using that anger to advance its own agenda than from violence.

The right has captured citizen anger and mobilized it to express intolerance against individuals and groups. Such organizing provides a release for feelings of anger and frustration. The right uses three specific forms of intolerance—stereotyping, scapegoating, and demonizing—to mobilize and organize recruits. These techniques are nearly always passed off as legitimate public education. The movement's leadership and professional activists design and promote the techniques; the followers and recruits are snared—usually willingly—by them.

The right's techniques of power politics initially troubled many conservative Christians. The leadership had to reassure them that it was God's will that they enter into a partnership with rightists who used scapegoating, stereotyping, and demonizing for the sake of political gain. Paul Weyrich mounted part of the effort to do so in 1983. Weyrich, the right's most canny and insightful strategist, saw the need to develop arguments that would draw conservative Christians into politics. His Free Congress Research and Education Foundation sponsored two lectures by two resident "experts," William H. Marshner and Enrique T. Rueda, to work out what can be done in politics that would meet God's approval. The lectures, published in booklet form, feature rambling justifications for all sorts of stealth tactics: lying in certain political circumstances is not lying but expressing "mental reservation"; spying is a proper action if the spy is following God's command; leaking information to the press is approved by God because the "unsaved" (liberals) are "clever, plenty of tricks up their sleeves, good at what they do." Christians have an obligation to match them.[20]

When the right mobilizes intolerance against a minority or an outgroup (such as lesbians and gay men, welfare recipients, or teenage offenders), it blames and demonizes the hated group and, at the same time, draws anger away from real sources of social ills. By displacing anger onto such decoys, the right allows for greater dominance by elites, while creating the impression of increased empowerment for those expressing their intolerance. For example, the Christian Right blames the declining quality of public education on "secular humanist" teachers. Blaming the teachers draws attention away from the complex social and economic problems facing public schools, students, and parents, including inadequate and uneven school funding.

Ironically, while elites benefit from this system of intolerance, the right often promotes an anti-elite message. The right's leaders, made up primarily of white, middle-class professionals and venture capitalists, have consistently invoked the theme of resentment against "elites," especially liberal policy makers and those who advocate for liberal causes. They fix blame for social problems on liberal policies and "big government," then claim that "elites" created both.[21] The anti-elite theme has helped to win over working-class followers within traditional Democratic Party constituencies. For instance, by blaming elites for advocating "profane" art, the right has succeeded in convincing many voters to reduce federal support for the arts and humanities. Similarly, the right has attacked the U.S. Department of Education, accusing it of forcing elite notions of humanism and relativism into public school curricula, and has tried to defund and close it.

The right has also targeted those it accuses of being aligned with liberal elites—the "undeserving" in society. It portrays social programs as a conspiracy among liberal policy makers, "corrupt" social workers (paid handsomely for their jobs), and "lazy" clients (on the dole at the taxpayers' expense). The meaning of this message is *constructed* by the right. In a step-by-step process, the right first cleansed its portrayal of the "undeserving" of *explicit* racial content, then used that portrayal to promote policies with *implicit* racial content. As a result, the right promotes racially discriminatory policies by marketing them to the public as "fair" or "color blind." The right has used this tactic of claiming "racial neutrality" in its attacks on welfare and on affirmative action, as well as to promote its "no special rights" argument in support of Colorado's anti-gay Amendment 2. In the case of welfare, while the right claims that the attack on welfare is not an attack on African Americans, the stereotypes of the "welfare queen" and the "welfare mother" play specifically to racial animosities. Personal responsibility, the central concept promoted by the right in its attack on welfare, serves as a racially neutral smokescreen that works hand in hand with the inflammatory stereotype of the "welfare queen" to create a respectable cover for an attack on poor people, especially poor people of color.

Stereotyping and scapegoating are time-proven techniques of right-wing organizing. They provide easy targets and reinforce an us–them dichotomy. They allow a movement to "hitchhike" on the fears and anxieties that are in the air at a particular historical moment.[22] And they help a protest movement fix blame for social ills on easily understood targets and lure recruits with the claim that the movement is defending them from these enemies. As a result, recruits both feel empowered and find an acceptable release for their anger.

RECRUITING CHRISTIAN EVANGELICALS

Skillful political strategists have organized and mobilized the right's protest movement at a time of public discontent. But the leadership needed to build a base of grassroots *activists* who were sufficiently motivated by political passion to deliver the new recruits that the movement needed. It found many of these within the ranks of Christian evangelicals. Though there is a wide range of opinions on both social and political issues among evangelicals, the research of James Guth and John C. Green shows that religiosity correlates with traditional moral values and patriotism.[23] When comparing Christian Right activists with Republican Party activists, Green finds that the Christian Right activists lag behind Republican Party activists in willingness to compromise, negotiate, and build coalitions. He emphasizes the important role of "Christian militancy"—a sense that Christians are under siege by hostile forces and must respond aggressively to defend themselves—in predicting intolerance among Christian Right activists.[24] Of the large number of evangelical Christians in the United States (approximately 30 percent of Americans by most estimates), members of one subgroup—fundamentalists—are most likely to be extremely conservative politically. From the mid-1950s until the early 1970s, conservative evangelicals were only sporadically involved in "worldly" politics.[25] Their concerns were primarily with private life and individual salvation. Further, important doctrinal differences among sectors of evangelical Christianity, primarily about the timing and conditions of the Second Coming, made it difficult for evangelicals to act in unison.

But, sensing that this constituency would be sympathetic to its message, the leadership of the New Right made a point of reaching out to conservative Christians, to mobilize them politically and link them with other sectors of its core constituencies.[26] Rev. Jerry Falwell, who became part of the New Right's leadership, played a central role in recruiting conservative Christians into the electoral arena. Falwell and others (including Ed McAteer and his organization, Christian Voice; the Religious Roundtable; the National Christian Action Coalition; and Intercessors for America) coalesced to form the New Christian Right and spread the message that if something were not done about contemporary society's corruption and immorality, the country would be lost before there could be a Second Coming. This message was effective in mobilizing and uniting Christian evangelicals. Recent research estimates that one-sixth of the electorate is either part of the Christian Right or sympathetic to it.[27]

It is a mistake, however, to give complete credit for the mobilization of evangelicals to individual national leaders. Although the national leadership was skillful, coordinated, and made masterful use of technology, grassroots ministers and preachers were equally important in the political mobilization of the Christian Right.[28] Well before the rise of Jerry Falwell's Moral Majority, conservative local clergy and laity had begun to emerge from their political isolation. In the mid-1970s, they had begun confronting issues close to home, in battles over abortion, school prayer, the Equal Rights Amendment, gay rights, or the IRS's stripping racially imbalanced Christian schools of their tax-exempt status. Preachers and ministers were increasingly prepared to give political direction to their church members, instructing them to oppose government interference and government secularism.

But how many evangelicals were conservative enough to follow the right's leadership? Researcher Clyde Wilcox has grouped evangelicals' opinions on issues, defining five "types" of evangelicals. Wilcox found the two most conservative types—"consistent conservatives" and "social conservatives"—to be the most likely converts to the Christian Right. A clear majority of white evangelicals fall into these two categories. On the other hand, the white mainline Protestants, Black evangelicals, and Catholics who comprise the two most liberal categories outnumber those who make up the two most conservative groupings.[29] These figures define the limits the Christian Right faces in mobilizing and recruiting Christian evangelicals. They also demonstrate broad support for liberalism among Christians.

The New Right's earliest recruitment messages of the 1970s and the 1980s appealed specifically to the moral beliefs and fears of conservative Christians. The messages focused on issues that troubled conservative Christians and that they associated with a "liberal" practice of Christianity. Abortion, decline of the family, gay rights, and the Equal Rights Amendment were explained as the result of the rise of secular humanism—the "enemy" which, by separating God from government, eliminates the religious dimension from the government's laws, programs, and institutions, including the schools.[30] Many national and local evangelical ministers and preachers have become activists and have mobilized their impressive leadership skills and resources in response to this message. These resources consist of money (the deep pocket of church giving); a captive audience; and a savvy understanding of the latest techniques of marketing and communication, including computerized direct-mail databases, the electronic church (television and radio), and telemarketing.

In the late 1980s, the Christian Right seemed to teeter. Prominent television preachers such as Jimmy Swaggart and Jim and Tammy Bakker were tainted by scandal and the rapid growth of conservative Christian televangelism temporarily slowed. Jerry Falwell became associated in public opinion with overreaching, political extremism, and religious intolerance. Support for Falwell's Moral Majority declined, and in 1989 it closed. Although President George Bush supported the Christian Right publicly, he delivered little in actual political spoils.

At precisely this low point in the Christian Right's fortunes, Pat Robertson announced the formation of the Christian Coalition, with the goal of organizing chapters in every state and running candidates in every district in the country. The Christian Coalition was built on the mailing list of Robertson's failed 1988 presidential candidacy, much as Richard Viguerie had built the New Right on the mailing list of the failed Goldwater presidential campaign.

As Executive Director of the Christian Coalition, Ralph Reed came to his job with a background in right-wing organizing. Though more pragmatic and less an extremist "loose cannon" than his boss, Pat Robertson, Reed too was capable of gaffes and missteps. Perhaps his greatest was to brag about the Christian Coalition's plan to run "stealth" candidates. Nevertheless, Reed (who left the organization in September 1997) deserves credit for building the Christian Coalition from its beginning budget of $200,000 to its 1997 budget of some $27 million, and a claimed membership of approximately 1.9 million.[31]

By taking its electoral agenda into the pews of conservative Christian churches (even including some Catholic churches), the right recruited and mobilized a "new" constituency. This was perhaps the leadership's most significant strategic decision. Christian evangelicals have proved to be among the right's most disciplined, uncompromising, and ideological ground troops. Though in the late 1970s the Christian Right could accurately be characterized as the tail attached to the New Right political dog, that tail arguably now wags the dog. Within the Republican Party, the Christian Right is so strong that in platform battles at the 1996 Republican Party convention, it exercised virtual veto power over mainstream Republicans, especially concerning stated positions on the "social issues."[32] It played a crucial role in dozens of close political races in 1994, some say serving as the "swing" constituency in the takeover of both Houses of Congress by Republicans for the first time in forty years, control of a majority of governorships, and major gains at state and local levels.[33] It played a central role in the Congressional impeachment of President Bill Clinton, mobilizing its troops to pressure Congress to punish Clinton through little-known organizations such as The Christian Alert Network (TCAN). TCAN's mission, "to inform individual Christian citizens on specific situations that adversely impact upon our basic Christian doctrine, religious freedom, and traditional families, and to encourage them to participate in the governmental process, in obedience to the Holy Scriptures and according to the intent of our Founding Fathers," illustrates how the right targets conservative Christians as potential political allies and mobilizes them in support of its political agenda.[34]

Those who study the right often debate whether the mobilization of conservative Christians was a result of the skillful deployment of vast resources or a result of the times, when the loss of good jobs and declining respect for religious people in an increasingly secular world created bitter, resentful recruits for a protest movement. We have seen that both are true. The Christian Right both benefited from a congenial historical moment and shaped and magnified that opportunity. Conservative

Christians, encouraged by their leaders to believe that their voices might be heard, developed a sense of political entitlement that has allowed them to move to a new level of political efficacy.

TRANSFORMATIVE ORGANIZING

In many cases, the right has simply copied the organizing techniques of its liberal/left enemies. The liberal "Alinsky model" of organizing, for instance, advocates reaching out to people by addressing issues that are close to home, then leading them to become more empowered by confronting political structures. The right also reaches out to people close to home—with values issues, economic promises, and family concerns. However, rather than stopping at empowerment, it consciously draws its grassroots constituency into its *movement*.

Conservative women, for instance, are drawn to right-wing women's organizations because those organizations are active on issues specific to the women's everyday lives, such as schools, childrearing practices, and day care. The right-wing women's organizations then teach them the right's political analysis, with the help of alarmist messages and misinformation delivered by trusted charismatic leaders. As a result, they acquire an understanding of, and commitment to, the right's broader agenda. The organizers' goal is to create right-wing women activists by validating politically uninvolved conservative women, giving them a sense that they are making a difference, and, through political "education," recruiting them into the larger movement.

This style of organizing is known as "transformative" organizing because the formerly uninvolved person, reached by a political organizer or inspired by a political issue, goes on to become a loyal member of an organization, church, or other group that is part of a political movement. Having an organizational victory during this process—a piece of legislation it supports is passed or its candidate is elected—can be a very positive experience for recruits, one that gives them a sense that their movement can make a difference. It was a substantial boost to the Eagle Forum, for instance, when the women under Phyllis Schlafly's leadership were able to stop the ratification of the Equal Rights Amendment in 1982.

Not all recruits travel the entire road to full movement membership. Those who are not "reached" so profoundly assume different degrees of membership. Just as liberals were accused of being "fellow travelers" with communists, even when they were not communists themselves, some conservatives who sympathize with the Christian Right lack a "belief" strong enough for them to identify as full-fledged members. Others may see themselves as members of the movement when working for a certain candidate or a certain issue, but then change their affiliation in other circumstances. Although not transformed into reliable movement activists, these recruits can play a crucial support role by lobbying for a specific issue or casting a particular vote.

RECRUITING YOUTH

A portion of the leadership of the contemporary right came out of Young Americans for Freedom (YAF), the largest and best-known right-wing college organization in the 1960s. YAF was an in-your-face, male-dominated strike force on college campuses, specializing in aggressive attacks on "liberal" student bodies. YAFers were arrogant, elitist, scornful of women and minorities—and proud of it.

Founded under the tutelage of William F. Buckley, Jr., YAF was greatly influenced by his *National Review* magazine. Most members supported Barry Goldwater's virulent anticommunism, and avidly supported the free market. They were not, however, uniform in their political ideology. YAFers were divided between "traditionalist" conservative ideology and libertarianism. Many of the libertarians were followers of Ayn Rand's radical individualism, known as "objectivism."

As a result of this split within YAF, the campus right in the late 1960s was divided and somewhat ineffective. YAF became a much smaller and less relevant organization, which has never been able to recover its former size. As the general tone of campus politics changed during the late 1970s and early 1980s, becoming more conservative and opening the door to a "new" campus conservatism, Old Rightist Reed Irvine, as well as other leaders of the New Right, stepped in to exploit this opening. Irvine founded Accuracy In Academia (AIA) in 1985 to "fight for academic freedom on campus" by tape recording or taking notes in the classrooms of "Marxist" professors and sending evidence of "inaccuracies" to the AIA national office in Washington, D.C. In a discussion of his plans for AIA, Irvine stated that "since young students may not have the knowledge or the time to carry out this function as carefully as would be desirable, we are asking mature adults to volunteer to enroll in courses near their homes to serve as auditors for Accuracy in Academia."[35] A few months after its founding, AIA was described by the American Association of University Professors (AAUP) as "better funded and more centralized than any right-wing student group in U.S. history."[36] At the same time, Campus Crusade for Christ was gaining strength on college campuses, with a parallel conservative religious message. A fundamentalist evangelical organization working nationally and internationally to promote a right-wing political agenda, with particular emphasis on anticommunism, Campus Crusade for Christ reported an income of over $105 million in its 1986 Annual Report.

With the second term of the Reagan Administration and the increased visibility of the New Right, the right's influence on campus grew steadily. But it wasn't just the national scene that influenced campus politics. It was also a concerted effort by the New Right to recruit conservative students, provide training and financial support to encourage their campus work, then give them movement employment so they could become lifelong activists, and perhaps even right-wing professionals.

In what seemed a time warp, the malicious style of the YAFers reemerged in the 1980s, as former Old Right students now trained the next generation of New Right students. The result was the same in-your-face, arrogant, elitist male style, but with up-to-the-minute technology and lots of money. The use of racist slurs in Dartmouth's right-wing student newspaper, the *Dartmouth Review* (under the leadership of editor Dinesh D'Souza), the mobilization of support for ROTC on campus, and the use of sexist humor to deprecate and harass feminists all echo the earlier YAF style.

Encouraging and subsidizing right-wing newspapers has been a major focus of the right's campus activity. By 1991, the right-wing Collegiate Network was able to list fifty-seven right-wing campus newspapers in its network.[37] *Campus Report*, a publication of Accuracy in Academia, claimed in 1995 to reach 100,000 students on campuses across the country. Young America's Foundation (not officially related to Young Americans for Freedom) publishes two newsletters, one titled *Campus Leader*, and holds annual National Conservative Student Conferences in Washington, D.C. All the major national right-wing student organizations also give fellowships and internships to promising students interested in carrying on the right's work. The Washington, D.C.–based Leadership Institute, founded by Old Rightist Morton Blackwell, maintains an employment placement service and an intern program that place institute attendees in prominent right-wing organizations.

In addition to student newspapers, the right supports campus chapters of College Republicans and organizes alumni to protest liberal professors' research projects or changes in the curriculum judged to "lower academic standards." It also funds the research of right-wing professors and often promotes their books. By mobilizing on these three fronts, the right has pressured and harassed women's studies and ethnic studies programs, demonized liberal professors, and defunded lesbian, gay, bisexual, and transgender campus groups. The right's general campus themes— opposition to "political correctness," multiculturalism, feminism, and gay rights—are supplemented by the specific themes students develop on individual campuses, such as support for apartheid or opposition to environmentalism.[38]

Just as YAF had been a feeder for young Republicans into the professional ranks of the Old Right, the right-wing campus activism of the 1980s and 1990s has been a recruiting ground for the New Right's future professionals. Richard Viguerie came out of YAF, then went to work for the national YAF headquarters before becoming a major leader of the New Right. Dinesh D'Souza and Ralph Reed are just the two most well known of a large number of the next generation of campus activists who have gone on to find employment and careers within the New Right.

This system of support for campus activism and mobilization of conservative alumni is not simply a spontaneous expression of a more conservative mood on campus. It results from the right's conscious strategy to direct vast resources of money, training, and materials to right-wing students on campus and alumni off campus, in a campaign to attack the "radicalized" colleges and universities. Once again, we can explain part of the right's success by its having caught a historical moment, when students, especially those who were politicized during the eight years of the Reagan Administration, were more open to its message.

THE ROLE OF MONEY

Money is now vital to politics, especially because the cost of electoral political campaigns has skyrocketed since the 1970s. Money is also vital to movement-building, especially the general operating support that pays the rent and salaries in nonprofit organizations. Liberals and leftists assume that the right has an unlimited supply of it, that the progressive movement has very little, and that this disparity explains the right's success. I rarely speak in public without being asked where the right gets its money. The question is motivated by a sense that the right's pockets are endlessly deep, and that an understanding of the source of its money would explain its effectiveness. Such an understanding might also explain exactly who is "behind" the right. The unspoken subtext is the constant shortage of money that many liberal and all progressive organizations feel on a day-to-day basis.

The right does have access to deep—and identifiable—pockets. The deepest pockets belong to twelve foundations, recently identified and researched by Sally Covington in an important report on right-wing foundation giving.[39] Prominent among them are the Lynde and Harry Bradley Foundation, the John M. Olin Foundation, the Scaife Family Foundations, the Smith Richardson Foundation, and the Koch Family Foundations.[40] The Adolph Coors Foundation, which played an important role in the early days of the New Right when Coors funded the start-up of the Heritage Foundation and Paul Weyrich's Committee for the Survival of a Free Congress, has retreated to a more balanced funding pattern in the 1990s, under public scrutiny and pressure. However, the Coors Foundation has recently spun off the Castle Rock Foundation, created specifically to fund right-wing organizations.

The funding of these twelve foundations is ideologically motivated and intentionally strategic. So, when Congress cut social welfare programs during the 1980s and 1990s, and called on foundations and churches to pick up the slack, right-wing foundations responded little or not at all. Humanitarian funding does not tempt these rightist foundations and their allied individual funders. Acting in seamless collaboration with the movement, right-wing funders focus on long-term goals, such as movement-building, leadership development, and recruitment.

With this kind of support, the right can afford to generously subsidize its most promising activists by providing secure movement jobs from their campus days on. The Heritage Foundation was originally established in part to provide a home for out-of-office right-wing Republican Senators and Congressmen. The right courts conservative professors and African American ministers with all-expenses-paid trips to conferences and overseas junkets.

An important strength of the right is that the movement's funding is not entirely dependent on the support of wealthy individuals and right-wing foundations. The right also raises enormous amounts of money from its own members and followers. For those of us who see the movement as a threat to democracy and tolerance, it is dismaying to see how broad its base of support is among average Americans. On a 1997 tour of the enormous three-building headquarters of Focus on the Family in Colorado Springs (tours leave hourly), my group was shown the huge room where 250 employees answer the more than 12,500 letters that come in each day to the organization and its head, Dr. James Dobson. The budgets of organizations like Focus on the Family or Promise Keepers, an evangelical Christian men's revival organization, which reached $110 million and $95 million respectively, are largely the result of clever marketing of organization "brand" products—such as magazines, pins, books, CDs, tapes, and T-shirts—and the relatively small donations of hundreds of thousands of followers. Focus on the Family publishes eighteen magazines. In its early years, Promise Keepers raised most of its budget from admission fees to its huge rallies and sales of a vast line of Promise Keeper paraphernalia. The massive number of individual donations to the Christian Coalition is a good example of a "small donor" grassroots fund-raising style that does not hesitate to demand financial support from those it recruits.

Centrist and left-of-center foundations and funding consortia also represent vast resources. They have less political impact than right-wing funders because they direct a substantial percentage of their money to humanitarian relief, both domestic and international. They support a large network of social service organizations, including shelters, legal clinics, and food pantries, often in collaboration with the state or federal government or private corporations. When we examine the funding that's "left" for explicitly liberal and progressive advocacy groups, training centers, media organizations, and think tanks, the amount of money available is substantial, but less than that tapped by the New Right for its movement-building. And when we focus on the progressive movement alone—organizations that go beyond liberal reformism to question the sources of poverty and injustice—the amount of foundation support available is a tiny fraction of that available to the right.

The right has been able to pursue the most expensive forms of organizing, including developing its own media outlets, creating endowed chairs at universities and colleges, building multimillion-dollar think tanks like the Heritage Foundation, and creating massive publishing and program bases like Focus on the Family. And right-wing foundations are often ideologically doctrinaire, unwilling to see any fault in their grantees and therefore stubbornly loyal to them. For example, when Bradley Foundation grantee Charles Murray published *The Bell Curve*, a book that "proved" that African Americans are inferior to "Caucasians" in intelligence,[41] he was asked to leave his post at the conservative Manhattan Institute for having gone too far. However, the Bradley Foundation, under the leadership of key right-wing foundation guru, Michael Joyce, stuck by Murray with a renewal of his $100,000-a-year grant when he went to the American Enterprise Institute.[42]

Funding by right-wing foundations has been oriented toward building a flourishing movement. Rightist foundations target only movement organizations, and provide them with resources adequate to support an institutional infrastructure that can exploit politically advantageous circumstances. In fact these foundations are so committed that they are sometimes willing to play the role of political activist themselves. For example, the Bradley Foundation created a National Commission on Philanthropy and Civic Renewal which "begins its work based on the fundamental principle 'less from government, more from ourselves.'" Bradley's stated purpose is to identify organizations that apply this principle. Calling the effort a "Commission" masks its politically motivated agenda and predetermined outcome. With this Commission, the Bradley Foundation is not simply a funder of the right, but itself becomes a right-wing organization, acting to influence other foundations' funding and promote the right's agenda. It is not simply the *amount* of money the right can control that gives it an advantage in its movement-building. That advantage also stems from the rock-ribbed ideological commitment to right-wing causes of its large donors (including foundations) and the self-generating nature of much of its ongoing income.

THE ANTI-CLINTON CAMPAIGN

Now that the right has consolidated its movement, the next step should be to expand its membership. But, because its leadership is focused on a narrow ideological agenda, the right is often unable to compromise in order to work with those who are not adherents. In the real world of electoral politics—which extends beyond the borders of the movement—the ability to engage in give-and-take is not just desirable but necessary. As the impeachment and trial of President Bill Clinton demonstrated, the right is single-minded when it sets itself on a political path. To its followers, this is adherence to political principle. But, to the majority of voters, it can appear unyielding and politically dogmatic.

Analysts of the "Monica Lewinsky Affair"—the pursuit of Clinton by Special Prosecutor Kenneth Starr and the Republican Congressional majority for having an affair with the young intern and subsequently lying about it—assign responsibility for the impeachment trial to various forces, from Richard Mellon Scaife, the ultraconservative funder, to the tobacco and gun lobbies, whose fortunes Clinton policies harmed. In a 1998 TV interview, Hillary Rodham Clinton blamed "a vast right-wing conspiracy" for the Republican effort "to undo the results of two elections." She was correct that a clique of right-wing believers mounted a no-holds-barred campaign to bring down Bill Clinton. This campaign's dogged work would naturally look to its victims like a vast conspiracy. But Ms. Clinton might more accurately have said that the right effectively mobilized its movement infrastructure in a campaign against her husband with the same tactics and resources it has brought to the anti-gay campaign, the anti-welfare campaign, or the campaigns against public education and affirmative action.

In the anti-Clinton campaign, the right circulated provocative videotapes, mobilized its own law firms, influenced media coverage, published research through its think tanks, and lobbied Republican legislators to adopt the campaign or "pay the consequences." The four "co-conspirators" named by Hillary Clinton—conservative televangelist Rev. Jerry Falwell, Senator Jesse Helms (R-NC), Senator Lauch Faircloth (R-NC), and Whitewater independent counsel Kenneth Starr—are just the tip of the iceberg of the rightist players who advanced the impeachment effort. She omitted a number of the most ghoulish of the anti-Clinton campaigners, such as Floyd Brown, whose Citizens United has relentlessly tormented the Clintons since 1992; Patrick Matrisciana, who made two widely circulated (300,000 copies) Clinton-bashing videos, *The Clinton Chronicles I* and *II*, and founded Citizens for Honest Government, which created a third video, *Bill Clinton's Circle of Power*; Linda Thompson, who made *The Clinton Body Count: Coincidence or Kiss of Death?*, a video that charges the Clintons with responsibility for the deaths of fifty-six people; Hugh H. Sprunt, author of "The Sprunt Report," which alleges that Vincent Foster was killed elsewhere and that his body was moved to Fort Marcy Park in Virginia; and journalists David Brock, Christopher Ruddy, and Ambrose Evans-Pritchard (a self-described "Tory hooligan"), who lent the illusion of careful research and responsible fact-checking to the more outrageous allegations of Clinton misdeeds.[43]

Organizations also played important roles. The *American Spectator*, the *Washington Times*, and *Insight* magazine ran a steady stream of anti-Clinton stories. Richard Mellon Scaife's so-called "Arkansas Project" magnified an Arkansas state trooper's allegation (later withdrawn) of Clinton's sexual misconduct; the right-wing Rutherford Institute became one of the legal counsels for Paula Jones; and Kenneth Starr and several lawyers for Paula Jones were members of the conservative Federalist Society.[44]

I believe, however, that calling these players a "conspiracy" implies that a group of individuals orchestrated and drove the anti-Clinton campaign. As analysis, this underestimates the breadth and depth of hatred for Clinton among the right's followers, and discounts the importance of the movement's infrastructure in mobilizing that hatred. As I attended the second day of Phyllis Schlafly's 1998 Eagle Forum Annual Conference, the "Starr Report"—Special Counsel Kenneth Starr's report of his findings in the investigation of the Whitewater scandal, the Paula Jones lawsuit, and the Monica Lewinsky sexual affair—was released to the public and excerpted in the *New York Times*. Its release infused an otherwise uneventful conference with excitement. Attendees clearly had a sense of being in the right place (Washington, D.C.) at an historic moment. Had I not been at the conference, I might have imagined that the anti-Clinton campaign was the creation of a small clique of clever, slightly mad conspirators who hated Clinton for their own personal reasons. Instead, I could see that this hatred is broad and passionate, and pervades the right's grassroots. Reading the Starr Report, with its salacious account of sexual peccadilloes, Eagle Forum members had an "I told you so" reaction. Soon after the Eagle Forum conference, I observed the same passionate hatred and sense of vindication at the Concerned Women for America Conference. A few weeks later the Christian Coalition "Road to Victory" conference prominently featured the anti-Clinton campaign. In all three instances, attendees received repeated encouragement to lobby their Congressmen and Senators and to "hold their feet to the fire" with threats of political retaliation if they didn't pursue impeachment to the limit.

To the grassroots warriors of the right's mass-based organizations, Bill Clinton embodies the moral degradation that has inspired their crusade. The right's leaders have educated them to see Clinton as a pot-smoking, draft-dodging, adulterous, criminally minded representative of the 1960s generation. When the time came for the right to mobilize against Clinton, its vast machinery was in place. Journalists nearly completely missed the story of this mobilization and the depth of feeling behind it. As with other right-wing campaigns, a passionate minority pursuing a demonized stereotype influenced public policy far beyond its numbers.[45] The key is that the minority was organized as a movement, with an infrastructure that can turn political passion into political clout. The impeachment process dragged on because the right's members insisted that it not be resolved until the final, bitter vote was taken.

THE FUTURE OF THE MOVEMENT

The reasons for the right's astonishing success are not mysterious. Its leaders have been skillful and effective in organizing a social and political movement at a time when economic and social conditions made the public open to its message. The right's strategy has been two-pronged.

It has focused on gaining electoral dominance and on building a stable, enduring movement. Its leaders have coordinated these two prongs so that they function collaboratively rather than competitively. Further, they recruited a previously unmobilized constituency (the Christian Right) to swell the movement's ranks. In the right place at the right time, the leaders pursued their extremist goals with the vigor of ideologues and the risk-taking of venture capitalists. Ironically, these very strengths may prove to be the right's Achilles' heel.

The impeachment fiasco has tarnished the right's image as a rock-ribbed force for morality. During the process, the right's players appeared obsessed, inappropriately partisan, and fanatical in their pursuit of a guilty verdict. The post-impeachment challenge, especially for the Christian Right, is to regain credibility as a voice against government waste and for family values, and to reposition the movement as a pragmatic force for change. After the impeachment trial, most U.S. voters see the right as vengeful, hypocritical, unresponsive, and slightly out of control—far from the pragmatic image put forth by Ralph Reed when he was the Christian Right's poster boy. Reed, former Director of the Christian Coalition, has become a symbol of pragmatism in the right's debate over the role of compromise within the movement. Unlike his former boss, Rev. Pat Robertson, Reed was always angling for ways to augment the Christian Coalition's power by increasing its membership and its influence in Congress. It was Reed who pushed for the Christian Coalition to back Robert Dole in his 1996 presidential race against Bill Clinton, although many in the Christian Right considered Dole too liberal on the social issues. Reed reached out to the African American community and shunned the anti-gay campaign as a "loser." Reed's successor, Randy Tate, a former (one-term) Republican Congressman from the state of Washington, is hoeing a more narrow ideological path for the Christian Coalition. During his tenure, however, the Christian Coalition has lost members and is not as powerful or effective as it was under Reed.[46]

The very end of the 1990s is a dangerous time for the right. The movement has enjoyed a prolonged period of success and has accomplished many of the goals on which its members generally agree. The next stage—pushing the "revolution" further—can highlight internal schisms and disagreements over tactics and even principles. We could read the results of the 1998 elections, when the Republicans did not make the substantial gains they expected in both the House and the Senate, as the beginning of a period of decline for the right. Following that "disappointment," much of the public showed only impatience with the Clinton impeachment trial. But, like a savings account that has, in the past, provided movement stability and durability, the right's infrastructure will continue to be an invaluable asset, even during "hard" political times.

Chapter 3

KITCHEN TABLE BACKLASH: THE ANTIFEMINIST WOMEN'S MOVEMENT

My first encounters with Phyllis Schlafly were in the late 1970s, when I lived in Chicago. Schlafly's organization, Eagle Forum, was then based in Alton, Illinois, where she and her husband Fred Schlafly lived. Illinois was one of the "swing states" that would play an important role in the ratification or defeat of the Equal Rights Amendment. As an activist who supported the ERA, I understood how important it was that the Illinois State Legislature ratify it. I couldn't understand why Schlafly's band of middle-class Christian women worked so doggedly to defeat the Amendment. It seemed irrational to me: Why would women work against their self-interest?

I soon realized that I was asking the wrong question. I was assuming that the self-interest of the women who belonged to STOP ERA, also headed by Schlafly, was similar to my own. I quickly learned that in order to understand these antifeminist women, I must see that their perceived self-interest was very unlike my own. Many STOP ERA members were Protestant evangelical and fundamentalist Christians, as well as conservative Catholics, whose religious beliefs led them to oppose equality for women. They feared the ERA would create a legal mechanism for the ongoing violation of God's will. As Schlafly told them, biblical law set the role of women as helpmates to their husbands—a message their pastors and ministers reiterated.

Though I could readily understand why women might oppose types of social change that would violate their religious beliefs, I was curious to know what made these anti–ERA women become *activists*, especially since their conservative religious beliefs would encourage activities within the church, but not in the public political sphere. Studying STOP ERA in the late 1970s, I found the answer to this question in a formula for organizing women that has worked for the right to this day. A charismatic woman, known for her savvy and wisdom and accepted and loved as a natural leader, recruits women around close-to-home issues (such as the potential for the ERA to result in coed bathrooms or daughters drafted into military combat), then gives them a home-oriented organizing model, such as prayer circles or chapters made up of small numbers of women. Meetings are often held around the kitchen table, allowing women to learn political lessons in small groups, from material provided by the charismatic leader. Gradually some women emerge and become trusted lieutenants, and the charismatic leader identifies and rewards them as such. As familiarity develops and momentum builds, the agenda of the organizing effort broadens to include the wider agenda of the right. The members thus become an arm of the right's larger movement.

Questions about conservative, antifeminist women have haunted me ever since they succeeded in defeating the ERA in 1982. Could pro–ERA forces have recruited them by directly addressing their concerns? Was it Schlafly's organizing style or her message itself that proved attractive? Why was it so easy for Schlafly to paint ERA supporters as the enemy? I did not see the ERA as a threat to antifeminist women, but as a help to all women. Why did we see things so differently?

I now understand that "seeing things differently" lies at the very heart of the right's antifeminist women's movement. The movement's leadership has identified opposition to the vision, policies, and programs of the feminist women's movement as a central theme of its backlash politics. The right's message of a return to "traditional values" has tapped the public's mixed feelings about recent changes in the role of women, and in the process, organized political opposition to feminist reforms. Right-wing women's leaders portray feminists as a threat to the family because they "promote" abortion, divorce, lesbianism, and, of course, the "sexual revolution."

This stereotyping and scapegoating of feminists (or "femi-nazis," to use Rush Limbaugh's term) accomplishes three goals. First, by denigrating feminists, the right further demonizes liberalism—the political sector most identified with legislation for women's rights. Second, the attack on feminists is a vehicle for promoting the right's vision of family values, serving as a major front in what Pat Buchanan has called the "culture war." And third, when the right positions itself in opposition to feminism, it attracts women who hold traditional secular or religious values to the larger rightist agenda. Organizing conservative women to oppose feminists has helped antifeminist leaders create a "women's auxiliary" of the right.

Rightist women leaders understand the political potential of antifeminist reaction because they recognize that the contemporary women's movement has been a profound agent for change in the social, political, economic, and cultural life of the United States. Feminists advocated, and in many cases won, a dramatic transformation in women's status by demanding reforms to increase their legal and economic power. This change sometimes appears superficial, because women continue to face sexist discrimination in so many settings, from the workplace to the legislature. But antifeminist women leaders fully appreciate the changes the feminist women's movement has brought about. By challenging the subordination of women to men, especially in the heterosexual nuclear family setting, feminism has challenged a bedrock value of both the Christian Right and the secular right.

In trying to roll back the gains of the feminist movement, rightist women leaders have generated a militant right-wing, antifeminist women's movement. The charismatic leaders of this important movement are often little known, and the right's male leadership frequently takes them for granted. These women leaders, however, do not protest. They seem content to serve as quiet, largely unheralded political helpers to the male leadership.

The antifeminist women's movement, though lacking public acclaim and recognition, is very important to the right's success. No political movement can achieve a major reversal in the country's political direction unless at least a sizable sector of women, especially middle-class women who have more access to power and money and more time to volunteer than do working-class women, supports it. When the right's leadership recruits sympathetic women, those women then are well positioned to serve as an "alternative" women's voice in countering the message of the feminist women's movement. Because they are women, they have greater legitimacy than men when they speak and organize against feminism.

It is disturbing to me, as a feminist, to see other women take the podium to denounce the goals I have worked for all my adult life. It is also powerful, demonstrating that the backlash against feminism is not entirely the creation of men protecting their privilege. The existence of women within the right's male-dominated leadership (though they are isolated in women's organizations) symbolically refutes feminism by showing that some women are willing, and even eager, to collaborate with the forces identified by feminism as the source of women's oppression.

No one voice speaks for the entire antifeminist women's movement. It has two distinct sectors: conservative Christian women whose activism in women's organizations is under the political umbrella of the Christian Right, and the secular activists who call themselves "equality feminists." Numerous other organizations of conservative women—from the evangelical Christian women's group Women's Aglow Fellowship International to the elite secular group Colonial Dames of America—are less tied to the political structures of the right, but also oppose the goals of the women's movement. And there are independent operators—right-wing media stars who have made careers of opposing feminism. Important distinctions exist among these antifeminist organizations and groups. In fact, they often have little in common except their shared hatred of liberalism, and especially of feminism, which they see as an expression of liberalism. Though they may hold each other in disdain because of political differences, class differences, or cultural clashes between secular and religious lifestyles, all these conservative groupings of women oppose feminism.

Four organizations dominate the right's antifeminist women's movement. Two are mass-based membership organizations—Phyllis Schlafly's Eagle Forum and Beverly LaHaye's Concerned Women for America (CWA)—whose members are primarily middle-class, Christian women with traditional values. Two other antifeminist organizations, the Women's Freedom Network and the Independent Women's Forum, organize primarily among professional women (especially within academia), are small, and focus on research, curriculum "reform," and media outreach. The members of all four organizations are predominantly white; the leaders are almost exclusively white.

The considerable achievements of the antifeminist women's organizations are often difficult to measure precisely. Much of the evidence of their political work's effectiveness is self-reported and anecdotal, described in their fund-raising pitches and public relations materials. A more objective indicator is the success of the organizations' public campaigns. Did they actually defeat a liberal initiative or roll back a feminist gain? Each of the four antifeminist organizations I have studied has participated in innumerable successful campaigns in support of right-wing causes, beginning with the defeat of the Equal Rights Amendment in 1982, and including support for the military buildup of the 1980s, attacks on the Department of Education and the National Endowment for the Arts, defeat of the Clinton health care reform plan, and attacks on sex education in the schools, the battered women's movement, and gay rights.

THE CONSERVATIVE CHRISTIAN ANTIFEMINIST WOMEN'S MOVEMENT

Phyllis Schlafly's Eagle Forum and Beverly LaHaye's Concerned Women for America are the right's answer to liberal mass-based women's organizations such as the National Organization for Women (NOW) and the National Abortion and Reproductive Rights Action League (NARAL). An integral part of the right, these organizations reflect the ideology and agenda of specific sectors of the right, and relate to the larger movement on an ongoing basis. Specifically, Eagle Forum acts as an arm of the Buchanan-Helms branch of the right, whose adherents are sometimes called "paleo-conservatives." This wing is so far right that it is barely contained within the New Right. CWA, on the other hand, is an arm of the Christian Right.

Phyllis Schlafly is the name most often associated with the antifeminist women's movement. She is the founder of Eagle Forum, the oldest and most widely known right-wing women's organization. After founding Eagle Forum in 1967, Schlafly went on to found STOP ERA in 1972. She reigned as grande dame of the antifeminist right until 1979, when Beverly LaHaye, a professional right-wing Christian organizer, launched her explicitly Christian women's organization, Concerned Women for America. In the 1990s, CWA is larger and more influential than Eagle Forum, and the two organizations compete for dominance of the antifeminist women's movement.

STOP ERA, Eagle Forum, and CWA all flourished during the early years of the Reagan Administration. As the right wing of the Republican Party—the institutional base of the New Right—consolidated its power under Reagan, social issues were at the center of its agenda. Much of the credit for crafting the antifeminist agenda belongs to Connaught (Connie) Marshner of the Free Congress Research and Education Foundation and Onalee McGraw of the Heritage Foundation, who broke analytical ground for the right's public policy on family values.[1] Drawing on the policy implications of Marshner's and McGraw's work, the Administration and its Congressional supporters pushed antifeminist and anti-gay legislative initiatives on many fronts. The most comprehensive piece of legislation they proposed was the Family Protection Act, which was repeatedly debated in Congress but never passed. Though the Reagan Administration and its Congressional allies were unable to deliver all of the changes demanded by the right's social agenda, they encouraged and gave succor to the right's family values initiatives, and did succeed in defunding abortion for low-income women.

PHYLLIS SCHLAFLY AND EAGLE FORUM

Phyllis Schlafly, a lawyer and intellectual, received much of her political education from her late husband, Fred Schlafly, who died in 1993. Fifteen years her senior, he was a prominent member of the Old Right who was obsessed with Old Right themes—paranoid anticommunism, bitter opposition to New Deal reforms, and rage over the "loss" of China and the Panama Canal.[2] The Schlaflys' politics mirrored those of the John Birch Society. Researchers have yet to settle just how closely affiliated with the notorious and discredited John Birch Society Phyllis Schlafly was in the 1960s and 1970s.

STOP ERA was not Phyllis Schlafly's first service to the right wing of the Republican Party. She had earlier written a book, *A Choice Not An Echo*, to promote Barry Goldwater's campaign for the 1964 Republican presidential nomination. The book is often identified as a crucial factor in building the support within the Republican Party that allowed Goldwater to capture the nomination.[3]

After Goldwater's overwhelming defeat, Schlafly founded Eagle Forum and led the 1977 campaign to oppose International Women's Year, which she painted as dominated by hateful "women's libbers" who did not represent the majority of American women. In this battle, she began to knit together the three principal themes of antifeminism: opposition to abortion, to equality for women, and to the ERA. During the 1970s, Schlafly developed—and delivered to the emerging New Right leadership—what Republican moderate Tanya Melich has called "the political gold of misogyny."[4]

But Schlafly soon became trapped in the political "no man's land" of women's issues, and later, children's education. Despite her five books on defense and foreign policy, she is seldom recognized by the right's leaders or the mainstream media for her knowledge of defense issues. In the 1970s Schlafly was nearly alone in defending and promoting General Daniel O. Graham in his "Star Wars" program to defend the United States from intercontinental missiles.[5] Rumors that Schlafly wanted to be Secretary of Defense in the first Reagan Administration were not even dignified with comment from the incoming Republicans, though she undoubtedly knows more about defense than many men who have served in that job.

The Republicans also never properly rewarded Schlafly for her role in defeating the ERA. The Reagan Administration threw only one crumb her way: a seat on the Commission on the Bicentennial of the Constitution. Perhaps Schlafly had done her job too well, and once the Republicans gained power, Schlafly's outspokenness became a political liability to her New Right male colleagues. She simply has been unable to join the club of the right's male leadership.

In reviewing Phyllis Schlafly's career during the 1980s, I am intrigued by how Schlafly failed to translate her success into real power, as well as how Beverly LaHaye succeeded in overtaking her. I believe the explanation lies both in Schlafly's complex character and in the somewhat old-fashioned nature of her right-wing politics. She has never taken the steps that are crucial in becoming truly influential in the Republican politics of the 1980s and 1990s. She has not aggressively pursued media exposure, and she has not been able to move beyond her political roots in the Old Right.

Schlafly enjoys occasional media coverage by dint of her status as the mother of the right-wing women's movement. However, unlike other New Right and Christian Right leaders, she has not created her own media outlet to circumvent the mainstream media. Her weekly radio program and occasional guest appearances are modest exposure by the right's standards. Schlafly's newsletter, a remarkably plain and simple four-page, two-color affair, *The Phyllis Schlafly Report*, has not changed its format in fifteen years. Although her photo does appear in the masthead, and she still writes the long feature article that is the newsletter's entire text, these promotions of herself as the leader and visionary of the organization lack the glitter of much of the New Right's style. Schlafly doesn't shrink from leadership or fame, but her appeal to her followers seems to lie in her patrician manner and dignified self-presentation. Her style is similar to that of the exclusive Daughters of the American Revolution. Eagle Forum, for instance, recently offered its members a ten-day cruise on the *Crystal Harmony*, "probably the most beautiful ship afloat," complete with seminars on board by Schlafly, at a cost per person ranging from just shy of $2,500 to nearly $10,000.

True to her roots in the Old Right, Schlafly has always been an isolationist, a ferocious anticommunist, a strong defense advocate, an unyielding foe of abortion and an opponent of free trade and big government. This particular mix of Old Right commitments (for which she gets strong support from her principal political sponsor, Senator Jesse Helms of North Carolina) has kept her from aligning perfectly with the ideological profile of the New Right. Schlafly shares the New Right's anticommunism, emphasis on family values, and hostility to government programs, but she has not abandoned her Old Right commitment to political isolationism and protectionist trade principles, both only weakly supported by New Right politicians.

Schlafly's politics are close to those of Pat Buchanan, another Old Rightist who has been unwilling to sign onto the New Right style. Both are vehemently anti-abortion (Schlafly, a Roman Catholic, was the national Chairman of the Republican National Coalition for Life) and adamantly opposed to "secular humanism." When Buchanan won the 1996 New Hampshire Republican presidential primary, Schlafly was quick to affiliate with him, appearing at his side at a news conference to endorse him.[6] Though much of Buchanan's brand of Old Right ideology has taken hold within the Republican Party, especially among the post–1996 "new Republicans," Schlafly herself continues to be marginalized.

THE ANNUAL EAGLE FORUM CONVENTION

I have learned a great deal about the Eagle Forum by attending its annual conventions. There, I have followed Phyllis Schlafly over the years with enormous interest, aware that in her role as charismatic leader, she must inspire considerable awe in her loyal followers. And I see that she does. Her carriage is erect, her hair is elegantly coifed, and her clothing is perfectly tailored. She is tireless, gracious, and approachable. When she walks down a hall, there is a certain hush of respect. Even I, her sworn political opponent, am aware that she is a formidable woman.

Eagle Forum conventions are serious, almost somber, affairs. They usually culminate on Saturday night with a hotel banquet, featuring a special guest speaker. In 1994, Phyllis Schlafly herself was the toast of the evening. On the occasion of her seventieth birthday, an impressive roster of the right's leadership turned out to toast her, including Jesse Helms, Senate Chair of the Foreign Relations Committee. In the audience, her Eagles (the most tried and true members wearing badges of honor in the form of eagle pins) celebrated their commitment to her organization and its ideology. In 1998, Schlafly again was featured at the banquet, this time as the evening's main speaker.

In a virtuoso performance that assured her audience that she was still the reigning charismatic leader, she spoke for well over an hour, without stopping for even a sip of water. She did a sweeping review of the history of the Republican Party since Dwight Eisenhower, repeatedly referring to Republicans who were not aligned with the Party's right wing as "the king makers." Schlafly passionately refuted the idea that her sector of the Party had ever sunk the Republican ship, especially at the national level.

Her thesis began with the assertion that Barry Goldwater was correct when he ran on a hard-right platform in 1964, and only lost because he was smeared and attacked by Republican king makers, as well as liberals. Schlafly went on to argue that Henry Kissinger was a tool of Nelson Rockefeller, and that there was something very fishy about how Nixon (also a betrayer of conservatives) was driven from office so that Gerald Ford ("who was never elected") could become President and appoint liberal internationalist Nelson Rockefeller as vice president ("not a coincidence!").[7] Schlafly ended her talk by describing the sort of man that "true conservatives" should support for president, describing an unnamed candidate who exactly matched Senator John Ashcroft (R-MO), at the time a possible candidate for the Republican presidential nomination in 2000.[8] Ashcroft, who subsequently withdrew from the race, was the featured speaker at the next day's closing luncheon.

At the 1994 Eagle Forum Convention, twelve of the fifteen principal speakers were men. By 1998 the ratio had improved; only thirteen of twenty-seven speakers were men, but four of the five *featured* speakers were men. Eagle Forum cannot attract "first string" speakers in a non-election year, so it must rely on those whose glory is either faded or tarnished, such as 1998 dinner speaker Hon. Edwin Meese III, former Attorney General under Reagan, or young men (and sometimes women) trying to break into the crowded ranks of the right's leadership. These younger speakers are still "inexpensive" because they are not yet so well known that they charge inflated speaking fees. Often their ambition and self-promotion dominate their presentations. The 1998 dinner speaker, Matt Drudge, who portrays himself as a rebel journalist and who claims to have "broken" the Monica Lewinsky story on the Internet's "Drudge Report," repeatedly bragged that 16 million people have visited his Web site and described himself as "having courage" and a willingness to "give my life for this country if I have to," implying that his work is so damaging to the powers-that-be that his life may be in danger.

Many of the workshops and keynote addresses at Eagle Forum conventions focus on issue areas identified as "women's issues," such as schools, health care reform, violence on television, or the latest misdeeds of feminists. A surprising number, however, stray far afield of these issue areas, into grand conspiracy theories, such as one promoted repeatedly at recent Eagle Forum conferences—the alleged international conspiracy behind the New World Order. This mammoth and complex conspiracy theory combines hatred of the United Nations, isolationism, anti-Semitism, and right-wing populist distrust of elites. For Old Rightists such as Phyllis Schlafly, the New World Order conspiracy occupies the central ideological place previously held by anticommunism.

President George Bush, never trusted by the right, adopted the phrase "New World Order" to describe U.S. international dominance after the fall of communism in eastern Europe and the Soviet Union. Growing numbers of those within the right now see this as code for the final arrival of One-World Government—a long-standing right-wing concept. According to this theory, One-World Government will prevail when the United States is finally robbed of all its sovereignty. At that time, rather than self-rule, we will have rule by the hated United Nations, which is seen as the center of the conspiracy. Aiding in this subversion are an array of co-conspirators, ranging from "traitorous Trilateralist elites" to "international (Jewish) bankers" and many co-conspirators within the United States who unconsciously play into the hands of the conspiracy. This theme is a favorite of Senator Jesse Helms (R-NC), and is one of the extreme positions that has kept him somewhat marginalized, even within the Republican Party. Phyllis Schlafly has written about it in *The Phyllis Schlafly Report*.

Interestingly, Schlafly herself does not publicly state the extreme positions taken by the speakers featured at her convention. She does, however, introduce each speaker, bestowing her approval on what the speaker is about to say, and implying that she herself has been moved and educated by the analysis we are about to hear.

BEVERLY LAHAYE AND CONCERNED WOMEN FOR AMERICA

Beverly LaHaye also promotes the "New World Order" conspiracy theory, but in a Christian context, in keeping with Concerned Women for America's explicitly Christian identity. Just as the Christian Right now dominates the right, Beverly LaHaye's CWA is now larger and more influential than the more secular Eagle Forum. Yet La-Haye is little known to feminists, and even less known to the general public. CWA's budget is at least eight times that of Eagle Forum. More than three times as many members attend CWA's annual conventions as attend those of Eagle Forum. CWA claims a membership of between 600,000 and 700,000, compared with Eagle Forum's claim of 80,000 members. Even though these figures are undoubtedly inflated, they accurately reflect the greater wealth and mobilizing power of CWA. It is sobering to compare these membership figures with the National Organization for Women's estimated membership of 250,000.

Beverly LaHaye reached the pinnacle of right-wing women's organizing by being in the right place with the right style, and knowing how to maximize her political impact through electronic media and slick public relations. Her style is that of a preacher rather than an intellectual. She organizes her followers in prayer circles, usually made up of seven women who meet "around the kitchen table." The CWA slogan is "Prayer, Praise and Action." Each of the triad is equally important, so that members are not simply encouraged to act—with specific instructions such as "Call your Congressman" or "Speak to your librarian"—but to become emotionally and spiritually engaged.

LaHaye is the wife of Dr. Tim LaHaye, a cofounder of the Moral Majority and a well-known leader within the Christian Right. For years, the LaHayes conducted profit-making Family Life Seminars with Christian couples, at which they honed their family values themes. They have long belonged to the network of Christian Right organizations that came into its own within the Republican Party during the 1990s. In fact, I would argue that they represent the far edge of the Christian Right. Both have served on the Board of Directors of the Coalition on Revival, an organization that promotes the idea that the United States should be governed by biblical law.[9]

LaHaye claims to have had a revelation in 1978 while she and her husband were watching Barbara Walters interview Betty Friedan on television. She reports that when Friedan claimed she represented many women in America, LaHaye leaped to her feet, declaring that Betty Friedan did not speak for her or her idea of womanhood.[10] The next year she launched Concerned Women for America to organize conservative Christian women to oppose "the feminists." This decision followed LaHaye's 1963 religious conversion, when she surrendered herself completely to God and became what she calls "a spirit-filled woman." She describes herself, before that conversion, as a "fearful, introverted person with a rather poor self-image." She has lectured on her transformation, developed her own analysis of four types of human "temperament," and teaches that bringing the Holy Ghost into your life can strengthen each type of temperament. The LaHayes' joint organization, Family Life Seminars, offers to analyze, for $29.95, the temperament of anyone willing to take a half-hour test.[11]

As a member of the Christian Right and the wife of an established Christian Right leader, LaHaye quite logically set out to organize Christian women, without regard for the exclusion of non-Christian women. CWA's religious style and language—that of evangelical and fundamentalist Protestants—is not altered to include Jews, Catholics, Hindus, Muslims, or others. However, I have seen Jewish and Catholic ideologues, who hold compatible right-wing political views, welcomed as speakers at CWA conventions.

LaHaye's unapologetic appeal to Christian women has made recruiting easier for her than it has been for Phyllis Schlafly. The women LaHaye recruits are already part of an existing Christian-based mass movement, and the family values message is deeply part of their daily religious experience. These women merely need to be educated about the threat to those values posed by liberals, then harvested for membership in the organization. LaHaye's background as the co-convenor of Family Life Seminars gave her the training in ministry that has been crucial for the task of founding a Christian Right women's organization. Not surprisingly, LaHaye's organizing style and tone is that of the church. CWA is an organization of heart and soul rather than intellect.

The contrast with Schlafly's style is evident in the CWA publication that parallels Eagle Forum's *Phyllis Schlafly Report*. CWA's monthly *Family Voice* looks like a magazine in booklet size. It is multicolor, printed on slick paper, and filled with organizational news and photographs. It is also a hard-hitting right-wing propaganda tool, full of political rhetoric, misinformation, and exaggeration. Perhaps its most important organizing feature is its visual focus on Beverly LaHaye, surrounded by leaders of the New Right and Christian Right, all bolstering her prominence and legitimacy. As charismatic founder and minister to the organization (LaHaye was once named President for Life), LaHaye's presence permeates the magazine. *Family Voice* prominently promotes LaHaye's half-hour daily radio show, which sociologist Sara Diamond estimates reaches an audience of 500,000.[12] Skillful public relations is key to CWA's success.

Beverly LaHaye's personalized style of public relations is captured in how she introduced her members to the 1980s war in Nicaragua, waged by the CIA–sponsored mercenaries called the "Contras" against the leftist Sandinista government. This Cold War struggle was far from the hearth-and-home interests that LaHaye uses to recruit members to CWA. It is unlikely that most of her members had more than a passing understanding of the war against Nicaragua. But LaHaye skillfully personalized the war, by traveling to Managua, the capital of Nicaragua, to meet with Violetta Chamorro, the matriarch of a prominent Nicaragua publishing and landowning family that split its support between the Sandinistas and the Contras. With video crew in tow, LaHaye documented her visit, especially her meeting with Chamorro, her Nicaraguan "sister" who sided with the Contras and "was fighting so bravely against communism," and who later was named CWA's Woman of the Year. After her return, LaHaye organized her members into prayer circles to assemble kits of toiletries and comfort items for the fighting men of the Contras. Violetta Chamorro was later elected president of Nicaragua.

By contrast, Phyllis Schlafly educated her members about the struggle in Nicaragua with long treatises about the dangers of communism and how President Reagan was fighting for "democracy." Her followers also were exposed to a right-wing reading of foreign policy, but on a more intellectual level.

LaHaye's hands-on, learning-by-doing approach has been a major strength of the right's organizing strategy. As the acknowledged charismatic leader, she provides the issue, the analysis of the issue, and guidance about the action that must be taken in response to the issue. The followers, grateful to be enlightened and led, become a mobilized, politicized, and dedicated political force.

CWA'S ANNUAL CONVENTION

The annual convention of Concerned Women for America is predictably bigger, more media-savvy, more stage-produced, more fun, and more explicitly Christian than the Eagle Forum convention. Christian songs and hymns are sung throughout the convention, and on Sunday morning there is a "Concert of Prayer." Each year I attend, I am struck by the high level of the convention's production values. The sound systems are professional and high-quality, the convention's logistics are flawless, and convention materials are slick and well prepared. As at Eagle Forum conventions, most of the principal speakers are men (eleven of the fifteen speakers at CWA's 1994 convention), but as is the case at Eagle Forum, this ratio is improving. In 1995, the number of male speakers (seventeen of twenty-five) was artificially inflated, because every declared Republican candidate for president came to speak, as well as House Speaker Newt Gingrich and Ralph Reed, the controversial former Executive Director of Pat Robertson's Christian Coalition.

LaHaye came to the New World Order conspiracy later than Schlafly, but she too endorses the theory that the New World Order conspiracy threatens our daily lives. At CWA's 1995 conference LaHaye praised and introduced Dr. Stanley Monteith, an orthopedic surgeon who publishes a conspiracy-minded right-wing newsletter called *HIV-Watch* and runs a radio show called *Radio Liberty*. Monteith traced the roots of the New World Order conspiracy to a nineteenth-century plan for a New World Order developed by British entrepreneur Sir Cecil Rhodes. In horrifying detail, Monteith described how the plan for international domination was then picked up by Andrew Carnegie, the American robber baron, and culminated in the Council on Foreign Relations and the presidency of Bill Clinton. Throughout his talk, Monteith referred to his research in "the secret files" as the source of his information. This long-standing right-wing conspiracy theory was enormously popular with the audience.

The 1998 conference was a time of change for CWA. Before its usual gathering of about 600 attendees at the Saturday evening banquet, Jim Woodall, long-time second-in-command and travel companion to La-Haye, announced that he would be leaving the organization. LaHaye herself stepped down as president earlier in the year, but clearly intends to retain her leadership role, now as Founder and Chairman of the Board. Carmen Pate, her successor as director of CWA, was warmly greeted by all and identified as "the person who now would travel with Mrs. La-

Haye." The unexpected bombshell was the dramatic announcement of a CWA spin-off organization, the Beverly LaHaye Center for Traditional Women's Studies. In a slick and professional fund-raising pitch featuring a video projected on two screens for the banquet audience, Woodall announced the new Center, describing it as "a research center dedicated to countering the radical feminist agenda" from "a biblically based worldview." While passing the hat for donations, Woodall gave details: The new Center would be adjacent to the CWA offices and would seek a Ph.D. as executive director. Donations were encouraged as a way to honor Beverly LaHaye.

But the evening was just beginning. The featured speaker was Dr. Margaret Nikol, holder of three Ph.D.s, musician, escapee from communist Bulgaria by way of East Germany, and dedicated Christian. In a speech that interwove hyper-patriotism to the United States, homophobia ("Homosexuality is an abomination"), Christian devotion, opposition to abortion ("Abortion is murder in the first degree"), singing, violin-playing, and stern criticism of Americans "who don't understand what they have," she cajoled and chastised a mesmerized audience. She ended her lengthy performance with a medley of patriotic songs, sung before a projected backdrop of a rippling American flag, followed by a fund-raising plea for money to print Bibles to send to Bulgaria. She urged the audience to buy her tapes, books, and CDs, on sale in the lobby.

While aggressively marketing her own and her husband's books, each year LaHaye uses the conference to promote a long-distance telephone service called Lifeline. Described as "the first long-distance carrier that is built on biblical values and centered around the Lord Jesus Christ," Lifeline donates part of the proceeds from its business to support CWA. LaHaye has promoted Lifeline as an alternative to AT&T's long distance service, which, she says, "has thrown its financial support behind numerous homosexual rights causes."

Both Beverly LaHaye and Phyllis Schlafly face the dilemma created by hierarchical, charismatic leadership; it is difficult for each to leave her organization without causing its collapse. Schlafly is still a dynamic and energetic leader, but she must yearn for a protégé who could replace her at the helm. LaHaye has signaled her exhaustion by stepping down as president of CWA. It will be interesting to see whether the two organizations ultimately will survive the departure of their leaders.

THE CONSERVATIVE CHRISTIAN ANTIFEMINIST WORLDVIEW

continue to struggle with the question: What motivates women to oppose efforts to attain legal protections and equal rights? I recognize that
antifeminist activists see their own self-interest differently from how I
see mine, but I cannot fully appreciate their view of the world until I
know the belief system that underlies their understanding.

I know there are undoubtedly as many explanations as there are antifeminist women. For many CWA members, their social conservatism
stems from their religious conservatism. A conservative reading of the
Bible defines a woman's role as subordinate to a man's, and the Bible is not
just a source of advice and guidance; it is an infallible mandate. Although
the women of Eagle Forum are almost assuredly Protestant or Catholic,
Schlafly teaches a more secular understanding of the world. Her defense
of traditional women reflects her Old Right politics. Her brand of political conservatism sees feminism as a liberal plot to advance socialism.

The activists of the antifeminist women's movement support a model
of behavior that derives from traditional Anglo-European principles of
individualism, Christianity, and self-restraint. In this model, they see
the blueprint for worthiness. Hard-working, church-going, responsible,
upright, heterosexual white people are the backbone of Western civilization, and account for U.S. progress and superiority. Concessions to
moral corruption, secularism, sexual "deviance," lack of personal responsibility, or multiculturalism threaten that society. In this worldview, traditional marriage, in which the husband is the provider and the wife
is the mother and homemaker, is not simply desirable; it is necessary,
because the breakdown of traditional gender roles leads to chaos. The
women of Eagle Forum and CWA feel that traditional marriage is ma-
ligned and denigrated by feminists.

The principles of the feminist women's movement both defy conservative Christian teachings and threaten the structure of the traditional
family. Perhaps most threatening of all, feminism rewrites the traditional marriage contract that assures women a permanent place of protection and support. To conservative women, feminist policies are a dangerous reordering of gender roles that leaves women insecure in a
menacing world. They see that often women's liberation has frightening
costs. They argue that a woman who steps outside her role is no longer in

a position to hold her husband to his role; that when a mother works rather than staying home with her young children, the children will bond more strongly with their day-care provider than with their own mother.

This worldview helps to explain the heated antifeminist rhetoric of the members of Eagle Forum and CWA. For the followers of the mass-based, right-wing women's movement, opposition to feminism is a holy war, and their demonization of feminists comes from the heart. I am stunned by the antifeminist rhetoric I hear at conventions. It often bears a closer resemblance to the language of hate literature than to simple political denunciation.

But the greatest demonization is reserved for "homosexuals." For conservative Christians, especially those who read the Bible literally, homosexuality is a practice condemned by God. Both Eagle Forum and CWA have ongoing campaigns against "militant lesbians" and "the gay agenda." When a feminist policy is under attack from either organization, it is usually smeared as lesbian-motivated. Any such tarring implies that the feminist position in question is anti-family, anti-Christian, and anti-male.

Right-wing women also see feminism as elitist; though feminists are morally inferior, they have influence and power to impose their own twisted, secular priorities. For conservative Christian women, the source of women's oppression is not men, but other women, specifically the women who control popular culture and have hoodwinked the unknowing public into supporting their selfish agenda. Their ally and financial underwriter is liberalism—which is seen as the handmaiden of socialism and communism.

Whipping up the latent resentments of conservative/traditional/ Christian women against feminists and their agenda serves a strategic purpose in right-wing movement-building. Right-wing leaders like Phyllis Schlafly and Beverly LaHaye appeal to women as wives and mothers, connect with them around their fears, then draw them into the right's broader agenda through education and hands-on activism. They educate them about how feminism is a threat to the family, about the "homosexual agenda," and about the elites in Washington who want to rob "us" and "destroy this country." For many conservative women, this is the path to becoming right-wing activists.[13]

EQUALITY FEMINISM

When I encounter "equality feminists," I ask slightly different questions from those I asked about the women of STOP ERA in the late 1970s. Equality feminists abhor all discussion of women as "victims," and refuse to accept that women as a class are oppressed. They believe in competing with men for status and success without regard to gender considerations, and they are viciously disdainful of women who consider gender a factor in their lack of personal achievement or career advancement.[14] Theirs are the success stories of modern capitalism. They made it the hard way and have no sympathy for those who haven't succeeded. In this case I cannot understand how professional women of considerable accomplishment, who operate in the public sphere and are quite obviously beneficiaries of the struggle for women's rights, can be so viciously opposed to feminism's arguments that they will dedicate their careers to opposing them.

I do know that equality feminists see themselves as a more mature stage of feminism—highly competent women who have demonstrated that they need no special treatment, such as affirmative action. They have a sophisticated relationship with the institutions of modern society, where they often occupy positions of power and prestige. They "pull their own weight," and do not want to be tainted by what they see as the whining and man-hating women's movement.

The roots of equality feminism are in academia, where many of the founders of this sector of the antifeminist women's movement are based. Some equality feminists are simply conservative women who have built their academic careers on the novelty of being antifeminist women. Some are former feminists who are disillusioned with the women's movement and are now its bitter enemies. And others, who are especially telegenic and who want to be known beyond their universities, have become media stars by providing "the other side" in discussions of women's rights.

The academic women who have published books and articles excoriating the "political correctness" and "victim blaming" of women's studies programs have attacked not just the work of feminist scholars but the practice of women's studies itself. Typical examples are Daphne Patai and Noretta Koertge, two academics who taught in women's studies programs, but have jointly written *Professing Feminism*, an angry attack on their former affiliation.[15] Elizabeth Fox-Genovese promotes a similar critique of women's studies in *Feminism Is Not the Story of My Life*.[16]

Off campus, alumni who oppose the acceptance of feminism and multiculturalism at their alma maters have formed organizations with names such as Ivy Leaguers for Freedom and the National Alumni Forum. These organizations give voice and clout to conservative alumni who want to reverse the increase in racial diversity and sexual permissiveness that has come to their (usually elite) campuses. In all cases, women's studies is a major target of the organizing.[17]

When conservative, professional antifeminists look for a compatible political women's organization outside their work settings, they are not comfortable with either the middle-class grassroots warriors of Eagle Forum or the evangelical Christian ladies of Concerned Women for America. Needing their own voice, they have generated two new organizations—the Women's Freedom Network (WFN) and the Independent Women's Forum (IWF). WFN takes itself very seriously as a combination research center and alternative antifeminist voice. IWF's style is more quirky and hip. Its reputation is built on its skill at working the media. The two organizations sometimes publish the same right-wing authors, but do not share the same leaders. In both organizations, the leaders and most of the members are white and middle- to upper-middle-class.

Rita Simon founded WFN in 1993 to promote a rightist political analysis of the role of women in society distinct from that of "old traditionalist" conservative women, especially the Christian women of Concerned Women for America. Simon writes that WFN "views women as competent, responsible individuals who do not need special protections and dispensations from the state. . . ." She goes on to say that WFN does not view women as victims, nor men as enemies. From her perspective, women's and men's views are "almost identical."[18] WFN publishes a quarterly *Women's Freedom Network Newsletter* and has published a small series of working papers, as well as a book-length collection of essays, *Neither Victim Nor Enemy*. WFN opposes the hard-fought legislation meant to protect battered women, the Violence Against Women Act;[19] maintains that women are treated too leniently by the judicial system in statutory rape cases;[20] and criticizes sexual harassment laws as increasingly "being transformed into a *lethal* weapon in some women's determination to secure the position of boss or doctor for themselves" (emphasis added).[21]

The Independent Women's Forum was founded in 1992. Though small, with a membership of fewer than 1,500, it is extremely effective in promoting its message. Its principal activities are publishing the *Women's Quarterly* and an "insiders'" newsletter titled *Ex Femina*, and maintaining a "Washington speaker series." IWF seems at times to exist purely to defend men and defame women. Representative articles from the *Women's Quarterly*, a magazine whose "shock jock" style seems a source of pride for its editor Danielle Crittenden, include an attack on women who suffer from multiple chemical sensitivities as "hysterical,"[22] a caricature of feminists who work against domestic violence as man-hating and simple-minded,[23] and a lament over the "casualties" in men's sports that have supposedly resulted from the provision in Title IX that women's sports be given proportionately equal funding.[24] With the American Enterprise Institute, IWF has co-published a book titled *Women's Figures: An Illustrated Guide to the Economic Progress of Women in America*, which "debunks" the "myth" that women earn 74 cents for every $1 earned by men. The authors argue that it is not gender discrimination that causes the "pay gap," but that women work fewer hours per week, have less work experience, and work at different (less demanding and less dangerous) jobs than men. In fact, the authors conclude, "American women enjoy the best and most rewarding job market in the world."[25]

While the Independent Women's Forum is known by TV talk shows and newsmagazines as a source for antifeminist spokespersons, the best-known equality feminists are independent operators, who have close ties to equality feminist organizations and have been supported by the right, but are media stars in their own right. At the head of the pack is Camille Paglia, a self-confessed attention-grabber based at the University of the Arts in Philadelphia. Part professor and part performance artist, Paglia has turned her loud, cranky critique of feminists as prudish misfits and victims into a media career.

Another critic of women's studies who has become a media star is Clark University's Christina Hoff Sommers, author of *Who Stole Femi-*

nism? The book's financial support and heavy promotion by conservative foundations won her appearances on countless television talk shows.[26] Sommers' media fame is matched by that of political commentator Laura Ingraham, who delights in playing the role of a dissident feminist, and Mona Charen, former associate director of the Office of Public Liaison in the Reagan Administration and now a syndicated columnist based at the right-wing newspaper the *Washington Times*. Laura Schlessinger, a former academic now known as "Dr. Laura," is an enormously popular right-wing radio personality, who advocates a tough line against working mothers.[27]

The ideology of the equality feminist sector of the right-wing women's movement mixes classical liberalism and rightist libertarianism. Classical liberalism, as distinct from New Deal liberalism, believes first and foremost in individual freedom. Like libertarianism, it is opposed to "big government" and supports the economic and political freedom of the individual above all. Rightist libertarianism opposes all government and maintains a permissive attitude toward nontraditional values and behaviors. Sometimes called "laissez-faire conservatives," equality feminists are less traditional on social issues, such as abortion rights and gay rights, than the Christian Right, but vehemently opposed to feminist solutions for economic and political problems, such as affirmative action, comparable pay, or mandatory day care.[28] IWF and WFN collaborate with like-minded organizations within the right, such as the Center for Equal Opportunity, an anti–affirmative action think tank established by former Reagan Administration official Linda Chavez, and the National Association of Scholars, a network of rightist scholars dedicated to restoring "an informed understanding of the Western intellectual heritage" within academia.

Equality feminists claim that they are objective—"neither right nor left"—but their sneering, disdainful, and aggressive style is reserved for feminism alone. A self-satisfied sense of superiority pervades their antifeminist "myth-busting." When they take on a "myth" such as women's relative reluctance to engage in violence, they seem to delight in countering it with stories and statistics showing women as perpetrators of crime and violence.

But equality feminists are not all grimness and nay-saying. They have a playful side, reveling in their nonconformity. They demonstrate their sexual hipness (distinct from humorless and anti-sex feminists) in satirical sexual send-ups and sex-role parodies. The *Women's Quarterly* is especially prone to titillating "political incorrectness" on the subject of women and sex. I might find such an in-your-face style appealing if it were not accompanied by a right-wing political agenda that rests on an assumption of a very smart and competent "us" sticking it to the feminists—the backward and wimpish "them."

As noted above, there is surprisingly little cross-fertilization within or among the sectors of the antifeminist women's movement. Each sector talks to itself, the media, and the sector of the right to which it relates. For instance, rightist academic women don't relate well to the Phil Gramm (R-TX), Trent Lott (R-MS), Jesse Helms (R-NC) anti-intellectual right-wing politics of the new Republicans. Their ambitions lie within academia, though they do promote their message publicly through the media.

In fifteen years of observation, I have never seen Phyllis Schlafly and Beverly LaHaye together in the same room. I have never heard or seen them refer to each other. I have never seen the Women's Freedom Network tell its members about Eagle Forum or Concerned Women for America. In fact, in *Neither Victim Nor Enemy*, Rita Simon, the organizational head and prime mover of WFN, misspelled Beverly LaHaye's name.[29]

THE EQUALITY FEMINIST WORLDVIEW

Equality feminists are so individualistic that they can hardly be said to share a worldview. Only a limited number of generalizations apply, and even those must be qualified. The Women's Freedom Network differs from the Independent Women's Forum in both style and content. Further, the Women's Freedom Network claims support from women who are not ideologically aligned with them, adding confusion to any attempt to map their ideological underpinnings.[30]

WFN's publication, *Neither Victim Nor Enemy*, is an attempt to explain the ideology behind the organization. Rita Simon edited the volume and contributes an essay. But, beyond a vague adherence to the title's message, it is hard to find much consistency among the volume's essays.

The authors share a radical individualism that does not see gender as a politically important characteristic. They all support the libertarian ideals of self-reliance, a minimal state, and free-market capitalism. They are ideologically distinct from the traditional women of the Christian Right because they support individual choice on social issues such as reproductive freedom and drug legalization. However, articles in the publications of both WFN and IWF contradict these generalizations.

One important basis for the antifeminism of equality feminists is their political opposition to liberalism and their almost religious belief that the free-market system will protect and promote them. It is little wonder that organizations such as CWA, with its conservative Christian beliefs, attract more women of color than does WFN, with its belief in the free market. Women of color have not been rewarded, indeed have hardly been included, in the free market. Further, the equality feminists' emphasis on formal education and membership in a profession excludes women of any race whose class status does not match that image.

Despite their elite, professional tone, equality feminists promote the lifestyle of what they call the "new traditionalist" woman. Thoroughly modern, she chooses to stay at home to raise her children, since she is too smart to fall for the idea that she can "do it all." She jokes about sex, answers frankly her children's questions about condoms, and is *never* a doormat to her husband.

As a feminist and a lesbian, I am under attack from both conservative Christian antifeminists and equality feminists, but I am more deeply offended by the equality feminists. I am offended by their elitism, especially when they promote themselves as intellectuals whose scholarly rigor is sharper than that of "fuzzy-headed," "sophomoric" feminists. I am put off by their hip, smug tone—whether delivering sarcastic critiques of received feminist wisdom, or spoofing with their in-crowd humor. They never acknowledge the hand-up they received from the women's movement, preferring to see their success in the male-dominated professional world as completely of their own doing.

But I am most offended by the fact that the equality feminists don't just attack feminists; they attack women—denigrating women and elevating men with equal vigor. They make the case that they are indistinguishable from men by demonstrating that women are not a defensible lot. They delight in painting women as just as aggressive, malicious, violent, deceitful, and oppressive as men. In some cases, they seem to imply that women are morally and ethically inferior to men.

Rather than representing a more mature version of feminism, as equality feminists claim, they strike me as a throwback to an earlier time, when very few women made it into the ranks of the professions and those who did were often contemptuous of other women. As is still often true, solidarity with other women is a formula for failure in a male-dominated workplace. Equality feminists have joined the male club, flashing their membership card at every opportunity and crossing the threshold of decency in the process. When they attack feminist work against sexual harassment by arguing that feminists exaggerate its importance (and men are oppressed as a result), they are absolutely in character.[31]

PROMISE KEEPERS

The model of family life promoted by Christian Right and secular right organizations depends on a caring husband and father who is a good provider and a faithful mate to his wife. The role of a traditional wife may require her to be subordinate, submissive, and secondary to her husband, but I understand its appeal for conservative women. It is part of a model of family life that guarantees one type of stability, security, and predictability in an uncertain world.

Throughout the 1980s and 1990s, when the traditional family model was heavily promoted by the right, I wondered if these husbands existed. Was there an enormous silent majority of family men who took their family responsibilities seriously and met the expectations created for them by right-wing antifeminist leaders?

Apparently not, because soon the leadership of the right identified the responsible male as the missing ingredient in the traditional family formula. At the outset of the Reagan Administration, right-wing economist George Gilder had promised that with marriage, children, and employment, men would be driven to be responsible.[32] But capitalism was making it hard to be an adequate provider; family life can be stifling for men as well as women; and sexist attitudes, which cross lines of class, race, religion and ideology, provide an ideal atmosphere for infidelity and shirking family responsibilities.

In this context, Promise Keepers (PK) has been a popular and effective addition to the right's infrastructure. Founded in 1990 with support from Focus on the Family and other Christian Right organizations, Promise Keepers is a mass-based evangelical men's organization known for its huge stadium rallies, attended by millions of men across the country. Its stated mission is to serve as "a Christ-centered ministry to unite men through vital relationships to become godly influences in their world." Its founder, former University of Colorado football coach Bill McCartney, came to the project with a history of anti-abortion and anti-gay activism.

Promise Keepers encourages men, when they attend a rally, to become born-again if they are not already, and preaches responsibility toward their families, guided by a literal reading of the Bible. PK is hostile to mainstream Protestant denominations, seeing true Christianity in independent fundamentalist evangelical churches. Though the Christian Right's political agenda is not explicitly promoted at PK rallies, the Promise Keepers serves much the same role as Concerned Women for America in providing a massive pool of recruits to that agenda. But PK uses none of the spiteful rhetoric of CWA. It is a softer, kinder version of Christian Right recruitment.

In 1997, at the height of its popularity and influence, Promise Keepers held a "million man march" called "Stand in the Gap" in Washington, D.C. Echoing the 1995 Million Man March called by Rev. Louis Farrakhan's Nation of Islam, PK organizers rallied a huge crowd of mostly white men and boys to its free, all-day outdoor rally. Speaker after speaker made veiled references to the millennium, and exhorted men to put their spiritual and domestic houses in order by being better husbands, fathers, and church members. Stand in the Gap was a media success, but it bankrupted Promise Keepers and launched an organizational crisis from which it is slowly emerging at the end of the 1990s.

Promise Keepers offers hope to conservative Christian women that it will make their husbands better family men. In return, Promise Keepers men require that their wives adhere to the traditional female role of helpmate. The PK leadership points to the Bible as the authority on the role of women, especially the famous quote from Ephesians 5:22–24: "A husband is the head of his wife, as Christ is the head and the Savior of the church. . . . Wives should always put their husbands first, as the church puts Christ first."

More than a dozen evangelical Christian women's organizations have appeared in the wake of Promise Keepers, such as Promise Reapers, Women's Ministry Network, and Women's Aglow Fellowship. Promise Reapers' principal activity is its newsletter *Adam's Rib*, designed to encourage, network, and support Christian women, especially the wives of Promise Keepers. Women's Ministry Network describes its purpose as "to enhance the efforts of Christian women and organizations whose calling is to evangelize, build up, or mobilize women across the globe, for the sake of the Gospel." And Women's Aglow Fellowship is a loose-knit organization of fundamentalist evangelical women whose culture, according to R. Marie Griffiths, a student of religion who spent two years researching Women's Aglow, is not unlike that of feminist support groups or rap groups.[33] Some women's evangelical groups are directly linked to Promise Keepers, and others are more independent. All are somewhat ephemeral, lacking the large budget and impressive organizing bureaucracy of Promise Keepers.

As is true of the men of Promise Keepers, it is hard to categorize the women who join organizations such as Women's Aglow, except to say that they are devout Christians struggling with living in a secular, materialistic world. Certainly they accept their assigned role as helpmates to their husbands. But they are not necessarily as vehemently antifeminist as the members of Concerned Women for America or Eagle Forum. Religion Professor Brenda E. Brasher, who conducted in-depth interviews with the women of two fundamentalist evangelical churches, concludes that "to Christian fundamentalist women, the restrictive religious identity they embrace improves their ability to direct the course of their lives and empowers them in their relationship with others."[34] One of Brasher's interviewees quotes Ephesians 4:25: "A husband should love his wife as much as Christ loved the church and gave his life for it."[35]

However, a strong commitment to the traditional family and to its centrality in material and spiritual life is true of nearly all conservative Christian women. So, when the Southern Baptist Convention amended its essential statement of beliefs in 1998 to include a declaration that a woman should "submit herself graciously" to her husband's leadership and that her husband should "provide for, protect and lead his family," huge numbers of conservative Christian women could support that amendment wholeheartedly.[36] Preparing women for that acceptance is an important part of the work of right-wing antifeminist women's organizations.

Perhaps irrationally, I am more at ease with the blatantly homophobic women of Concerned Women for America than with the slick, savvy (but much less homophobic) women of the Independent Women's Forum. Members of each group see themselves as morally superior to me and feel they have correctly analyzed the source of my political wrongheadedness. Sometimes I am unnerved, even frightened, to see what intense intolerance flows from the traditional and religious beliefs of women of the Christian Right. But I can be equally unnerved to see equality feminists take the style and language of feminism and twist it to attack feminism, women, and the larger progressive struggle. They are privileged white women who have built careers on either denigrating or patronizing other middle-class white women, and who ignore low-income, victimized, and marginalized women of all races. When men have friends like these, they can be comfortable with their sexism. The antifeminist women's movement will always be there to support them.

Chapter 4

CONSTRUCTING HOMOPHOBIA:
THE RIGHT'S ATTACK ON GAY RIGHTS

've been called a racist, a sexist, and homophobic. I wear those labels as badges of honor." This statement was made by David Bradley, a right-wing member of the Texas State Board of Education when he spoke at the 1998 annual conference of Eagle Forum. To this audience, which applauded his statement, Bradley is a hero—an audacious fighter for traditional Christian values in the face of the "sell-out" politics of conservatives like Texas Governor George W. Bush.

David Bradley, who is proud of his homophobia, is a minor figure when compared with the professional right-wingers who have built their careers on opposing gay rights. He is relatively unknown outside Texas, unlike Gary Bauer, Rev. Donald Wildmon, Rev. Louis Sheldon, Paul Weyrich, Rev. Jerry Falwell, Dr. James Dobson, or Rev. Pat Robertson, whose campaigns against homosexuality are national in scope. But Bradley's words are important precisely because he is *not* a national figure. He is an example of the grassroots mobilization of the Christian Right. By bringing the right's revolution to a state administrative body, he and several other Christian Right colleagues on the Texas State Board of Education caused chaos and political paralysis. He has disrupted Board of Education meetings with various publicity stunts, such as publicly ripping the cover off an algebra book that he considered "mediocre." He consistently unites with four other Republican "social conservatives" on the Board to block secular curricula, protesting, for instance, textbooks that promote Darwin's theory as the explanation for evolution.[1]

Hundreds, perhaps thousands of David Bradleys work today at the state and local level. Although some promote the entire range of conservative Christian values, it is rare to find any "pro-family" conservative Christian who does not place opposition to gay rights high on his or her list of "issues not to be compromised." And they work in a highly charged and contested environment of public opinion. With the exception of the issue of abortion, no issue divides the U.S. public more starkly than homosexuality.[2]

The right has made its attack on gay rights a centerpiece of its "traditional values" agenda, which now rivals the right's anti-choice campaign for importance within the panoply of social issues. This attack takes many forms: state and local level anti-gay initiatives; laws that prohibit gay marriage or domestic partnership; opposition to lesbians and gay men in the military; and opposition to school programs that attempt to reduce homophobia. Further, the Christian Right has mounted two broad-based movements that use softer rhetoric and a less confrontational style to oppose homosexuality—Promise Keepers and the "ex-gay" movement.

Lesbians and gay men became a serious target of right-wing organizing in the 1970s, when activists within the gay rights movement gained greater visibility and began to frame gay rights as an issue of personal freedom.[3] The right responded by developing a counter-movement to oppose gay rights. Its central strategy has been to mount anti-gay ballot initiatives at the state and local levels. These ballot questions, all aiming in one way or another to restrict the civil rights of lesbians, gay men and, more recently, bisexuals, have kept the right's anti-gay agenda in the public spotlight. The earliest such referendum was in Boulder, Colorado, in 1974, where a municipal gay civil rights law was repealed. In the 1970s and 1980s, local gay civil rights laws were overturned by referenda in St. Paul, Eugene, Wichita, Duluth, Houston, and a number of other cities and towns. Since 1990, the pace has accelerated, with contradictory results. St. Paul and San Francisco, where referenda had overturned earlier gay civil rights laws, saw new gay rights laws upheld. Colorado's anti-gay Amendment 2 passed in November 1992, but was struck down by the U.S. Supreme Court in 1996. Statewide anti-gay initiatives were defeated in Oregon (in 1992 and again in 1994) and in Idaho. At the same time, anti-gay forces in Oregon shifted their focus to the local level, passing anti-gay ballot questions in twenty-six (mostly small) towns in 1993 and 1994.

A mix of gay rights advances and setbacks has continued throughout the 1990s. In 1998, Maine became the first state to repeal its gay rights law, but Florida's Miami-Dade County Commission voted to reinstate the gay rights protections that Anita Bryant had successfully overturned in 1977. Local governments across the country passed two gay rights bills, but defeated five. By 1999, according to the Human Rights Campaign, eleven states had passed anti-discrimination laws protecting lesbians and gay men. It seems that, though every advance is contested, the extension of civil rights protections to gay people is slowly gaining political ground.

By the end of 1999, no doubt more states and localities will witness struggles over new anti-gay legislation; more legal challenges to successful anti-gay ballot questions will percolate up to the Supreme Court; and the map of local pro- and anti-gay legislation will have changed in subtle ways. The attack on gay rights is a popular and effective issue for the right. For that reason, it is unlikely that it will be abandoned within the foreseeable future. More likely, the right will further institutionalize its anti-gay attack by strengthening the institutions that carry it out.

HISTORICAL BACKGROUND

The gay rights movement in the United States is often traced to June 27, 1969, in New York City, when police raided a Greenwich Village bar, the Stonewall Inn, and bar patrons rebelled in protest.[4] Seven years later, in 1976 in Dade County, Florida, Anita Bryant led the first religious campaign against gay rights. Run by Bryant, her husband Bob Green, and a fellow rightist named Ed Rowe, who went on to head the Church League of America briefly and later, Christian Mandate, it opposed a vote by Dade County commissioners to prohibit discrimination against gay men and lesbians in housing, public accommodation, and employment. By promoting a successful referendum to repeal the commissioners' vote, Bryant's campaign gained strength and notoriety.

Anita Bryant inspired a similar 1977 campaign in California, where California State Senator John Briggs, who had worked with her in Miami, sponsored the "California Defend Our Children Initiative," in reaction to a 1975 California law preventing local school boards from firing teachers for homosexuality. This binding initiative, on the general election ballot in November 1978, provided for charges against school teachers and others advocating, encouraging, or publicly and "indiscreetly" engaging in homosexuality. It prohibited the hiring and required the firing of lesbians and gay men if the school board deemed them "unfit." The initiative failed, but California Defend Our Children Executive Director Rev. Louis Sheldon, now head of the Anaheim-based organization Traditional Values, would remain a leading figure in anti-gay organizing.[5]

Bryant's anti-homosexual campaign ended in 1979 with the collapse of her two organizations, Anita Bryant Ministries and Protect America's Children, which were hampered by a lack of political sophistication. Contemporary techniques now used to influence the political system—direct mail, computer technology, religious television ministries—were not available to Bryant. Also, since few religious fundamentalists and evangelicals were then interested in the political sphere, they were not active in political campaigns such as hers. Bryant herself was plagued by personal problems, especially a divorce, and her organizations were not able to respond effectively to a pro–gay rights boycott that targeted Florida's orange industry because she was a major spokesperson for the industry.

With the 1980 election of Ronald Reagan, the New Right launched a more sophisticated anti-gay campaign under the umbrella of the "traditional values" agenda. This "second" anti-gay campaign has been far more successful than those of the 1970s. Planned at the national level and carried out by at least fifteen large national organizations, this campaign has reflected an in-depth understanding of the political system and has drawn on innovative techniques and shrewd strategies.

THE NEW RIGHT'S ANTI-GAY CAMPAIGN

The New Right's anti-gay organizing has had several marked successes. It has constructed local-level anti-gay campaigns that appear to be exclusively grassroots efforts, when they actually are guided by major national organizations. It has increased the impact of each New Right organization's efforts by building networks and coalitions among them and by coordinating political campaigns. In many cases, it has camouflaged the religious basis of its organizing by highlighting the more secular theme of "defense of the family." And it has used stereotyping of lesbians and gay men, whom it characterizes as white and middle-class, to insert a wedge between the gay rights movement and low-income people and people of color, irrespective of income level.

An important event in launching the New Right's anti-gay campaign was the publication of Enrique T. Rueda's massive 1982 book, *The Homosexual Network*, a hostile examination of the organizations, activities, and ideology of the gay rights movement.[6] Rueda directs much of his critique of homosexual organizations at their liberalism. A native of Cuba and a Catholic theologian, he is also interested in the moral dimension of homosexuality and the offense against the Church that he sees in its practice.

In 1987, the Free Congress Foundation, which had sponsored Rueda's book, condensed and updated it to include the AIDS crisis. In its earliest days, AIDS in the United States was almost exclusively confined to the gay male community. The new book, *Gays, AIDS and You* by Michael Schwartz and Enrique Rueda, stands as a formative work in the right's analysis of homosexuality in the context of the AIDS crisis. Its introduction illustrates clearly the link between the book and the spate of subsequent anti-gay initiatives:

> The homosexual movement is nothing less than an attack on our traditional, pro-family values. And now this movement is using the AIDS crisis to pursue its political agenda. This in turn, threatens not only our values but our lives. . . . They are loved by God as much as anyone else. This we believe while affirming the disordered nature of their sexual condition and the evil nature of the acts this condition leads to, and while fully committed to the proposition that homosexuals should not be entitled to special treatment under the law. That would be tantamount to rewarding evil.[7]

Significantly, Rueda wrote his two important critiques of the gay rights movement at the suggestion of, and under the sponsorship of, Paul Weyrich and the Free Congress Foundation, which Weyrich directs. FCF's early and important work on the issue of homosexuality foreshadowed a national campaign to highlight homosexuality as a threat to the well-being of U.S. society. Weyrich, a cofounder of the Heritage Foundation, was more astute than many in the New Right in his early appreciation of the potential of anti-gay themes in building the success of the movement. But he was not alone in understanding the appeal of this issue in right-wing organizing.

As early as 1978, Tim LaHaye, "family counselor," author, husband of Beverly LaHaye of Concerned Women for America, and prominent leader in both the pro-family and religious right components of the New Right, published *The Unhappy Gays*.[8] In 1983, Jerry Falwell's Moral Majority sent out at least three mailings that highlighted the threat of homosexuality and AIDS. In a similar vein, Robert G. Grant's organization, Christian Voice, used the threat of homosexuality as a major theme in a late-1970s fund-raising letter that began, "I am rushing you this urgent letter because the children in your neighborhood are in danger." [9] And Phyllis Schlafly of Eagle Forum, grande dame of the pro-family movement, made heavy use of the accusation of lesbianism in her early 1980s attacks on pro–Equal Rights Amendment organizers.[10]

Another significant figure during this period was anti-gay activist Dr. Paul Cameron, who was director of the Institute for the Scientific Investigation of Sexuality in Lincoln, Nebraska, in the early 1980s, and is now chairperson of the Family Research Institute in Washington, D.C. Cameron has encouraged punitive measures against people with AIDS. In 1983 the American Psychological Association removed Cameron from its membership rolls "for a violation of the Preamble to the Ethical Principles of Psychologists."[11] Despite being discredited by reputable social scientists, psychologists, and psychoanalysts, Cameron has served as an "expert" on homosexuality at numerous right-wing and religious right conferences, and was hired as a consultant on AIDS by California's William Dannemeyer, then a Republican Assemblyman.[12] Cameron has been supported by the Free Congress Foundation, which, in 1983, distributed copies of his Model Sexuality Statute.

As the 1980s unfolded and the New Right achieved substantial gains on economic, military, and foreign policy issues, abortion continued to be the central issue in its traditional values agenda.[13] Although the campaign against homosexuality was not a major focus in the mid-1980s, the New Right never repudiated it. Within the New Right there was ideological agreement that homosexuality should be met with alarm and loathing and that the gains made by the gay rights movement were a threat to "family values."

COLORADO'S AMENDMENT 2

In the late 1980s, three issues reinvigorated the New Right's anti-gay activism: the gay rights movement's success in obtaining gay rights ordinances, bills, and initiatives at the local level and in state legislatures; the promotion of school curriculum reform and school counseling programs that reflected a greater acceptance of lesbians, gay men, and bisexuals, such as Project 10 in Southern California; and public funding of what the right has termed "homoerotic" art. In each of these areas, anti-gay activists have represented their efforts to roll back gay rights advances as grassroots efforts, mounted by outraged citizens stirred to action by local manifestations of "gay power." While local groups did and do exist, their power and effectiveness is enormously enhanced by the technical assistance provided by the right's *national* organizations. It is good political strategy to claim that voters in any particular state suddenly realize that gay rights threatens their well-being and then create an anti-gay initiative in order to face down the "gay agenda." What actually occurs, however, is that a small group of local rightists launch an anti-gay effort that powerful national organizations then supply with training, money, and a host of right-wing perks, such as legal advice and nationally known speakers, making it appear more spontaneous and widespread than it is.

Colorado's Amendment 2 provides a case study of the effective involvement of national right-wing groups in a state-level initiative. It also served as a testing ground for the right, which enabled the movement to experiment with such themes as "no special rights." Many of the right's tactics in the Amendment 2 campaign have become standard fare in anti-gay organizing.

Amendment 2 was a statewide ballot initiative designed to amend the

Colorado Constitution. The Amendment would have repealed existing gay rights ordinances in various Colorado cities and forbidden passage of such ordinances in the future, at the local or state level. In the early 1990s, it was a major national story, occupying a central place in the media's coverage of the right's "family values agenda." Jim Woodall, former vice president of Concerned Women for America, has called it "the *Roe v. Wade* of the homosexual issue."[14] Placed on the ballot in Colorado in 1991, it was passed by the voters in 1992. A challenge to its constitutionality, *Evans v. Romer*, was quickly brought by a legal team headed by Denver attorney Jean Dubofsky, with crucial help from Suzanne Goldberg of the Lambda Legal Defense and Education Fund. Although Colorado Governor Roy Romer personally opposed Amendment 2, Colorado's attorney general was legally required to defend the Amendment's constitutionality before Judge Jeffrey Bayless of the Colorado District Court.

As executive director of Political Research Associates, I was asked by the legal team bringing the challenge to serve as an expert witness on the role of the right in supporting the amendment. Political Research Associates prepared a background paper that detailed the strategies and tactics used by the right and analyzed the ideological roots of the right's arguments. I testified at the nationally televised hearings held on the legal challenge.

It was clear, starting with the hearing's opening arguments, that I was considered to be the "wild card" of the upcoming testimony. Much of the testimony by other witnesses was fairly predictable: the mayors of Aspen, Denver, and Boulder would testify that they opposed the overturning of their cities' gay rights ordinances; the psychologists for the state would testify that gay sexuality was pathological; psychologists for the challengers would testify that gay sexuality was "normal" and should not be a basis for discrimination. But, among the attorneys for the state, there seemed to be general nervousness over what I would say.

After I survived a challenge to my status as an expert by the attorney representing the state, one of the attorneys for the challenging legal team questioned me. Using the PRA background paper as a guide, he asked pertinent questions about our research findings, allowing me to describe the role played by national right-wing organizations in mounting

Amendment 2, as well as to establish that a religious agenda motivated the local organizers.

Shortly after the conclusion of the hearings, Judge Bayless struck down Amendment 2, a decision upheld in 1996 by the Supreme Court. When handing down his decision, he stated that he had not taken any of my testimony into account. However, we were able to get into the public record a fairly complete description of the national forces behind the Amendment and statements made by anti-gay organizers that revealed their hidden right-wing Christian agenda. Now, a number of years later I see, as I only suspected then, that Amendment 2 established the organizing template for the right's subsequent anti-gay initiatives. The right still uses the practice of demonizing lesbian, gay, bisexual, (and now, transgender) people—whipping up resentment and fear among voters, and camouflaging the conservative Christian basis of its opposition to gay rights in state- and local-level anti-gay organizing.

Colorado for Family Values (CFV), the local sponsor of Amendment 2, was founded by Coloradans Kevin Tebedo and Tony Marco. It became almost inactive following the overturning of Amendment 2, but in the late 1990s it has made a comeback. In 1992, it promoted itself as a grass-roots group, although its tactics, success, and power largely resulted from support from the right's national anti-gay campaign. Five of the national organizations active in anti-gay organizing were represented on CFV's executive and advisory boards: the Traditional Values Coalition, Focus on the Family, Summit Ministries, Concerned Women for America, and Eagle Forum. Rev. Pat Robertson's Christian Coalition was not officially represented on the board of CFV, but had a strong presence in Colorado and was ubiquitous nationally in anti-homosexual organizing. These same players are the organizational leaders of the Christian Right's anti-gay campaign at the end of the 1990s.

Colorado for Family Values has maintained adamantly that national religious or political groups did not coordinate its strategy.[15] However, according to People for the American Way, a Washington, D.C., organization that monitors the right: "The Religious Right's anti-gay vendetta is not, as its leaders often claim, a spontaneous outpouring of concern about gay issues. Theirs is a carefully orchestrated political effort, with a unified set of messages and tactics, that is deliberately designed to foster division and intolerance."[16] A review of the involvement of national organizations in Colorado's Amendment 2 campaign supports this analysis.

REV. LOUIS SHELDON'S TRADITIONAL VALUES

Traditional Values (often called the Traditional Values Coalition), based in Anaheim, California, is headed by Rev. Louis Sheldon, a former aide to Pat Robertson who shares much of Robertson's interest in the legal codification of moral issues. In 1988 he led the opposition to Project 10, a counseling program for lesbian and gay adolescents in the Los Angeles school system. In 1986 and 1988, he endorsed a California anti-homosexual initiative sponsored by far-right extremist Lyndon La-Rouche that sought, in effect, to require quarantine for people with AIDS. Sheldon himself has been accused of advocating "cities of refuge" for people with HIV infection.[17] He was a veteran of anti-gay campaigns well before he supported Amendment 2.

Rev. Sheldon convened a 1990 conference in Washington, D.C., that he billed as a "national summit meeting on homosexuality." A dominant theme of the conference was that homosexuals have, since the 1960s, been seeking "special protection over and above the equal rights already given to all Americans." This theme would later appear in Colorado as the central theme of Colorado for Family Values' promotion of Amendment 2.

FOCUS ON THE FAMILY

The 1991 arrival in Colorado Springs of Dr. James Dobson and his organization, Focus on the Family, was an important catalyst for Colorado for Family Values. CFV had already led a successful campaign against a local gay rights ordinance. Focus on the Family, however, brought to Colorado Springs a tremendous influx of resources and sophisticated political experience. It arrived with 750 employees (and has since added another five hundred) and an annual budget of nearly $70 million, including a $4 million grant from the El Pomar Foundation to buy fifty acres in Colorado Springs. Focus on the Family is indeed a national organization. While it had no official ties to CFV, it offered "advice," and several Focus on the Family employees, such as public policy representative Randy Hicks, have served on CFV advisory boards.[18] Focus on the Family gave CFV an in-kind donation worth $8,000.

With a background in pediatrics, James Dobson is best known as an advocate of traditional discipline and corporal punishment for children. However, his organization has also been heavily involved in anti-homosexual organizing. In 1988, Focus on the Family activated a dormant Washington, D.C., arm called the Family Research Council, headed by Gary L. Bauer. The Family Research Council distributed a "homosexual packet," available through Focus on the Family, which contained the lengthy document, "The Homosexual Agenda: Changing Your Community and Nation." This detailed guide for activists includes a section titled "Starting an Initiative." In October 1992, the Family Research Council separated from Focus on the Family for tax purposes, in order for FRC to have more freedom to lobby.[19] Its director, Gary Bauer, has since become the leading anti-gay voice within the Christian Right.

SUMMIT MINISTRIES

Summit Ministries of Manitou Springs, Colorado, is a little-known Christian Right organization whose work is national in scope. Founded in the early 1960s, it specializes in educational materials and summer youth retreats. Its president is Rev. David A. Noebel, formerly a prominent preacher in Rev. Billy James Hargis's Christian Anti-Communism Crusade. Noebel is on the advisory board of CFV. As early as 1977, he authored *The Homosexual Revolution,* in which he claimed that "homosexuality rapidly is becoming one of America's most serious social problems." He has also written several books claiming that rock and roll and soul music are part of a communist plot to corrupt U.S. youth. Summit Ministries later published *AIDS: Acquired Immune Deficiency Syndrome: A Special Report,* coauthored by David Noebel, Wayne C. Lutton, and Paul Cameron.[20] Virtually every issue of the *Journal,* Summit Ministries' monthly newsletter, has contained several anti-homosexual entries.

Noebel's history with Rev. Billy James Hargis's Christian Anti-Communism Crusade helps to explain the friendly relationship between Summit Ministries and the John Birch Society. Noebel was a member of the John Birch Society until at least 1987, and for many years Summit Ministries took out full-page advertisements for its summer youth retreats in *Review of the News* and *American Opinion*, two John Birch Society publications. Both the Christian Anti-Communism Crusade and the John Birch Society were Old Right organizations of the 1950s. Asserting that communism was rampant in the United States, both organizations believed that communists manipulated the civil rights movement, that the National Council of Churches promoted communism, and that communists controlled the United Nations. In 1962, Rev. Billy James Hargis purchased an old resort hotel in Manitou Springs, which, renamed The Summit, became a retreat and anticommunism summer college.[21]

Summit Ministries is also politically close to Dr. James Dobson and Focus on the Family. Dr. Dobson leads seminars at Summit Ministries, and his endorsement of Summit's work was prominent in the ministry's 1992 material promoting its thirtieth anniversary.

CONCERNED WOMEN FOR AMERICA

Touting itself as the largest women's organization in America, CWA has, since its founding, described homosexuality as a sin. Its literature consistently associates feminism with lesbianism in an attempt to smear feminists in the eyes of conservative Christians. CWA was represented on the Colorado for Family Values advisory board by the president of its Colorado chapter, Bert Nelson.

CWA distributes a pamphlet written by Beverly LaHaye, titled "The Hidden Homosexual Agenda," which rallies Christians with the call: "Homosexuality is not at all normal. It is sin. The Bible clearly tells us not to practice such immorality. . . . Now is the time for Christians to stop the hidden homosexual agenda."[22] CWA also repackaged a treatise by Tony Marco, titled "The Homosexual Deception: Making Sin a Civil Right," as a pamphlet and widely distributed it. Marco, cofounder of CFV, had filed the treatise with the State of Colorado as evidence supporting Amendment 2.[23] In this case, to give a local activist his due, we see the local group creating material that a national organization then used—a reversal of the usual pattern.

Former Vice President Jim Woodall was the resident CWA "expert" on "the gay agenda" in the 1990s. In his workshops on the subject, he promoted an image of lesbians and gay men as predatory "recruiters" of young children into "the homosexual lifestyle." Folded into the workshops were excerpts from *It's Elementary*, a video by film-makers Deborah Chasnoff and Helen Cohen, which documents classroom teachers working with elementary school children to demystify homosexuality. In August 1998, CWA sent a direct-mail appeal opposing President Bill Clinton's Executive Order 114478, which added "sexual orientation" to categories the federal government may not use as a basis for discrimination. In her appeal, LaHaye argued that the Executive Order would force the federal government to employ and give "special job protections" to people who have sexual orientations other than homosexual, such as "people who: make lewd phone calls; expose themselves to others; and engage in prostitution."[24]

EAGLE FORUM

Phyllis Schlafly's Eagle Forum, based in St. Louis, Missouri, is another national organization whose local affiliate was represented on the advisory board of CFV. Schlafly is known for her successful campaign against the Equal Rights Amendment, where she used the threat of homosexual and lesbian privileges as a central tenet of her opposition. She maintained that the ERA would promote gay rights—leading to the legitimization of same-sex marriages, the protection of gay and lesbian rights in the military, the voiding of sodomy laws, and the protection of the rights of persons with AIDS.[25] Eagle Forum continues to play a role in opposing gay and lesbian rights.

THE CHRISTIAN COALITION

While not playing as direct a role in the Amendment 2 campaign as these five, other national groups have been active in the right's broader anti-gay campaign. The most prominent of these is Rev. Pat Robertson's Christian Coalition. Robertson, longtime host of the cable television program *The 700 Club* and prominent leader within the Christian Right, ran unsuccessfully in the 1988 Republican presidential primaries. In October 1989, he used the 1.9 million names he had collected during his 1988 campaign to identify 175,000 key activists and donors and launch the Christian Coalition. Under the leadership of its first director, the youthful and dynamic Ralph Reed, the new Coalition's stated goal was "to build the most powerful political force in American politics."

The national Christian Coalition headquarters urged the 175,000 "key" activists to establish Christian Coalition chapters in their precincts. The organization identified five goals: 1) Build a grassroots network using professional field organizers and training schools; 2) construct a lobbying organization to work at the national and state levels in every state and Washington, D.C.; 3) create a mass media outreach program; 4) create a legal arm to defend the gains made in state legislatures from challenge by the American Civil Liberties Union; and 5) develop a prayer network to unite all evangelical and pro-family voters.

Christian Coalition training tapes teach activists to fight those forces pursuing "an agenda of chaos." An early videotape used homosexual scenes to illustrate the moral decline of America. Although opposition to homosexuality has always been a commitment of the Christian Coalition, it was the 1990 political battle over a gay rights initiative in Broward County, Florida, that moved the anti-homosexual agenda to prominence within the organization. In its literature, the Christian Coalition took credit for "spearheading" the initiative's defeat. It claims to have "led the charge" and "won a major political victory." Robertson called on Christian Coalition members to "duplicate this success in your city and state and throughout the nation." [26]

By 1992, the organization had grown dramatically. Ralph Reed claimed 250,000 members in forty-nine states and $13 million in the bank. The Christian Coalition launched an election year get-out-the-vote effort which included "in-pew" registration at churches, the distribution of up to 40 million "voter guides," and the use of computer-assisted telephone banks to help elect favored candidates in key races.[27]

Reed didn't hide the fact that he worked surreptitiously. "I want to be invisible," he told one reporter. "I do guerrilla warfare. I paint my face and travel at night. You don't know it's over until you're in a body bag. You don't know until election night." [28]

Colorado for Family Values is not an affiliate of, nor is it funded by, the Christian Coalition. However, the Oregon Citizen's Alliance, the group leading the anti-homosexual initiative campaigns in Oregon, is a Christian Coalition affiliate. And even in Colorado, the Christian Coalition played an indirect but important role in supporting the Amendment 2 campaign. The National Legal Foundation of Chesapeake, Virginia (a conservative Christian legal organization founded by Pat Robertson and funded by Robertson's Christian Broadcasting Network, but no longer affiliated with Robertson), gave advice to Colorado for Family Values as early as 1991, long before Amendment 2 was on the ballot. The consultation was intended to help CFV formulate ballot language that would survive legal and political challenges. By the end of 1992, the National Legal Foundation had taken over much of the legal work of CFV.[29]

Several other right-wing organizations are active in the anti-gay movement. These include the Berean League, which is based in St. Paul, Minnesota and publishes Roger J. Magnuson's *Are Gay Rights Right?* Tony Marco used this widely discredited book in the treatise he wrote for Colorado for Family Values. The Berean League also issued a three-page document, "Some Things You May Not Know about Homosexuality," which was circulated in Oregon during the 1992 campaign to promote Oregon's anti-gay Measure 9.

The American Family Association, headed by Rev. Donald Wildmon and based in Tupelo, Mississippi, has an annual budget of $7 million and focuses primarily on profanity, adultery, homosexuality, and other forms of what it deems anti-Christian behavior and language on television. Wildmon has specialized in boycotting the corporate sponsors of TV shows that he dislikes. He also has mobilized his membership against the "pro-gay bias" of the National Endowment for the Arts.[30] In the late 1990s, Wildmon collaborated with Assemblies of God and other Christian Right organizations to boycott the Disney Corporation for films made by Disney and its subsidiaries (*Priest, Dogma, Chasing Amy, Pulp Fiction, Color of Night, Clerks, Chicks in White Satin, Lie Down with Dogs,* and *The House of Yes*), a book published by Disney-owned Hyperion Press (*Growing Up Gay*), and annual "gay and lesbian days" at Disney World— all evidence of Disney's "anti-family" values.[31]

The Rutherford Institute of Manassas, Virginia, a nonprofit legal defense organization that played a role in representing Paula Jones in her lawsuit against President Bill Clinton, spearheaded a 1992 suit in Hawaii to block implementation of the state's new gay rights law. Though it has adopted a more moderate persona in the later 1990s, the Institute has been associated with the far-right fringe of the Christian right; its speakers bureau has included R. J. Rushdoony, a prominent Christian Reconstructionist, who claims the text of the Bible provides the only legitimate basis for civil law. The most zealous wing of Reconstructionism has called for the death penalty for homosexuals, adulterers, and recalcitrant children.

THE "NO SPECIAL RIGHTS" WEDGE

Whereas in the 1992 hearing I testified about the role right-wing organizations played in promoting Amendment 2, another major theme of that hearing was whether the right to be gay is a protected civil right. The state, acting in defense of the Amendment, called several witnesses who testified that homosexuality is a choice, and therefore those who choose it should not be protected from discrimination. The plaintiffs, challenging the Amendment, called witnesses who testified that a gay sexual orientation is predetermined, either biologically or psychologically. Homosexuality, in this case, is an innate characteristic and merits civil rights protections.

This testimony highlighted an important theme in the right's attack on gay rights—the assertion that lesbians and gay men are seeking "special rights" or "special protections." This was the guiding premise behind Anita Bryant's campaign, was raised again by Enrique Rueda in *The Homosexual Network* and *Gays, AIDS and You*, and eventually emerged as the major slogan of the anti-gay ballot campaigns in Colorado, Oregon, and in ongoing anti-gay measures.

The right's distinction between civil rights and "special rights" is meant to establish a contrast between "deserved" and "undeserved" rights. The right argues that, while people of color "suffer" from a characteristic that they cannot freely choose, lesbians and gay men choose a behavior of which society disapproves and must, therefore, live with the consequences—discrimination against them. To justify this mean-spirited withholding of civil rights, the right has created a myth that there is a scarcity of civil rights. Right-wing leaders argue that to recognize the civil rights of an undeserving group diminishes the meaningfulness of protections for other, deserving groups. They raise the specter of multiple undeserving groups, all applying for civil rights protections, causing the very concept of civil rights to become meaningless.

The right's argument is flawed and hypocritical. There is no scarcity of civil rights. People who are gay, for whatever reason, have the right to seek protection from discrimination by arguing that it is their civil right to be gay. Further, civil rights are not assigned only on the basis of physical characteristics that "show." Discrimination often is legally forbidden on the basis of race, ethnicity, religion, or disability, irrespective of whether there are visible manifestations of these protected characteristics. What the right actually objects to is the "immorality" and "sin" of homosexuality, a judgment based on conservative religious beliefs or simple anti-gay bigotry. While anyone has a right to hold homophobic views, the right would have the United States extend legal protections to those who discriminate against lesbians and gay men.

Gay rights ordinances do not provide "special rights," but a guarantee of equal rights for lesbians and gay men. Knowing that to be true, CFV used the slogan "No special rights" only in its public material, not in the legal language of Amendment 2. That decision was made on advice of its legal counsel, the rightist National Legal Foundation (NLF), which advised the group to stay away from the "No special rights" language in formulating the Amendment because it would not pass constitutional tests, but instead to use it as the centerpiece of its publicity campaign. [32] Coloradans were bombarded with advertisements and flyers that drummed home the purposefully misleading message that Amendment 2 simply reversed the unfair granting of "special rights" through gay rights ordinances.

A widely distributed video titled *Gay Rights, Special Rights* uses the "No special rights" theme in an especially cynical way. The Traditional Values Coalition produced the video in conjunction with Jeremiah Films. By featuring "experts" testifying that granting rights to homosexuals diminishes the rights of African Americans, it implies that there are only limited civil rights to go around, and that homosexuality is a *choice*, whereas skin color is immutable. When right-wing "promotional materials" portray equal protection for lesbians and gay men as granting civil rights to "immoral" individuals, the intention is to drive a wedge between the gay rights movement and people of color, and imply that the two are mutually exclusive. [33]

Gay Rights, Special Rights also portrays lesbians and gay men as an economically privileged group, almost all of whom are white, middle-class professionals. The right portrays lesbians and gay men as wealthy professionals with no childrearing responsibilities and lots of disposable income in order to make them even less deserving of "special rights" and less appealing to working-class and other voters who have little disposable income. In a voice-over on the video, Rev. Louis Sheldon says, "Homosexuals are not . . . homeless people, under bridges, in food lines. These are high income people who want to push their agenda."

In 1992, CFV's Tony Marco claimed in a report published by Focus on the Family that "homosexuals have an average annual household income of $55,430, versus $32,144 for the general population, and $12,166 for disadvantaged African American households." This incorrect characterization of lesbians and gay men as wealthy is intended to inflame sentiment against gay rights. It is impossible to collect comprehensive data on lesbian, gay, bisexual, and transgender people when so many remain in the closet. Anti-gay groups and publications base their data on skewed samples—primarily on surveys taken by gay magazines and magazines that are purchased by higher-income people.[34] More broadly representative research suggests that gay people do not earn more than heterosexuals, and that lesbian, gay, and bisexual people appear to earn less than heterosexuals.[35]

Future anti-gay initiatives will undoubtedly continue the use of the "No special rights" slogan that has proved so effective in both nurturing homophobia and burnishing the image of the anti-gay right. The slogan allows the leaders of the right's campaign to present themselves as the defenders of "deserving" people, such as people of color and working-class people. The tacit implication—that people of color and working-class people are not lesbian or gay—helps create and maintain a wedge of resentment between groups who might otherwise be political allies.[36]

CAMOUFLAGE OF THE CHRISTIAN AGENDA

Three of the four national New Right organizations playing the highest profile role in organizing in support of Colorado's Amendment 2 were explicitly Christian organizations. However, these organizations highlight the religious principles undergirding their anti-homosexual politics only when they are targeting other Christians. When organizing in the wider political arena, they frame their anti-gay organizing as a struggle for secular ends, such as "defense of the family."

This is an important aspect of the religious right's organizing. Since the mid-1980s, when the heavy-handed style of Jerry Falwell's Moral Majority became less popular, the Christian Right has cast its campaigns in terms not so obviously linked to the Bible. Ralph Reed of the Christian Coalition refers to the soft-pedaling of the religious message as "stealth" campaigning.

In the case of the anti-gay campaign, both the secular right and the Christian Right have offered slanderous depictions of "predatory" behavior by "diseased" lesbians and gay men. Various anti-gay campaigns have accused gay people, especially gay men, of eating feces, molesting children, and destroying the family. Many of these characterizations are "documented" by the work of Dr. Paul Cameron and Roger J. Magnuson.[37] Oregon's 1992 anti-gay initiative equates homosexuality with "pedophilia, sadism or masochism." In some explicitly religious attacks gay people are seen as the pawns of Satan. Such representations are widely accepted among many people involved in anti-gay organizing.

Though the right doesn't usually mention the religious basis of its anti-gay fervor, occasionally it becomes explicit. In 1992 Bill McCartney, former football coach and member of the advisory board of Colorado for Family Values, said at a press conference that homosexuality was a "sin" that is "an abomination of almighty God." [38] McCartney went on to found the Promise Keepers. Former Colorado U.S. Representative William Armstrong, who describes himself as having had a "life-changing experience" when he became religious, was chairman of the advisory board of CFV.[39]

Kevin Tebedo, CFV Executive Director, has made the clearest statement of the religious basis for the work of CFV. In a Colorado Springs church, Tebedo said that Amendment 2 is "about whose authority takes precedence in the society in which we live. . . . Is it the authority of God? The authority of the supreme King of Kings and Lord of Lords? You see, we say we should have the separation of church and state, but you see, Jesus Christ is the King of Kings and the Lord of Lords. That is politics; that is rule; that is authority."[40]

In spite of the obvious role of conservative Christian principles in its values, Colorado for Family Values does not refer in its literature to Christianity, biblical admonitions on homosexuality, or religious principles. A large CFV packet of information, dated January 1992, does not mention a religious basis for CFV's work. Finally, the CFV Mission Statement does not mention religion.

In her extensive examination of the legal arguments presented by both the majority decisions and minority dissents in each of five decisions on Amendment 2 handed down by various courts at the state and federal levels, researcher Didi Herman concludes, "Anti-gay measures in the United States are, at their heart, orthodox Christian measures. Arguably, when they become legislation, the establishment clause (the First Amendment, prohibiting the establishment of one religion) is violated." Herman goes on to point out that, ironically, the framers of the constitution are revered by the Christian Right, who ignore the founders' intent to control the passions of the Christian majority of their time and not to institutionalize Christianity as state practice.[41]

NEW PLAYERS/NEW STRATEGIES

The public apparently has tired of the cloak-and-dagger methods of the Christian Right, its good versus evil themes, and the constant negativity of its message. Many journalists read the Republicans' weak showing in the 1998 mid-term elections as a referendum on the harsh style of the Christian Right, its image as a slash-and-burn movement, and a successful campaign by liberals and progressives to paint it as "extremist." But the Christian Right, always adaptable to changes in the political climate, has fashioned a "softer" face in response to evidence of mainstream disenchantment with its acrimonious style.

THE EX-GAY MOVEMENT

Nearly every right-wing organization that played a role in Amendment 2 has signed on to the right's new kinder and gentler anti-gay campaign —ex-gay ministries and reparative therapy. Ex-gay ministries have existed since the 1970s, consistently promoting the notion that through a personal relationship with Jesus Christ, lesbians and gay men can "leave the homosexual life." Reparative therapy, also a long-standing option for "unhappy homosexuals," is a discredited psychological practice that counsels lesbians and gay men who are unhappy with their sexual orientation to help them become straight. The two approaches make up the ex-gay movement.[42]

Until the late 1990s, the ex-gay movement was only a shadowy part of the right. Many Christian and secular right-wing organizations had kept at arms length even those lesbians and gay men struggling to be straight. Gay people sympathetic to the right's politics—overwhelmingly middle-class, white men—have often been treated as an embarrassment, as was the case when Presidential candidate Bob Dole returned a campaign donation made by Log Cabin Republicans, an organization of gay Republicans.

All this changed in July 1998, when the ex-gay movement made a splashy and expensive appearance in the national media with full-page ads in the *New York Times*, the *Washington Post*, the *Chicago Tribune*, the *Wall Street Journal*, the *Los Angeles Times*, and *USA Today*. The ads featured various human-interest personalities, including two stalwarts of ex-gay publicity—Anne Paulk, a white former lesbian who is now in a heterosexual marriage and is a leader of the ex-gay movement, and African American football star Reggie White, a Christian Right spokesperson for the anti-gay campaign. The ads touted the effectiveness of repentance and redemption as Christian "paths out of homosexuality." A predictable spate of media coverage followed their appearance.

The leading ex-gay ministry is Exodus International, a Seattle-based network of more than a hundred individual ex-gay ministries in the United States and internationally. Until the late 1990s, the most notable public story about Exodus was the 1978 defection of two of its founders, Gary Cooper and Michael Busee, who fell in love, left the organization, and, in the early 1990s, went on the talk show circuit to criticize the ex-gay movement.

The umbrella organization for the practice of reparative therapy is the National Association for the Research and Therapy of Homosexuality (NARTH), an organization formed to oppose the 1973 decision by the American Psychological Association to no longer classify homosexuality as an emotional or mental disorder. A network of self-identified "reparative therapists," the organization has aggressively promoted its discredited methods, including placing in major newspapers op-ed pieces that are thinly disguised ads for reparative therapy. Joseph Nicolosi, an early practitioner of reparative therapy, testified in support of Colorado's Amendment 2 during the legal challenge before Judge Jeffrey Bayless.

The ex-gay movement could have tried to pass itself off as an independent, consumer-driven movement with no formal connection to the Christian Right. The newspaper ads, however, make no such claim. They were co-sponsored (at a total cost of over $200,000) by fifteen organizations, including the Christian Coalition, Concerned Women for America, and the American Family Association—Christian Right organizations that had been active in the Amendment 2 campaign. A fourth sponsoring organization, the Family Research Council (FRC), is a lead organization in the right's late-1990s anti-gay campaign. FRC is a spin-off of Focus on the Family, another Christian Right organization that had played a central role in the Amendment 2 campaign.

The ex-gay movement repackages a slogan popularized by Anita Bryant's anti-gay campaign: "Love the sinner, hate the sin." It opens the door to Christian acceptance of homosexuals, so long as they give up, or are trying to give up, the "sin." Giving its homophobia a gentler face, however, is only one of the strategic roles that the ex-gay movement plays for the right. Equally important, the ex-gay movement reinforces the "No special rights" argument. If lesbians and gay men can change, their sexuality is not immutable. The ex-gay movement rebukes gay rights by asserting that gay sexuality is a choice. As such, the right argues, it is not a candidate for civil rights protections.

The right lost no time in deploying its new strategy. In 1998 "family values" forces sponsored a referendum on the Maine ballot to overturn the state's anti-discrimination law. The right campaigned effectively for the referendum through its "Truth Tour" organized by Parents and Friends of Ex-Gays (P-FOX), an ex-gay organization founded in 1995 by Anthony Falzarano—an ex–gay activist based in Washington, D.C.—to counter the effectiveness of Parents, Family, and Friends of Lesbians and Gays (PFLAG). By showcasing ex-gays and parents of ex-gays, the Christian Right bolstered its argument that, because homosexuality is simply behavior-based, it should be protected from discrimination no more than other behavior-based groups, such as smokers. The anti-gay referendum was approved by Maine's voters.

FAMILY RESEARCH COUNCIL

Gary Bauer of the Family Research Council mobilized P-FOX to serve the right's political agenda, providing it with organizational and financial support and sponsoring a press conference in October 1996 to bring P-FOX to the attention of the media. By the end of the 1990s, Bauer has become a star of the Christian Right. A former member of the Reagan Administration, where he served on the White House staff and worked under William Bennett at the U.S. Department of Education, Bauer is a combative and uncompromising strategist. He is considered by some within the right to be an impractical purist and by others to be the hero of the movement. All would agree that he is currently the most active leader in the Christian right's anti-gay campaign.

Bauer has placed himself and FRC at the center of the right's anti-gay campaign. His close relationship with Dr. James Dobson affords him the backing of Dobson's 2.1 million-member, $113 million Focus on the Family empire. *U.S. News and World Report* has called Dobson the leading right-wing figure in the country, stating that he has far "greater reach than either Jerry Falwell or Pat Robertson at the height of their appeal."[43] Bauer is also close to Paul Weyrich, whose importance within the right has not diminished in more than twenty years.

The Family Research Council plays the partisan political hardball that Focus on the Family avoids. This both affords Focus on the Family cover for its tax-exempt status and allows for the smooth coordination of two fronts in the right's family values agenda. Bauer lobbies Congress on issues such as abortion, homosexuality, school prayer, and funding for the National Endowment for the Arts, while Dobson's Focus on the Family serves as a publishing and counseling center to help families restore themselves through conservative evangelical Christian principles. More confrontational and uncompromising with elected representatives than is the Christian Coalition, both Dobson and Bauer are seen by some within the Republican leadership as inexperienced in dealing with Congress.[44] Bauer further irritates some members of Congress with his Campaign for Working Families, a political PAC he created to support "pro-life" and "pro-family" candidates. He often acts as an ideologue who is willing to alienate the Republican Party.[45]

In 1995 FRC broke ground on its new $5 million dollar headquarters in Washington, D.C.[46] In 1998, FRC could boast a membership of 455,000 and a budget of $14 million.[47] Gary Bauer has stated that he would like to see a "self-assured Christianity" in this country. That Christianity includes vehement opposition to gay rights. Bauer is constantly before the public with his anti-gay message—appearing on the lecture circuit, at press conferences called by FRC and other Christian Right organizations, and on television talk shows. Material currently being distributed by FRC includes briefing papers on the anti-gay Defense of Marriage Act (DOMA) and the "high-risk situation" of children of gay parents, as well as papers debunking any research that supports gay rights, including the high rates of gay youth suicide and the existence of a gene found only in gay people. FRC also has published a booklet titled "The Bible and Homosexuality." Nearly half the booklet is devoted to how the "homosexual Christian movement" has "ensnared" churches in debate over gay rights, especially within Protestant denominations. The author concludes: "One of the major grounds of contention in this debate is the ecclesiastical blessing of same-sex unions. . . . If the church allows the integrity of marriage to be compromised and fall by the wayside, with it will collapse the integrity of the family as the cornerstone of human civilization."[48] The booklet provides a list of ex-gay ministries.

ANALYZING THE RIGHT'S ANTI-GAY CAMPAIGN

The leaders who have been steadfast in targeting "practicing homosexuals" have shifted strategies and tactics as new political opportunities open and others close. Each time the right responds to a gay-rights ordinance, or mounts an offensive action to roll back gay rights, such as DOMA, it can call on its vast network of organizations to respond readily with money and support. As a result, the movement can take maximum advantage of a political opportunity, such as President Clinton's attempt to end discrimination against lesbians and gay men in the military.

Some right-wing leaders' arguments are cynical and disingenuous. I have already mentioned one example: the legal advice given by the right-wing National Legal Foundation to Amendment 2 organizers, stating that the language of "special rights" should not be used in the amendment itself because it would not hold up legally, but should be used heavily in "public education" about the Amendment. Another example is the right's depiction of AIDS as the "gay plague," meant to add fear of disease to the already strong fear and sexual anxiety that homosexuality raises among many heterosexuals.[49] The right demonizes lesbians, gay men, bisexuals, and transgender people—never an accepted minority—

and uses them symbolically to create support for its conservative Christian protest movement.

Whether or not this campaign succeeds in its goal of rolling back gay rights, it works well for the right's movement-building. Nearly every right-wing conference I have attended has featured a workshop on "the gay agenda," demonstrating the importance of the issue to the right's organizing. I find in conversations with attendees at these workshops that, though they may find battling "the gays" distasteful, they want their organizations to do that work.

Whipping up fear of "predatory," "child molesting," "flaunting" homosexuals is also a good right-wing fund-raising tactic. When Beverly LaHaye sent an alarmed 1998 direct-mail piece to her members about a pro-gay Executive Order issued by President Bill Clinton, her enclosed donation slip asked the member to "help Concerned Women for America pressure Congress to rescind President Clinton's Executive Order immediately." When the Springs of Life Ministry released the anti-gay video *The Gay Agenda* in 1992, the tape grossed $1.5 million in the first year.[50]

Campaigns also build internal movement cohesion. Because movements are dynamic, leaders rise and fall in prominence. Despite shifts in leadership, the movement's organizations must continue to work together and coordinate their activities in order to maintain an effective campaign. After Ralph Reed left the Christian Coalition, for instance, Gary Bauer emerged as the new, young, ambitious, go-getter "family values" man. Like Reed, Bauer understands the importance of networking. Along with Phyllis Schlafly and Beverly LaHaye, he has been instrumental in creating and setting the agenda for the House of Representatives' Conservative Action Team. He played a similar role in creating another House network, the Family Caucus. The family values agenda and its anti-gay campaign draw together and coordinate a wide range of allies from the movement's pro-family organizations, pushing them to work together on an issue that may not be their central focus.[51]

But the anti-gay campaign is not simply a political ploy to rally the movement, raise money, and win new recruits. It stems from a sincere belief that homosexuality is an abomination because it is a sin against God. The right's secular and religious leaders and strategists embellish that belief with other demonizing assertions: lesbians and gay men are wealthy and influential in government, the media, the arts, and in popular culture, and they pursue a "hidden agenda" that goes far beyond acceptance of the "gay lifestyle" to include recruitment of children and destruction of the family.

Less obvious in the anti-gay campaign is the right's hatred of "secular humanism," which the right uses as shorthand for all that is evil and opposed to God. Secular humanism is a worldview based in reason and science rather than religion. It places humans in charge of their own destiny, rather than assuming that God controls the universe. We can trace the distrust of secular humanism to the turn-of-the-century American nativist right, which believed in a secular humanist conspiracy to undermine the United States. The right linked the purported conspiracy to its extreme fear of communism's undermining effect on both Christianity and the Christian family.[52] Today, the right is focused on liberalism and its "assault on the family," rather than on communism. It is, for the right, the basis for feminism, liberalism, atheism, and immorality. The right sees secular humanists as the morally permissive people who support and approve of gay rights and with whom it is engaged in what Pat Buchanan, at the 1992 Republican National Convention, called America's "culture war." As Paul Weyrich has described it, "Well, first of all, from our point of view, this is really the most significant battle of the age-old conflict between good and evil, between the forces of God and the forces against God, that we have seen in our country."[53]

HOMOPHOBIA AND HATE CRIMES

The brutal 1998 murder of Matthew Shepard, a white gay University of Wyoming student who was driven to a remote site by two men and two women his own age, then beaten and left tied to a fence to die, was widely covered in the mainstream press. The next day the *New York Times* carried a story in which Steven Schwalm, spokesperson for the Family Research Council, responded to the crime by saying, "Hate crime laws have nothing to do with the perpetrators of violent crimes and everything to do with silencing political opposition."[54] Both the Christian Right and the secular right devote enormous resources to spreading the message that homosexuality is a sin, a perversion, a threat to U.S. culture, and a threat to children, and the leadership does nothing to discourage its right-wing followers from acting on it in violent ways.

Matthew Shepard's murder was a tragic and horrifying act. But his murder was not as uncommon as nearly all of the mainstream media coverage implied. While not new, "gay-bashing" is now better documented, and, based on that documentation, has increased markedly since the late 1970s. Hate crimes against lesbians and gay men reported in 1997 increased 8 percent over those reported in the previous year, while overall serious crime decreased.[55] Anti-gay hate crimes are the third largest category of hate crimes, representing 14 percent of those reported (with racist hate crimes accounting for more than 50 percent of all hate crimes). Most researchers agree that the anti-gay hate crimes reported are just the tip of the iceberg, as most such crimes go unreported.[56]

Hate crimes were identified as a special form of violence in the 1980s, when activists demonstrated that the racist and anti-Semitic violence committed by far right hate groups has its own motivation and impact.[57] Most people would agree that Klan violence or neo-Nazi skinhead violence, when directed at a group's stated enemies, is motivated by hate. Hate crimes (sometimes called "bias-motivated crimes" because they are the result of prejudice and bigotry) inflict more than physical damage to people and property. They "send a message" intended to terrorize the targeted group.

Anti-gay hate crimes send a clear message: People who transgress conventional sexual and gender roles in appearance or behavior risk violent punishment, or, at the very least, verbal assault. Anti-gay hate crimes serve to silence and control the gay community, and make it dangerous to be publicly and visibly "out."

The message of anti-gay hate crimes overlaps strikingly with the right's message. The right's demonizing and scapegoating of gay and lesbian people create a hospitable environment for individual bigotry within a climate of what psychologist Gregory Herek calls "cultural heterosexism."[58] By opposing "special" protections for lesbian and gay people, the right's leadership encourages discrimination against anyone who does not stay "in the closet," anyone who, because of stereotypes, appears to be lesbian or gay, or anyone whose gender presentation flouts societal norms. To be quiet and invisible, or to work toward becoming "ex-gay" is the right's formula for protecting these people from society's homophobia.

Many lesbian, gay, bisexual, and transgender people feel that the right's attack on them is directly linked to anti-gay hate crime violence. In some cases we can easily see that link. If the perpetrators express their motivation while committing the crime—most often verbally—or carry out the crime as an act of hate group membership, their motivation is clear. But it is often difficult to establish a direct link between a homophobic hate crime and the vicious anti-gay rhetoric of right-wing groups. "Unaffiliated" individuals, many of them juveniles, who are not hardcore ideologues, commit the great majority of reported hate crimes. Most are drunk or thrill-seeking or egged on by peer-group pressure. But we can assume that all feel that what they are doing is, on some level, either justified or condoned by the larger society.

But the right's leadership takes no responsibility for the increase in anti-gay hate crimes. Its leaders deny any connection between their rhetoric and the increase in anti-gay violence. Since the term "hate crimes" came into existence in the mid-1980s, the right has fought every effort to focus attention on them or to bring special sanctions to bear on those who commit them. Senator Jesse Helms (R-NC) mounted a vigorous opposition to the Federal Hate Crimes Statistics Act of 1990, which simply mandated hate crime data collection.[59] Nonetheless, gay rights activists have successfully worked to pass hate crimes legislation in forty-five state legislatures and the U.S. Congress. Usually the measures involve some form of "penalty-enhancement" for designated hate crimes.[60]

Although the right has not been alone in opposing hate crimes legislation, its motivations are particularly suspect because it so often opposes legal protections for the groups victimized by hate crimes. While homophobia certainly has a life of its own in U.S. culture, the right's anti-gay campaign encourages and legitimizes violent actions.

Research suggests that hate crimes tend to be excessively brutal when compared with similar types of crime.[61] In a three-week period in 1998, for example, the New York City Gay and Lesbian Anti-Violence Project collected reports of twenty-seven anti-gay bias crimes against both men and women. In addition to chasing their victims and calling them "faggot" and "dyke," attackers used knives, bricks, bottles, and clubs. One victim was beaten unconscious, another lost an eye, another was slashed and required eight stitches, another was kicked down the subway stairs. Some attacks occurred on the street, others in parks, others on subway trains. Victims were walking their dogs, exercising, or sitting in their cars. The most common location for an attack was outside a gay bar, presumably a place where it is easy to find potential targets.[62]

Often it is difficult to establish what was in the minds of the perpetrators, except to say that issues of sexuality and gender are at the center of homophobic hate crimes. Penalty-enhancement may be an imperfect instrument in discouraging spontaneous hate crimes. But just as hate crimes send a message to victims and their communities, designating hate crimes with special penalties sends a message that society will not tolerate the violent or threatening expression of prejudice and bigotry. Hate crimes warrant a special category that sets them apart from others. A society that does not respond to a *pattern* of crime against one of its member groups could justifiably be accused of condoning that pattern.

I feel equally threatened by the right's anti-gay campaign and the increase in hate crimes against lesbian, gay, bisexual, and transgender people. I find it particularly infuriating to see the right stereotype, vilify, and scapegoat my gay community, one that is unusually rich in its racial and cultural diversity. Equally infuriating is the right's use of religious beliefs as the basis of its anti-gay campaign. I cannot either recognize my community in this campaign's distorted depiction or relate to the right's version of Christianity—one that justifies prejudice. What I do recognize is a campaign that is good for movement-building. I expect to see the right continue its anti-gay campaign as long as "homosexuality" remains a fruitful issue for the movement.

have benefited from affirmative action, first in admission to graduate school, and later in obtaining teaching positions at three different colleges. And, in each case, the institution benefited from my presence, specifically because I am a woman. In graduate school, I was the class representative to the faculty meetings, making a department with just one woman faculty member appear "inclusive," and providing a sorely lacking feminist perspective on department policy. In political science departments, I invariably taught a women's studies course in feminist political theory or women and politics, allowing the departments to respond to student demand for such courses without hiring a full-time faculty member with formal credentials in women's studies. I know that affirmative action helped me to overcome discrimination that would have denied me nearly every advancement in my working life but I am comfortable with the balance between the advantages I received and what I gave.

I also know that, to many white people, affirmative action is palatable because it helps white women, as well as men and women of color. The strategy of emphasizing its benefit to white women can therefore be an effective strategy for defending affirmative action. But the political struggle over affirmative action is really about race, not gender.[1] The right attacks affirmative action primarily on the grounds of race, even when the attacker is a person of color.

Although the right masks the racial animus behind its attack on affirmative action, that attack provides an instructive case study of the subtlety and effectiveness of the right's "new" racism. Affirmative action has been high on the right's hit list since the mid-1960s. Its virtual defeat in the policy arena and in the voting booth exemplifies how a well-funded and highly coordinated political movement has engineered a retreat from the goal of decreasing economic and social inequality and has redefined fairness to apply only to the individual, not to the group. Similar to its campaign against welfare or its attack on lesbians and gay men, the right incubated the campaign against affirmative action in the 1960s and 1970s, designed its implementation in the 1980s, and brought it to fruition in the 1990s.

When the early architects of affirmative action developed it as a policy to benefit African Americans, who had mounted a strong civil rights movement to demand an end to racial discrimination, the right reacted almost immediately. Later, when other people of color and white women began to benefit from affirmative action, many white people continued to see affirmative action as a program to benefit African Americans.[2] The right often frames the issue to reinforce that perception, perhaps because, in the United States, African Americans are the principal target of white racism, and benefits for Blacks, especially if they are cast as "special" benefits, are politically unpopular among many white voters.

In the 1980s, the first decade of the right's electoral power, its strategists refined the ideological basis for the attack on affirmative action and developed various tactics for rolling it back. During the same decade, Ronald Reagan's appointment of at least half the entire judiciary ensured that the U.S. Supreme Court and the lower courts would abandon their role as a bulwark against reactionary initiatives. In the 1990s, having refined its arguments and softened the terrain of public opinion, the right struck its blow in the legislative arena. The result has been a triumph for the "new racism" and enormous setbacks of the gains for the civil rights movement.

AFFIRMATIVE ACTION AS AN EXTENSION
OF THE CIVIL RIGHTS MOVEMENT

The right is correct when it claims that affirmative action is a government-imposed extension of the 1964 Civil Rights Act. Although affirmative action was not included in the Civil Rights Act, very soon after the Act was passed, the government was compelled to develop it, reflecting the urgent demand for justice from the civil rights movement.[3] Lyndon Johnson, president in 1964, put the power of his office behind a liberal vision of affirmative action. His strategy was to mandate it throughout the executive branch of government, thereby making it government policy.

When the 1964 Civil Rights Act passed, the Johnson Administration relied on the Equal Employment Opportunity Commission (EEOC), which had been created to enforce Title VII, the employment section of the Act. Jobs and promotions would then be based on the principles of meritocracy, with open competition and the "best" person, determined in a non-discriminatory way, winning. In those more optimistic times, civil rights supporters of all races thought that the removal of racial discrimination would allow Black people to "win" their proportionate share of jobs and promotions. I was one of a great many white people moved by the vision of Dr. Martin Luther King, Jr., when he called for a society in which people are judged not by the color of their skin, but by the content of their character. It is particularly painful to see the right appropriate King's words and use them to attack affirmative action.

Right-wing authors seldom note that Dr. King understood that eliminating discrimination would not be an adequate corrective to a history of racist oppression. In his 1964 book, *Why We Can't Wait*, King wrote:

> Whenever this issue of compensatory or preferential treatment for the Negro is raised, some of our friends recoil in horror. The Negro should be granted equality, they agree; but he should ask for nothing more. On the surface, this appears reasonable, but it is not realistic. For it is obvious that if a man is entering the starting line in a race three hundred years after another man, the first would have to perform some impossible feat in order to catch up with his fellow runner.[4]

King was correct. It quickly became clear to civil rights activists and supporters within the Johnson Administration that the 1964 Civil Rights

Act alone would not eliminate discriminatory practices in hiring and promotion, and even when it did, Blacks and other people of color would be unable to compete with more-advantaged white applicants because the playing field of preparation and past opportunity was not level. Further measures were necessary, and the Johnson Administration responded with Executive Orders, Justice Department lawsuits, and Department of Labor regulations. In 1965 Johnson issued Executive Order 11246, which required affirmative action only from employers who held contracts with the federal government, included sanctions for those who did not, and ultimately created the Office of Federal Contract Compliance (OFCC) within the Labor Department.[5] During this period, the unions practiced exclusionary apprenticeship and membership policies, especially in the building trades. Johnson and the Democratic Party did not confront this discrimination head-on (except for those employers holding federal contracts), since the unions were heavy supporters of the Democratic Party. Nevertheless, the right quickly labeled the Johnson Executive Order "reverse discrimination."

Ironically, during the Nixon Administration, the OFCC oversaw four "special area programs" or "home town plans" that culminated in the famous "Philadelphia Plan," which both strengthened and refined affirmative action. The Philadelphia Plan required federally supported projects to establish minimum standards for racial fairness in contract bidding. It defined the correct standard as a percentage of racial minority employees that corresponded to a "target" percentage or "goal." It thereby established an important new benchmark for federal antidiscrimination policy.[6] Though Nixon was lukewarm on affirmative action, his appointees at the Labor Department supported the Philadelphia Plan. To the Administration, it had the further appeal of being opposed by the unions, many of whom supported the Democrats.

In 1970, the Department of Labor issued guidelines designed to end discrimination against women in jobs that were paid for with federal funds. In 1972, Congress passed the Equal Opportunity Act and several other measures that expanded the scope of antidiscrimination protections for women and people of color, and Nixon signed it into law. In 1973, a milestone Consent Decree was concluded in a joint agreement between AT&T and three government agencies—the EEOC, the Labor

Department, and the Justice Department. The Consent Decree created the "AT&T Model Plan," in which the Bell System agreed to pay damages and change its employment policies in response to a finding that 95 percent of those employed as low-paying operators or clerical workers were women, and, of higher-paid craft workers, 95 percent were male and only 6 percent of those were Black. Virtually no white women or African American women or men were in managerial positions.[7] At AT&T, the Civil Rights Act of 1964 had had little impact on patterns of hiring and promotion. The AT&T Model Plan brought the power of the federal enforcement mechanism to bear on employment practices within the private (albeit subsidized and regulated) sector.

The Nixon Administration advanced the cause of affirmative action despite its firm ideological opposition to it. While the steps above represent progress for civil rights groups and women's groups, a 1972 *New York Times* survey found that the Nixon Administration "has all but abandoned efforts to force federal contractors to hire more blacks, other minority workers, and women." The survey found that personnel at the Federal Office of Contract Compliance were "demoralized" and were not enforcing the 1969 Philadelphia Plan.[8] Enforcement did not improve until the Carter Administration came into office in 1976 and extended antidiscrimination protections. Its Labor Department developed regulations that set goals and timetables for hiring women on federally funded construction projects on a trade-by-trade basis.[9]

AFFIRMATIVE ACTION AND THE "NEW RACISM"

Much like members of a family, the different sectors within the electoral right—the New Right, neo-conservatives, paleo-conservatives, the Christian Right, and new Republicans—see race differently, often quarreling among themselves and sometimes changing their positions over time. Outside the family are the political neighbors, the far right activists who carry guns and advocate violence against people of color, Jews, abortion providers, and "homosexuals." Though not welcomed by the electoral right, they do influence the Republican Party's right wing.

All sectors of the right assert that racism is a thing of the past: specifically, that both legally sanctioned (*de jure*) discrimination and the informal practices of *de facto* discrimination have been corrected. Right-wing strategists and intellectuals either deny or ignore the existence of institutional racism—the systematic encouragement and toleration of racial inequality in a wide variety of sectors, such as housing, education, and employment.[10]

Throughout the 1980s, press coverage of the New Right did little to expose the right's denial of ongoing racism. The press did cover the racist and anti-Semitic activities and ideologies of the far right, and especially the Identity movement in the West and the farmbelt, the Posse Comitatus in Wisconsin, white supremacist activity in the South, and organizing by the Rev. Sun Myung Moon and neo-fascist Lyndon LaRouche. But the New Right's leadership distanced itself from these far right activities. The movement intended its very title, *New* Right, to state its abandonment of the far right's racial agenda. Paul Weyrich, one of the most prominent New Right leaders, wrote in March 1984, "Conservative in the black community means racist and that is understandable. The leadership on the right, however, bears no resemblance to the reactionary Southern icons of the past. . . . I am sure there are people who call themselves conservatives who are prejudiced. But the leaders are far from it."[11] When journalists reported a New Right Republican making a racial slur, quick denunciation by right-wing leaders and an apology from the perpetrator usually followed.

Journalists, wanting to write about New Right racism, found themselves without a "smoking gun" to document the movement's racism. Further, the New Right embraced, published, and promoted a cadre of intellectuals of color who developed and refined an intellectual base for an attack on the civil rights movement. Such tactics proved effective in obscuring the New Right's racism.

New Right Republicans and their allies in the Reagan Administration came to office in 1980 with a clear agenda of rolling back the gains of the civil rights movement. But they did not promote the Old Right's form of white supremacism—based on the assertion that whites are biologically superior to Blacks. They renounced that position and instead promoted what sociologist Amy Ansell has called "the new racism," a term that captures the contemporary right's more subtle style of racism.[12] Its trademarks are the abandonment of a commitment to equality and a redefinition of the principle of fairness. The new racism declares group identities to be irrelevant. From the right's perspective, the logic is simple: There is no more racial discrimination; therefore race is not a characteristic that should be acknowledged in hiring or promotion; therefore people should be judged on the basis of "merit" alone. Affirmative action based on race or gender becomes both inappropriate (because group identities have no significance) and unfair (because it does not consider *only* the qualifications of each individual applicant). This right-wing argument masterfully captures the themes and language of the civil rights movement and twists them to defeat the movement's goals.

Two well-known intellectuals who are at the heart of this practice are Harvard history professor Stephan Thernstrom and his wife, Abigail Thernstrom. Self-described "1950s liberals," they are more accurately rightist libertarians who have focused on affirmative action as the greatest of liberalism's mistakes. In their widely reviewed 1997 book, *America in Black and White*, they argue that Black progress is chronically underestimated, and racial attitudes in the United States have improved so dramatically that it is now "dangerous" to promote affirmative action, which often hurts Blacks. Their personal mission is to promote "color blind" policies as the only true reflection of the original intent of liberal racial programs. Although Abigail Thernstrom doesn't like to be considered a conservative, she is a senior fellow at the rightist Manhattan Institute and has served on the boards of three movement organizations—the Institute for Justice, the Center for Equal Opportunity, and the Cato Institute. The Thernstroms' research for their book was supported by grants from at least three rightist foundations, as well as by a grant of $180,000 from the John M. Olin Foundation to promote the book.

Abigail Thernstrom outshines her husband as an established voice of opposition to affirmative action. She has been a high-profile opponent of race-based programs since the early 1980s, and *America in Black and White* is her second book on the necessity for color blind policies. The Thernstroms' next book is to be a study of the growing gap in academic performance between Black and white students in grades K–12.[13]

By asserting that racism is a thing of the past, the right can justify dismantling the programs and policies put in place as a result of pressure from the civil rights movement. For example, welfare programs, affirmative action programs, protection of the rights of criminal defendants, bilingual education, and services for immigrants are all policy initiatives that the right has painted as serving "undeserving" individuals at the expense of "deserving" taxpayers. The right maintains that the effects of these policies are race-neutral, while at the same time using vicious racial stereotypes to fan whites' racial resentments. The result has been a virtual war by the right against people of color, waged behind a smokescreen of race neutrality.

For the most part, people of color have not been fooled. Writing about African Americans, UCLA sociologist Lawrence D. Bobo states:

> All too often, a major subtext of campaigns about reducing welfare and fighting crime is a narrative about generally retaining white status privilege over blacks, and specifically about controlling and punishing poor black communities. This thinly veiled racial subtext of American politics is not lost on the black community. It feeds a growing suspicion and distrust among African Americans that white-dominated institutions may be moving toward overt hostility to the aspirations of African American communities.[14]

By his own survey research into the nature of white racism, and his analysis of the research of others, Bobo has found that the right's "new racism" has now permeated public opinion. While support for Jim Crow racial practices has declined steadily since the 1940s, it has been replaced by the right's formulation: People of color are responsible for their own disadvantaged circumstances because racism is no longer a social problem. Bobo also finds that the white public is increasingly reluctant to support any role for government in correcting what racism may still occur. This is especially true in the case of programs such as affirmative action that attempt to address racism not as a problem of individual prejudice, but as a problem of a racist society that systematically discriminates against certain groups.[15]

WEAK AND STRONG AFFIRMATIVE ACTION

In rightists' attacks on affirmative action, the terms "affirmative action," "preferential treatment," and "reverse discrimination" are often used interchangeably. This clever political ploy blurs the distinctions between different types of affirmative action and helps to create the mistaken impression that all affirmative action involves quotas. By further suggesting (repeatedly and incorrectly) that whites, in particular white men, experience "reverse discrimination" as a result of affirmative action "quotas," the right's leadership has created a now widely held belief that affirmative action is harmful and unfair to white people.[16] According to the right, it is time now for white people to mount a movement to protect *their* "civil rights."

But there are several ways of seeing affirmative action and several ways of practicing it. For those who support a "color blind" approach to racial equality, such as U.S. Supreme Court Justice Clarence Thomas, there is no place in hiring or promotion for any consideration of race. The only acceptable form of affirmative action, therefore, is outreach to, and recruitment of, candidates of color and white women. This "weak" affirmative action does not ensure that these candidates will get to be represented in the workplace. It only opens up the opportunity for every-one to compete for jobs, often in settings where people of color and/or white women have been excluded from competing in the past.

"Weak" affirmative action has strong bipartisan support. Even the New Right could not attack the practice of creating equal access for job *applicants*. Weak affirmative action does not promote consideration of race as a factor in the actual *hiring* process. "Strong" affirmative action, however, challenges the "color blind" principle of fairness in an attempt to go beyond open competition for jobs. Its goal is to achieve a more eq-uitable race and gender distribution among employees and in their promotions.

"Strong" affirmative action requires that employers set up timetables to meet targets or goals for hiring people of color and white women in order to increase their presence in the workplace. To meet these targets, goals, or, in some rare cases, quotas, an employer may choose a candidate of color or white woman who is qualified over another qualified white male candidate. Some proponents of "strong" affirmative action advo-cate hiring minorities in percentages equal to their proportion in the larger population. The right consistently fails to distinguish among types of affirmative action and portrays all affirmative action as "strong."

One point of contention in "strong" affirmative action is whether the "hand up" it gives to people of color and white women should apply only to those who have suffered quantifiable discrimination, or to all who belong to a group that has been discriminated against in the past. Affirmative action opponent Carl Cohen has framed this distinction as "redress for injury" versus "entitlement by color."[17] The right opposes any affirmative action practice that bestows preference on the basis of race or gender, absent proof of individual past discrimination. Rightists sometimes argue that affirmative action is unfair because it penalizes whites who themselves never discriminated and sometimes argue that it rewards people who never were actual victims of discrimination. In making the latter argument, rightist authors often underscore their assertion that racial discrimination is a thing of the past.[18]

Examples of strong and weak affirmative action are found in the AT&T Model Plan. In accordance with the 1973 Consent Decree, AT&T practiced strong affirmative action for six years, until it was able to break down racial and gender stereotypes and integrate the workforce by race and gender. Its hiring and firing policies then reverted to weak affirmative action—essentially a policy of nondiscrimination.[19]

THE NEOCONSERVATIVE CRITIQUE

We see the purposeful blurring of the distinction between weak and strong affirmative action in the first widely distributed salvo in the right's attack on affirmative action, neoconservative scholar Nathan Glazer's 1975 book *Affirmative Discrimination*. Glazer articulated nearly every argument in the backlash attack on affirmative action, and to this day critics have added little to it. Glazer played a familiar neoconservative role: to develop the intellectual arguments that subsequently evolve into a full-scale right-wing campaign. This pattern has been particularly common to matters in which race is central, such as welfare "reform."[20]

My own interest in researching the right began with a fascination with neoconservative thought. As early as the mid-1970s, it seemed clear to me that neoconservatism represented a compelling redesign of Old Right ideas. Most neoconservatives started their political careers as leftist or liberal Democrats, then switched their allegiance to the Republicans, in part because they were deeply opposed to communism. Their former Democratic Party affiliations gave them a reputation as moderates, with a thoughtful and mature vision born in idealism but tempered by experience.

I quickly learned that neoconservatives were, and still are, punitive toward the poor, snide when attacking any category of people they consider muddle-headed or softhearted, forgiving of dictators as long as they are anticommunist, and condescending toward their fellow rightists. No one book more accurately captures the nasty tone and right-wing content of neoconservative thought than Glazer's *Affirmative Discrimination*. And no book better illustrates how important neoconservatives have been to the development of the contemporary right's ideas.

Glazer presented himself as a scholar who opposed racism and claimed some mildly liberal credentials. But his tone and language belie this liberal veneer throughout the book, including his use of the inflammatory title, *Affirmative Discrimination*. Glazer embraced the role of liberal heretic, nowhere more so than when he argued that by 1973, racial discrimination in the labor market was no longer an issue, therefore affirmative action was no longer needed. This is his most lasting (and shameful) contribution to the anti–affirmative action position.

Glazer also contributed nearly all the ideas that were to become the right's critique of affirmative action, especially that it violates "the first principle of liberal society" by tampering with equality of opportunity. He argued that by recognizing group rights above individual rights, affirmative action reestablishes a basis for discrimination and therefore is not an extension of the civil rights movement. Glazer reviewed instance after instance of bureaucratic rigidity in the application of affirmative action guidelines to support his one-sided argument that affirmative action will lead to discrimination rather than bring society relief from it.[21] In this argument-by-anecdote, Glazer built his case that:

- Affirmative action addresses a problem that no longer exists, because, as of 1973, there were no more patterns of discrimination in the labor market.

- Affirmative action violates the rights of the individual to be treated in a "color blind" way. Here Glazer pioneers another tactic, used by many who followed him, by going back to the Civil Rights Act of 1964 to point to an injunction in the Act against forcing any employer to grant preferential treatment. Affirmative action, he argues, defies this injunction by favoring one group over another, thus forcing employers to show preferential treatment to members of one group.[22]

- Affirmative action creates a white backlash. "Compensation for the past," Glazer says, "is a dangerous principle. It can be extended indefinitely and make for endless trouble."[23]

- If a hiring process is based on judging applicants' "qualifications," one cannot prove that a group has been discriminated against on the basis of race just because members of that group do not appear in certain job categories in numbers equal to their numbers in the larger society. When the goal becomes "statistical parity" between a group of employees and the larger society, the original intent of affirmative action—to refrain from discriminating and to announce, when advertising the job, that the employer does not discriminate—has been superseded by "quotas." Instead, Glazer argues, perhaps the members of one group just "qualify" for jobs more frequently than the members of another.

- Affirmative action does not help the most disadvantaged members of minority groups, those it was presumably designed to help, because the benefits accrue to all members of a category, whether those members are, in fact, targets of discrimination or not.

Racist assumptions run throughout Glazer's argument. If, as he maintains, there is no more discrimination in the labor market, yet many African American and other people of color remain locked out of jobs, he can only be arguing that whites are better at meeting job qualifications. The explanation lies either in the genetic inferiority of racial/ethnic minorities or in the institutional racism that results in poor preparation for jobs, poor educational opportunities, low quality housing, and poor health care, all of which contribute to a lowered ability to compete for jobs.

But Glazer explicitly critiques and dismisses the notion of institutional racism. He says, "This term has not been subjected to the analysis it deserves. It is obviously something devised in the absence of clear evidence of discrimination and prejudice. It suggests that, without intent, a group may be victimized."[24] Glazer sees institutional racism as an empty concept, a device used to explain differences in hiring patterns of people of color and whites, and an assertion based on no evidence.

Glazer himself would not say that the failure of people of color to "keep up" with whites in the labor market results from genetic inferiority. Nevertheless, his attack on affirmative action is a crucial paving stone on the path to genetic determinism.

In *Affirmative Discrimination*, Glazer is concerned about the disruption of the status quo, a system of rewards in hiring and promotion that he sees as maintaining high standards—rewards based on qualifications and high levels of performance. He implies that creating statistical parity means opening jobs for "unqualified" people of color, and he is particularly worried that a white backlash will result when whites resent "those of lesser competence and criminal inclination" who will benefit from affirmative action. Glazer never entertains the corollary argument that the current employment of white males "of lesser competence and criminal inclination" is a matter for policy discussion. He argues that improving access for people of color will lower hiring and promotion standards and discriminate against whites, ignoring the possibility that it would improve the workplace, increase fairness in the larger society, or expand the talent pool by including those who have been excluded.

Glazer's assertion that whites are harmed by affirmative action has become widespread public opinion. Analyzing data from the National Opinion Research Center (NORC) in 1990 and 1994, sociologist Orlando Patterson concludes that, whereas 70 percent of whites surveyed believed that affirmative action was harming white people, only 7 percent had experienced "reverse discrimination," and only 16 percent knew of someone close to them who had. Patterson goes further to conclude that "the vast majority of Euro-Americans are actually quite content with the affirmative action programs *with which they are acquainted at their own workplaces*" (italics in original). Here we see the effects of what Patterson calls the "concocted controversy" over egregious harm done to whites by the practice of affirmative action.[25]

Although *Affirmative Discrimination* has been called "the bible of neoconservative thought" on affirmative action, Glazer has had a change of heart in the late 1990s, and began to support affirmative action, to the fury of his neoconservative colleagues.[26] He argues that affirmative action is necessary to preserve the legitimacy of American democracy.[27] As a result, Nathan Glazer is enjoying another run in the public spotlight, as the defender of affirmative action, making precisely the same arguments about equal opportunity for people of color that he spent much of his career denying and blocking.

BLACK CONSERVATIVES INSERT A WEDGE

Throughout the late 1970s, 1980s, and 1990s many other rightists built on Nathan Glazer's influential text. A number of these critics of affirmative action are people of color; of all those, "Black conservatives" are the greatest in number and in influence. Nearly every prominent critic of affirmative action who is a person of color is male. Linda Chavez, former director of the U.S. Commission on Civil Rights in the Reagan Administration and now head of the Center for Equal Opportunity, an organization dedicated to opposing affirmative action, is the rare exception. Most of the critics of color have asserted, like Glazer, that the civil rights movement succeeded in dismantling the racial barriers of the Jim Crow era, making affirmative action policies unnecessary.

Black conservatives Thomas Sowell, Walter Williams, Shelby Steele, Glen Loury, and Stephen Carter, as well as other scholars of color, such as Dinesh D'Souza and Linda Chavez, play a politically important role in the right's attack on affirmative action. Criticisms of civil rights goals and support for the dismantling of affirmative action by a person of color, especially a Black person, whom affirmative action was originally intended to benefit, legitimize the racially hostile white critique of affirmative action. The New Right leadership has been acutely aware of this racial dynamic. It is no accident that, at the same time that Clarence Thomas complained that Black conservatives were barely accepted within the white New Right establishment, Black conservative intellectuals who attacked affirmative action were widely published in New Right outlets.[28]

Black scholars who oppose affirmative action are not necessarily part of a political movement. They prefer to label themselves as "conservative" rather than as full members of the New Right. Some Black conservatives have attained prominence within mainstream media outlets and have written for liberal, as well as rightist, presses and periodicals. But many of them have documented ties to the right, are supported by right-wing institutions, and speak within right-wing venues. Equally important, their ideas have become central to the New Right's analysis of civil rights, not only in the area of affirmative action.

Thomas Sowell and Walter Williams are two Black conservatives whose careers illustrate the links between Black conservatives and the right. Both men became identified with the New Right after movement organizations began to supplement their incomes, publish their work, especially in neoconservative publications such as *Commentary* and *The Public Interest*, and adopt their ideas and arguments.

Sowell, who was a student of libertarian economist Milton Friedman at the University of Chicago, is the most widely published of the Black conservatives. He is a free-market purist who emphasizes self-reliance and opposes government intervention in any form, and is a social traditionalist who dissents from the civil rights movement's liberal ideology.[29] For many years, Sowell has been a professor of economics at UCLA, and a senior fellow at the right-wing Hoover Institution on War, Revolution and Peace.

Sowell was an early critic of affirmative action. In 1975, the same year that Nathan Glazer published *Affirmative Discrimination*, the American Enterprise Institute, a rightist think tank where Sowell was an adjunct scholar, published his slim booklet titled *Affirmative Action Reconsidered*. Sowell's booklet was not widely circulated and is narrowly focused on academia, but many of his arguments are the same as those promoted by the higher-profile Glazer. Sowell asserts that affirmative action violates the spirit and intent of the 1964 Civil Rights Act, and that job discrimination in academia had become a thing of the past before affirmative action was instituted. Sowell, like Glazer, ignores institutional racism.[30]

Walter Williams, a widely published conservative economist, joins Sowell in arguing that the key to "minority group" progress is economic success. He criticizes the civil rights movement, with its emphasis on political clout, for offering African Americans false promises of progress. Especially egregious, according to Williams, is the damage done to Black economic progress by government affirmative action programs, which violate free-market principles of supply and demand, and harm minority groups by interfering with the very mechanism (the free market) which holds the most promise for economic success for poor communities.[31] Williams's work, especially his 1982 book, *The State against Blacks*, has received support from right-wing sources, including the Hoover Institution, the Heritage Foundation, and the Scaife Foundation.[32] The book is a publication of McGraw-Hill's New Press, but is identified as a "Research Book" of the rightist Manhattan Institute.[33]

Black conservatives adamantly assert that their beliefs are not contrary to the interests of people of color.[34] But, in part because their work is so useful to the right's attack on affirmative action and on other gains of the civil rights movement, the majority of Black leadership has furiously denounced them. No two Black conservatives have been more denounced than Justice Clarence Thomas and Ward Connerly, a member of the University of California Board of Regents and spokesperson for Proposition 209, California's 1996 anti–affirmative action initiative. Although both men have themselves benefited enormously from affirmative action programs, as have most of the critics of color discussed here, their opposition to it seems to be the central principle driving most of their career decisions.[35]

I am often tempted to dismiss Black conservatives as opportunists who have attained notoriety by holding iconoclastic ideas for which they were rewarded by career advancement. But I know that to take Black conservatives and other conservatives of color seriously is the only way to develop an effective response to their arguments. When I look to progressive scholars of color for their "read" of Black conservatives, I am compelled by the analysis of sociologist Deborah Toler. In one of the earliest studies of Black conservatives, Toler sees contemporary Black conservatism as consistent with a long-standing "Black bourgeois mythology" that has long asserted that middle-class African Americans are different from (and superior to) the Black majority. To establish this difference, Toler argues, members of the Black bourgeoisie insist they do not manifest the attitudes and behaviors associated with negative Black stereotypes, but instead identify with the positive attitudes and behaviors associated with white stereotypes. As a result, a sector of the Black bourgeoisie has been characterized by political conservatism and an acute sensitivity to white opinion.[36] The progressive African American scholar Cornel West sees Black conservatives similarly. According to West, the members of the Black bourgeoisie who align themselves with the right are engaged in a middle-class identity crisis, as they both seek white approval and distinguish themselves from "the state of siege that rages in working-poor and very poor communities."[37]

Glen Omatsu, discussing Asian American neoconservatives, sees a similar link between class status and conservative politics among Asian American conservatives. But Asian American conservatives, in addition to distinguishing themselves from working-class Asian Americans, distinguish themselves from other communities of color, which they see as lacking their own high level of commitment to education, achievement, and traditional values. Often they blame quotas, which set *upper* limits on the admission of Asian Americans to colleges and universities, and on affirmative action programs for African Americans, Latinos, and American Indians, whom they see as "less qualified." Asian American conservatives are largely professionals who speak to other professionals, and ignore the great need for affirmative action on the part of large numbers of poor Asian Americans.[38]

BLACK CONSERVATIVES EXPAND THE CRITIQUE

In many respects, Black conservative scholars have added little to the critique as it had been laid out by Nathan Glazer in 1975. But their voices have incrementally increased the power of the anti–affirmative action critique. As African Americans, they have mounted an attack on the civil rights leadership, a step that some white New Right leaders were reluctant to take because they realized that to appear too hostile to the civil rights movement would provoke accusations of racist intent. Black conservatives also have argued that affirmative action has, in fact, harmed Blacks by imposing a stigma on those hired under affirmative action guidelines; that affirmative action benefits only the "best and brightest" of African Americans, leaving the most disadvantaged behind; and that self-help and free-market capitalism are the only effective methods of advancement for disadvantaged people of color.

Black conservatives also agree with Glazer's assertion that affirmative action harms the self-esteem of those who benefit from it. In his 1984 book, *Civil Rights: Rhetoric or Reality?*, Thomas Sowell claims that there is an "invidious and acute" danger in affirmative action for "minorities" and women because it undermines their self-confidence and instills a message of dependence on the civil rights and women's liberation movements.[39] Shelby Steele, making much the same argument in his 1990 book, *The Content of Our Character*, attracted even greater attention and was more successful in inserting the "damaged self-esteem" perspective into public debate. Steele claims that policies of "racial preference" for Blacks cause "a kind of demoralization, or put another way, an enlargement of self-doubt. Under affirmative action the quality that earns us preferential treatment is an implied inferiority."[40] Elsewhere, Steele describes affirmative action as a "Faustian bargain" for Blacks, who are demoralized by the inferiority implied by preferential treatment.[41] Right-ist sociologist Charles Murray claims that Black students' self-esteem is harmed when affirmative action encourages them to attend schools for which they are not qualified.[42]

But in *The Shape of the River* (1998), the most comprehensive study to date on the experience of students of color admitted to institutions of higher education under affirmative action programs, Derek Bok, former president of Harvard University, and William G. Bowen, former president of Princeton University, find no evidence of harm done to the self-esteem of African American students. "Black students do not seem to *think* they have been harmed as a result of attending selective colleges with race-sensitive policies. Were it otherwise, one would assume that the ablest Black students would be resentful of these policies and colleges that adopted them."[43]

When Black conservatives discuss Black self-esteem and affirmative action, they most often illustrate their arguments with anecdotes drawn from their own middle-class experiences or those of other intellectuals and professionals of color. They do not make clear the proportion of Black people who have benefited from affirmative action and do not have feelings of stigma or unworthiness. Nor do they address the experience of blue-collar workers, whose access to jobs in the building trades, within the rank-and-file of large corporations, and within government agencies has increased dramatically as a result of affirmative action.[44] Black conservatives seem to argue that access to a good job with a good income is of no concern to Blacks when compared with the threat to their self-esteem that affirmative action represents. Black conservatives analyze two groups: middle-class Black professionals and poor urban Blacks. They do not discuss how twenty years of affirmative action minority contract and set-aside programs have benefited working-class people of color.

The moderately conservative Randall Kennedy, African American professor of law, refutes the "damaged self-esteem" argument, arguing that whites disparage Blacks, whether or not they are the beneficiaries of affirmative action. Kennedy points out that it is difficult to distinguish white disparagement of Blacks based on affirmative action from the disparagement that results from ongoing racism. Further, he says that the absence of Blacks from colleges and other important social institutions where they historically have been excluded has itself had stigmatizing consequences. Their absence encourages whites to assume that they are not qualified for membership or employment in any but service jobs in these institutions. And finally, he argues that most Blacks understand affirmative action to be a very minor benefit in the larger scheme of their experiences: that it only modestly compensates for past exclusion, and is a very mild departure from a romanticized and incorrect notion of a pure meritocracy of the past when "merit" was defined by whites.[45] Further, the conservative "self-esteem" critique encourages a shift in focus from the racism and sexism that pervades many workplaces to the feelings of low self-esteem allegedly experienced by those who benefit from any form of affirmative action.[46]

Another Black conservative contribution, made by both Thomas Sowell and Shelby Steele, is the argument that the civil rights agenda, especially "preferential treatment" policies, has harmed African Americans by benefiting the middle class at the expense of the urban poor, a result predicted by Glazer. Black conservative scholars get intellectual support for this argument from two men who would not identify themselves with the New Right: William Julius Wilson, a well-known African American sociologist at Harvard, and Ken Auletta, a white professional journalist. Wilson argued in his 1978 book, *The Declining Significance of Race*, that it is class, not race, that now holds many Blacks down.[47] Building on this thesis, Wilson maintains in *The Truly Disadvantaged*, published in 1987, that the origins of a Black "underclass" lie in African American male joblessness.[48] Although Wilson acknowledges that middle-class African Americans are dramatically more economically successful as a result of the civil rights movement, he emphasizes the growing gap between middle-class and poor African Americans.

The concept of an inner-city "underclass" first appeared in sociologist Gunnar Myrdal's 1963 book, *The Challenge of Affluence*, referring to a poor, unemployed, economically redundant and discarded group—primarily African Americans.[49] Journalist Ken Auletta added to Myrdal's concept an elaborate schema of pathological behaviors with his 1982 book, *The Underclass*.[50] Both Wilson and Auletta argue that the existence of a dysfunctional, socially aberrant underclass is evidence of the failure of liberal policies to help the poor move out of poverty.[51] But Sowell, Steele, and other Black conservatives take the argument to its right-wing conclusion: blaming the civil rights movement itself for *creating* the plight of the urban poor "underclass."

The Black conservative antidote to the damage done by liberal programs is "self-help" or Black capitalism, which renounces government "interference" through social programs, which are characterized as "handouts." Both Sowell and Williams promote this free-market ideology; Black writer and activist Robert Woodson has converted it into action. Woodson has attempted to take his ideas to the street level through his Washington, D.C.–based National Center for Neighborhood Enterprise.

Woodson has been a resident fellow at the American Enterprise Institute and has served as chair of the Council for a Black Economic Agenda, which focuses on "rebuilding Black neighborhoods by giving residents more spending money and investment capital."[52] He evokes a very positive, even romanticized, image of Black community strength and individual entrepreneurship during the nineteenth and early twentieth centuries, especially the work of Booker T. Washington, who founded the National Negro Business League in 1900. Woodson credits Black independence and "self-worth" for the Black community's remarkable ability to maintain its own institutions and its own political clout in the face of tremendous repression. In the Roosevelt Administration's introduction of New Deal programs to address economic distress, Woodson sees "the creation of a professional class of social policy bureaucrats and a corps of sociologists, psychologists and social workers who, in effect, formed a social service industry with its own social status, goals, and interests, a situation that often worked against the interest of the poor."[53]

Woodson's analysis is a compelling one, and corresponds to similar critiques of the social service establishment made by progressives. However, when he takes the next step, to develop policies that address Black poverty, he concludes that the answer lies in unfettered capitalism. Completely denying any role for government aid programs, he assigns all hope for the community to Black business.[54] Arguing that social programs destroyed the Black community's greatest asset, its autonomy, Woodson places too much faith in the conservative snake oil of the free market. In that market, success depends on access to capital, credit, and contracts. Woodson fails to address the institutional racism that so often denies Black-owned businesses those essential tools.

FANNING THE WHITE BACKLASH

While Black conservatives played an enormously influential role in refining the intellectual arguments against affirmative action and giving them increased legitimacy, the books of two white scholars, George Gilder and Charles Murray, took these positions into mainstream public debate and received widespread media attention during the Reagan Administration. Gilder's *Wealth and Poverty* and Murray's *Losing Ground* reframed the Old Right's explicit racism into the coded discourse of the new racism. By calling for the legislative rollback of *all* anti-poverty programs, including welfare, housing subsidies, job training, and affirmative action, they were in tune with both Reagan Administration policy and an ongoing shift in public opinion regarding poor people, especially poor people of color. By breaking out of academic intellectual circles and becoming best-selling authors, Gilder and Murray were able to reach the white legislators and opinion makers who were crafting the rollback of affirmative action.

In *Wealth and Poverty* (1981), Gilder popularized many of the arguments incubated in the late 1960s and 1970s in the pages of relatively obscure right-wing publications, especially the Old Right *Human Events* and the neoconservative *Public Interest*.[55] According to Gilder, poverty is caused by liberalism and its wrong-headed thinking about values and family structure. He is particularly disdainful of the "equal rights conglomerate," especially the EEOC. Gilder argues that governmental bureaucracy is a universally evil influence on a society that would do a far better job of creating wealth and eliminating poverty if it abolished all government programs and adopted the free-market model of Milton Friedman and his "Chicago School" of Economics.[56]

In *Losing Ground* (1984), Charles Murray builds on Gilder's arguments. He points to the increase in government transfer programs and the simultaneous increase in "social problems" as evidence that liberalism has made poverty and crime worse. He accuses liberal whites of "excessive solicitousness" and "condescension" toward Blacks in maintaining that Blacks are owed a debt, and that when they fail to succeed, it is because the system is stacked against them. In discussing affirmative action and set-aside programs, Murray holds a typical take-no-prisoners position: "My proposal for dealing with the racial issue in social welfare is to repeal every bit of legislation and reverse every court decision that in any way requires, recommends, or awards differential treatment according to race, and thereby puts us back onto the track we left in 1965."[57]

Quite understandably, New Rightists Gilder and Murray became the darlings of the Republican policy establishment. Backed and promoted by the New Right's think tanks, they benefited from their media savvy. The Manhattan Institute supported Murray as a senior research fellow when he published *Losing Ground*. It raised $125,000 to promote his book and paid him a stipend of $35,000. Most of the money came from two prominent funders of New Right organizations, the Scaife Foundation and the John M. Olin Foundation. The Manhattan Institute has also supported George Gilder.[58]

Gilder and Murray point to the "dependency" caused by liberal programs and the "culture of poverty" these programs encourage as responsible for poverty. From this perspective, poverty is the fault of the individual poor person, whom they often portray, in anecdote and example, as an undeserving, unmotivated, dependent, and sometimes rapacious person of color. Although Gilder and Murray certainly did not *cause* the Reagan Administration's legislative attack on the poor, their books were crucial to popularizing an image of a poor person as both Black and "undeserving." And this image, in turn, enhanced the backlash against programs such as affirmative action that the right painted as "favoring" Blacks and other "undeserving" people of color.

In keeping with the new racism, Gilder and Murray, like Nathan Glazer and the Black conservatives, present themselves as "true" civil rights advocates, conservatives who take Blacks seriously and treat them fairly, as individuals who must stand or fall on their own merits. In their attacks on liberalism, their critique of liberal attitudes toward Blacks and other people of color is often on target. Their accusations that white liberals patronize voters of color, use people of color as tokens, and relate to people of other races in a paternalistic, rather than power-sharing, style all too often portray liberal arrogance in action. By exposing these short-comings in liberal race attitudes, Gilder and Murray become more effective agents of the right's backlash appeal to white voters. What reveals the hypocrisy of their arguments is their denial of existing racism, their dismissal of the need to level the playing field, and their sneering disdain for the ongoing struggle for equal rights.

AFFIRMATIVE ACTION, THE NEW RIGHT, AND THE REAGAN ADMINISTRATION

During Ronald Reagan's presidency, most Administration policy initiatives and decisions were either derived from, or informed by, such right-wing think tanks as the Heritage Foundation, the Committee for the Survival of a Free Congress (now the Free Congress Foundation), and the American Enterprise Institute. Nowhere was this more obvious than in the area of affirmative action. The "color blind" argument—that one should ignore race because it is not a legitimate consideration in hiring, admission to colleges, or job promotion and affirmative action—quickly became the ruling ideological position within the Administration. Its members denounced racial group preference as a bad means for achieving equality, maintaining that racial minorities do not have legitimate collective interests. Results, the Administration argued, do not have to be equal, so long as employers and educational institutions provide equal opportunity to compete for jobs and admissions.

Rightist Reagan Administration appointees implemented many of the policies that rolled back affirmative action enforcement. Many of them were strategically placed in the bureaucracies responsible for administering and enforcing civil rights protections in general and affirmative action in particular. Reagan appointed Black conservative Clarence Pendleton as head of the U.S. Commission on Civil Rights, and another Black conservative, Clarence Thomas, as chair of the EEOC. White rightist William Bradford Reynolds was appointed Assistant Attorney General for Civil Rights in the Justice Department, where he defined all affirmative action as "quotas" and insisted that discrimination could not be charged without proof of "intent."

Such a position was difficult to hold publicly because the Reagan Administration portrayed itself as a friend of civil rights. But while wanting to maintain this image, the Administration agreed politically with New Right leaders in their push for a complete rollback of all programs except those that addressed cases of discrimination on an individual basis. To simultaneously satisfy the need for a pro–civil rights image and pursue an anti–civil rights agenda, the Reagan Administration defunded the civil rights enforcement arms it controlled.[59]

The Bush Administration continued this policy with greater momentum and success, as the Supreme Court and the lower courts became increasingly dominated by Reagan and Bush appointees. The Reagan and Bush Administrations accounted for half of the appointments to the Supreme Court, virtually guaranteeing a rightist tilt to its decisions. The departure of Justices Harry Blackmun, William Brennan, Thurgood Marshall, and Byron White deprived the Court of its liberal civil rights supporters. The Reagan/Bush appointments of Anthony M. Kennedy, Sandra Day O'Connor, Antonin Scalia, and Clarence Thomas, and Reagan's appointment of William Rehnquist as Chief Justice, have reversed the court's previous liberal bent.

The Reagan Administration's policies on affirmative action exemplify the "new racism." Despite that Administration's pro–civil rights rhetoric, its policies rolled back both the practice of affirmative action and the enforcement of civil rights laws. In addition to opposing affirmative action, the Reagan Administration initially supported tax exemptions for the private, segregated academies set up in the South to avoid legally mandated integration in the public schools. It supported South Africa at a time when U.S. Blacks and others were urging a boycott of its apartheid regime. It opposed school busing, a strong Voting Rights Act, and the celebration of Martin Luther King, Jr.'s birthday as a national holiday. It pursued a policy of "states' rights," a phrase that surely had enormous appeal for the Old Right southerners who had used it to justify segregation in the 1950s and 1960s.

George Bush, who accurately perceived his need for the support of the New Right and the increasingly powerful Christian Right, often promoted programs and policies that blocked the advancement of people of color, despite his reputation as less "racially insensitive" than Reagan. The Bush Administration carried out the policies of the Reagan Administration, including the smear of women receiving welfare as "welfare queens" (stereotyped as lazy and sexually promiscuous Black women); opposition to race-conscious electoral districting that increased the chances of Blacks winning office; the appointment of conservative judges hostile to civil rights; and support for the death penalty, without regard for its disproportionate use against people of color. Like the Reagan Administration, the Bush Administration saved its most florid and explicit rhetoric for the attack on "preferences and quotas." During both Administrations, opposition to affirmative action played an important role in the New Right's strategy of appealing to a white ethnic and southern backlash against civil rights and against the Democratic Party.

THE BELL CURVE

During the Bush Administration, a split occurred within the electoral right. The extreme right of the New Right took the humorous name "paleo-conservatives," to distinguish themselves from the "softer" members of the New Right. Prominent paleo-conservatives include Pat Buchanan, Senator Jesse Helms (R-NC) and Allen Keyes, African American talk show host and political candidate.[60] No book has stated the paleo-conservative case on race in a more incendiary fashion than *The Bell Curve* (1994), coauthored by Charles Murray and the late Richard Herrnstein. For more than 800 pages, the authors make the case that race and class inequalities in society can be explained by differences in genetically determined intelligence, not by institutional racism, unequal opportunity, or differences in social and economic circumstances.[61]

On the topic of affirmative action, *The Bell Curve* is consistent with Nathan Glazer's *Affirmative Discrimination*, written twenty years earlier, and with many of the arguments made by Black conservatives. In two chapters devoted entirely to this topic, Herrnstein and Murray argue that affirmative action defies the reality of a gap between the elite and the rest. They assert that people find their "natural" place in society based on IQ. When affirmative action violates the "natural" assignment of a place, the result is negative stereotyping and lowered self-esteem. The authors argue that affirmative action is no longer needed because, before the Civil Rights Act of 1964, Blacks had already attained "job fairness," meaning jobs that match their IQs.

The Bell Curve is a departure from the New Right's renunciation of explicit racism. Its assumptions update the work of an independently wealthy nineteenth-century Englishman, Francis Galton, who coined the term "eugenics"—the study of hereditary characteristics that may improve or impair the racial qualities of future generations, either physically or mentally.[62] In the U.S., the premiere organization dedicated to preserving the idea and practice of racial eugenics is the Pioneer Fund, which funded the two most notorious contemporary eugenicists, Arthur Jensen and William Schockley.[63] Pioneer Fund head Harry F. Weyher regretted not funding Herrnstein to write *The Bell Curve* and acknowledged that "we'd have funded him at the drop of a hat, but he never asked."[64]

The Bell Curve became a widely reviewed bestseller, with most commentators condemning it on both intellectual and political grounds. One of the better-known exposés of the authors' slippery use of statistics is Stephen Jay Gould's "Mismeasure by Any Measure," which details both the book's erroneous use of statistics and the fallacy of its central assumption that intelligence can be measured by the use of *g*, a "general factor" of intelligence.[65] A group of six scholars collaborated on a book-length critique of *The Bell Curve*'s social science and politics, and a vast array of journalists and writers, representing the many racial and ethnic identities slandered by the book, wrote masterful denunciations.[66] Even some paleo-conservatives, such as Pat Buchanan, John McLaughlin, and Rush Limbaugh have criticized *The Bell Curve*, though other rightist publications gave it generally favorable reviews. Shockingly, reporters in some mainstream publications gave the book neutral or mildly sympathetic reviews, including Malcolm Browne, science reporter for the *New York Times*.[67]

The Bell Curve embarrassed the leadership of the New Right, which attempted to distance the movement from it.[68] But it is a mistake to characterize the book as outside the ideology and public policy of the contemporary right. *The Bell Curve* is, instead, a logical progeny of the New Right's arguments against affirmative action. Its difference is in style, not basic assumptions or conclusions. The same indignation aroused by *The Bell Curve* should apply to New Right and neoconservative arguments that racial discrimination is a thing of the past, institutional racism does not exist, and race is no longer a factor in the lives of people of color. For if that is the case, then when people of color do less well in achievement tests or are not promoted in their workplaces as quickly as white people, no explanation remains except *The Bell Curve*'s explanation that they are "naturally" inferior.

New Rightists and neoconservatives are more than willing to state (and promote) the assertions that racial discrimination is exaggerated, or even a myth, and that institutional racism is the imaginary and unconfirmable creation of liberal intellectuals. But they want to disassociate themselves from the logical conclusion that the persistent inequality between white people and people of color is a result of the "inferiority" of people of color. When the President's Advisory Board on Race concluded in 1998 that "whites and Asians enjoy greater advantages economically and have better access to health care," and that "the social and economic progress of Blacks slowed between the mid-1970s and early 1990s, the economic status of Hispanics has declined in the last 25 years, and American Indians are the most disadvantaged ethnic group by far," the right remained silent.[69] Unwilling to state the racist conclusions of its own assertions, it could offer no explanation except the conclusions of *The Bell Curve*. Yet the right's leadership adamantly denies racist intentions.

Certainly, many liberals have also shied away from naming institutional racism as the cause for lower average test scores among people of color. For example, Derek Bok and William G. Bowen, in *The Shape of the River*, present evidence that African American students lag behind white students in grade point average. These self-described supporters of affirmative action and liberals on matters of race speculate that such factors as the number of books at home, opportunities to travel, or the nature of the conversation around the dinner table may explain the gap. They, too, do not point to institutional racism.[70]

NEW REPUBLICANS, NEW TACTICS

In 1994, after a Republican electoral sweep created a Republican majority in both Houses of Congress, the incoming Republican "freshmen" were so far to the right of the New Right that they were dubbed "new Republicans." Anti–affirmative action efforts increased dramatically, and have taken three forms: statewide initiatives banning affirmative action, lawsuits, and national anti–affirmative action legislation. To pursue these strategies, a number of new organizations whose principal purpose is to defeat affirmative action have appeared.

In November 1996, California voters passed the first successful statewide anti–affirmative action initiative, Proposition 209 or the California Civil Rights Initiative (CCRI), banning the practice of affirmative action in state employment, education, and the letting of contracts. Another blow to affirmative action in 1996 was the decision in *Hopwood v. Texas*, in which a three-judge panel of the Fifth Circuit Court of Appeals struck down an affirmative action admissions policy at the University of Texas Law School.[71] Lawsuits have since been filed in several other states challenging affirmative action practices in college admissions. At the national level, a Congressional bill, "virtually written by Clint Bolick of the Institute for Justice," would eliminate federal affirmative action. Initially known as the Dole-Canady Equal Opportunity Act, it has become simply the Canady Equal Opportunity Act.[72]

In all these instances, the right exploited the language of civil rights to turn back civil rights advancements. It appropriated the term "civil rights" and used it to refer to the rights of white people.[73] National organizations whose names might be taken to signal a liberal agenda, such as the American Civil Rights Institute, the Institute for Justice, the Center for Individual Rights (a nonprofit law group that helps students sue colleges over admission), and the Center for Equal Opportunity, exist to roll back the gains of the civil rights movement, especially affirmative action.[74]

In mounting its campaign against affirmative action, the new Republicans correctly identified a certain amount of grassroots opposition to affirmative action. Then, following a pattern developed in other right-wing campaigns, such as the anti-gay Amendment 2 campaign in Colorado and the campaigns against welfare recipients and immigrants, the organized right directed public attention to the issue, and defined it by using misleading language and distorted "statistics." The right's funders, strategists, adherents and politicians all collaborated to advance the campaign, putting their political and economic resources in support of the redefined issue.

In the case of California's Proposition 209, Republican Governor Pete Wilson, a presidential candidate at the time, used the Proposition

209 campaign to promote himself as a card-carrying member of the right. Ward Connerly, a businessman and member of the University Board of Regents (which controls the University of California system of campuses, a central locus of the struggle over affirmative action in California), provided an African American voice of leadership by heading the principal pro–Proposition 209 organization, Yes on Proposition 209. Connerly went on to form the American Civil Rights Institute, whose mission is to replicate the Proposition 209 campaign in other states.[75]

California's Republicans and traditional right-wing donors played a major role in bankrolling the Proposition 209 campaign, contributing approximately $1 million. Well-known right-wing funders also supported the effort, including media mogul Rupert Murdoch, who contributed $750,000; Howard F. Ahmanson, Jr., who contributed $350,000; and Richard Mellon Scaife, who contributed $100,000. Altogether, Yes on Proposition 209 raised $5,239,287, while its main opponent, the Campaign to Defeat 209, raised $2,185,086.[76]

The story of the passage of Proposition 209 illustrates the complex interaction of the right's effective political strategy, the political will of the players involved, and the skillful manipulation of language to exploit the negative mood of the voting public. One example of this interaction is the naming of Proposition 209, "The California Civil Rights Initiative," which gave voters no clue that it would eliminate affirmative action rather than support civil rights. Voter confusion over the intent of the initiative was widespread. The right applied the same strategy in Washington State's 1998 anti–affirmative action Initiative 200, known as I-200, which passed in November 1998.

In each state, the attorney general is responsible for giving the voters an impartial account of ballot initiatives. However, California's Republican Attorney General Dan Lungren, who had often and candidly expressed his opposition to affirmative action, wrote a required summary of Proposition 209 that omitted any indication that it would eliminate affirmative action. Despite a court challenge to this sleight-of-hand, the wording was ultimately retained.[77]

For a number of reasons, affirmative action supporters were not able to turn back Proposition 209. Because California Democrats hold varying views on affirmative action, the right was able to successfully use it as a "wedge" issue to split the Democratic Party's coalition. The right also had good political timing, since Proposition 209 was on the ballot just when President Bill Clinton, running for reelection, was unwilling to take a forceful stand on behalf of affirmative action lest he lose Democratic votes and give a political advantage to his opponent, Senator Bob Dole. The Democratic National Committee and the Democratic State Central Committee of California contributed less than half as much money to defend affirmative action as the Republican Party contributed to defeat it.[78] Afraid to take a forceful position in defense of affirmative action, the Democratic Party chose to keep its distance from an initiative that would profoundly and negatively affect some of its most loyal constituents, but was supported by others. In Jesse Jackson's words at the time, "The Republicans are wedging while the Democrats are hedging."

The outcome of these rightist efforts is mixed, and the ultimate fate of affirmative action is unclear. Certainly it is weakened, perhaps fatally. Nevertheless, on November 4, 1997 voters defeated a local anti–affirmative action initiative in Houston, and, two days later, the House Judiciary Committee voted to delay consideration of the Equal Opportunity Act (the Canady bill). Many supporters of the anti–affirmative action campaign seem shocked by the drastic effect of their work. For example, in California and Texas law schools, 1997 admission of Black students dropped 80 percent and 83 percent, respectively. So, affirmative action languishes, receiving only weak support from the Democratic Party, and opposed by a well-financed campaign conducted by the Republican Party and the organized right. As a widely accepted public policy, affirmative action may not be dead, but it has been stopped in its tracks.

WHERE WERE THE DEFENDERS OF AFFIRMATIVE ACTION?

Although liberals were the architects of most affirmative action policies, they seem unwilling to mount a spirited defense of it in the face of the right's multipronged attack. The right's use of the "color blind" standard to attack affirmative action has not been adequately challenged, and liberals have not argued the existence of institutional racism to explain the need for affirmative action. Liberal Democratic Party officeholders, who have access to the resources and media exposure necessary to conduct effective public education, have, for the most part, been unwilling to expend political capital in defense of affirmative action.

Much of this lack of a liberal defense reflects changes in the Democratic Party and the weakness of liberalism in general during a period when it has been under relentless attack. Six of the most prominent liberal senators lost in the 1980 election as a result of the New Right's vicious anti-liberal smear campaign conducted by the National Conservative Political Action Committee (NCPAC), its Executive Director Terry Dolan, and a core of about a dozen right-wing organizations that made up the New Right.[79] Those liberals remaining in Congress became reluctant to "go out on a limb" for any but a few carefully chosen issues. Affirmative action was not a strong contender.

Part of the New Right's strategy to lure white southerners and northern ethnic voters to the Republican Party was to argue that the Democratic Party had become the vehicle for "minority interests." The accusation worked well for the right. As Democratic voters crossed over to vote Republican, the progressive wing of the Democratic Party lost almost all influence within the Party, the liberal wing became weak, in numbers and in influence, and Democratic centrists became the dominant sector of the Party.

Democratic centrists argued that, if it were to survive, the Democratic Party must acknowledge that much of the white electorate had tired of any national effort to promote equality for people of color and (less so) for women. By electing Ronald Reagan, then George Bush, they argued, a plurality of white voters had sent a clear message that they were finished with two decades of racial progress, programs designed to empower the poor and marginal in society, and questions about the superiority of white, western European culture. The message that the major issues of racial discrimination in housing, employment, and promotion have been addressed by civil rights legislation and are now a thing of the past clearly has resonated with many white voters, because it speaks directly to their fatigue with social change and their growing resentment of advances by people of color.

Those liberals who have defended affirmative action have not been able to popularize even the most uncontested arguments in its favor: for instance, that preferences of various sorts are often used in selection processes—such as benefits for veterans, or college admission for athletes and the children of alumni and alumnae. What makes those practices acceptable, especially in the case of veterans and athletes, is the widely held judgment that these recipients are "appropriate" and "legitimate."[80] Most white Americans do not extend the same benefit of the doubt to "average" people of color.

Further, while many white liberals are willing to argue that racial diversity at college and in the workplace has social value in habituating people of different races to each other, other white liberals (and even many progressives) have not been willing to present the cultures of people of color, or the hidden history of women's contributions, as unique, valuable, and strengthening components of "American culture." White liberal opinion makers have not argued forcefully that often these cultures and contributions have been unacknowledged, or sometimes excluded, from mainstream cultural outlets. Apparently, for many white liberals, this message transcends the mandate of the civil rights movement they support and ventures too far from white America's self-image.

Most of those people who have mounted a strong defense of affirmative action are progressive rather than liberal, have little influence with centrist Democratic Party officeholders, and have only limited influence with liberals. Scholars such as Amy Ansell, K. Anthony Appiah, Ronald Dworkin, Christopher Edley, Jr., Amy Gutmann, Manning Marable, Salim Muwakkil, Stephen Steinberg, and Cornel West, who have spoken and written about the continuing need for affirmative action programs as the unfinished work of the civil rights movement, have not been able to parlay their arguments into the political clout necessary to hold elected officials accountable.[81] Within critical legal studies, the work of Derrick Bell, Kimberle Crenshaw, Richard Delgado, Charles Lawrence III, Mari Matsuda, Patricia Williams, and many others, has broken the mold of traditional legal discourse to create new forms of debate regarding the importance of, and necessity for, affirmative action.[82] But, once again, this scholarship, though it has advanced our understanding of the necessity for affirmative action, has not translated into a strong campaign of public education to counter the right's "color blind" paradigm.

The right has constructed a double assault on liberalism's rationale for affirmative action: denying the existence of institutional racism, and confining the debate over fairness exclusively to individual rights. Liberals were left with two tasks: to prove that institutional racism exists, which they showed slight inclination to do; and to go beyond individual rights to argue that society must accept occasional individual unfairness to promote social justice. Liberals, it seems, lacked either a belief that institutional racism exists or the political courage to make it their message.[83] When the scholars mentioned previously have argued that institutional racism is still prominent in the lives of people of color, and that sometimes the larger social good of correcting systemic injustices must take precedence over individual rights, the resulting debate has been confined primarily to an academic audience.

Ironically, many of the corporations which were initially forced by the federal government to create affirmative action programs now stand out as defenders of those programs, while elected politicians and right-wing activists are successfully dismantling affirmative action programs in the public sector and in higher education. A number of corporations have simply continued their existing affirmative action programs despite the right's attack. And, with the majority of public bureaucracies in the hands of conservative state- and local-level Republicans, it is within the corporate sector that there seems to be an appreciation of the value of diversity in the workplace and the advantages of tapping the entire breadth of the U.S. talent pool—pragmatic rather than moral arguments. So long as the moral justification for affirmative action remains muddled in the public's mind and infected with disinformation from the right, it appears that support for affirmative action will hang on most strongly where it is good for business.

CLASS-BASED AFFIRMATIVE ACTION

Some liberals and progressives, understanding that affirmative action as now conceived is unpopular with the public and likely to be under ever-increasing attack, are proposing that class replace race as a new basis for affirmative action. They reason that if affirmative action were based on class rather than race, it would apply to all races, and that race-neutrality would presumably calm the white backlash that has plagued race-based affirmative action. There is strong evidence that when social programs are universally applied—that is, when they apply to everyone who falls into a specific measurable category, such as low-income people—public opinion polls indicate more reliable support for them than when they favor only one segment of a group, such as low-income people of color.[84] Class-based affirmative action also would address the increasing poverty of the "truly disadvantaged" by giving them a better chance for admission to educational opportunities, employment, and promotion. It carries moral weight by addressing the *actual* victims of current discrimination and lack of opportunity. Under class-based affirmative action, a young Clarence Thomas would qualify, but his son or daughter would not.

Class-based affirmative action addresses a long-standing theme of progressive social justice work: the grossly unequal distribution of power and money in the United States, which the Republican agenda of low taxes and minimal social programs has now exacerbated. A final virtue of replacing race with class is that it may encourage coalitions across race. Class-based affirmative action might, therefore, breathe new life into the progressive movement by focusing it on a goal that minimizes intra-movement differences, and uniting it around progressives' common commitment to address unfair privilege.[85]

The arguments for class-based affirmative action assume that its race- and gender-based version has disproportionately helped those best able to take advantage of it (primarily middle-class white women and middle-class people of color) and has left the weakest (of all races) in society behind. Harvard sociologist William Julius Wilson has been especially persistent in asserting that only middle-class African Americans benefit from affirmative action. Because we don't have adequate research on affirmative action, Wilson's assertion has received wide acceptance. However, it seems unlikely to be correct, since so many affirmative action programs apply to working-class jobs in fire, police, and other municipal service jobs, and in both skilled and unskilled contracting work.[86]

Nonetheless, the gap between the middle class and the poor clearly is growing (not to mention the increasing gap between the rich and the middle class), and, despite affirmative action's dramatic successes, the circumstances of the extremely disadvantaged have not improved markedly. Obviously much more is needed. Social programs in areas such as education, job training, employment, and food assistance, which often are proposed by Black conservatives as an alternative to affirmative action, are unlikely to be funded, given the current anti-poor attitudes among much of the voting public. So, a simmering debate among liberals and progressives is whether the "more" that is needed should be affirmative action programs that are class-based.

Advocates for both race-based and class-based affirmative action assume that race and class can be determined by scientific means. But each year scholars publish more research about how race is mutable, socially constructed, and unscientific. A growing body of literature, especially studies of the historical transformation of groups from one racial or ethnic categorization to another, testifies to how racial categories can be assigned for political and social purposes. So long as race remains the basis for affirmative action (and gender for women—a less problematic categorization, though not without its own ambiguities), the lack of a scientific basis for racial classification will remain an issue.[87]

The same ambiguity applies to class. Many social programs that are means-based require an applicant to prove the need for service or assistance. Numerous accounts detail the difficulties and indignities suffered by people who must provide "proof" of their need. As with race, generalizations are possible; for instance, all those without high school educations are less advantaged than those who have college degrees. But individual variations allow injustices to occur. Both race and class are blunt instruments of measurement.

Nevertheless, although a class-based affirmative action program seems to comport with basic principles of fairness, the *consequences* of the shift from race-based to class-based affirmative action would make clear that class should not replace race as the primary determinant of compensatory actions. Because racial discrimination persists in the United States, and institutional racism pervades our society, the elimination of race-based affirmative action programs would again deny many people of color access to jobs, contracts, promotion, and admission to higher education. The introduction of class as the basis for affirmative action would not correct that exclusion because race discrimination persists across classes (as class discrimination persists across races). Even when a child faces positive life chances based on income or education, that child can be disadvantaged relative to a white child of the same income and education, simply because of skin color.[88] Class should be allowed only as a factor to be considered *with* race.

Where race-based affirmative action has been eliminated, such as in California after the passage of Proposition 209, the number of people of color admitted to institutions of higher education has fallen dramatically.[89] If class were substituted for race in affirmative action policies, the result would be similar. Because there are so many more white people than people of color in the United States (whites outnumber Blacks 8 to 1), and there are more white people who are poor than there are poor people of color (low-income whites outnumber low-income Blacks 2.5 to 1), the use of class-based affirmative action would help far more poor whites than poor non-whites. Further, in the case of higher education, white students from low-income families score higher on SAT tests than do Black students from low-income families.[90]

Although, in seeking equal opportunity for all, race may not be the only proper basis for affirmative action, class should not be the only basis either. "Class" does not take color into account, and color is a complicating factor across class. "Class" also does not take gender into account, although gender discrimination excludes women from opportunities and promotions and results in their receiving disproportionately low pay.

A formula for affirmative action that takes race, gender, and class into account would be complicated to administer and may not be substantially more popular with the voting public than the current race- and gender-based policies. It may open the door to demands for affirmative action considerations from a broad range of groups that suffer discrimination and lack opportunity. Because race is so prominent in the hierarchy of American prejudices, the hostility to affirmative action "preferences" may persist in a "reformed" affirmative action that considered class as well as race and gender. But it would improve the fairness of affirmative action and better, if imperfectly, serve the goal of compensatory justice.

When rightists insist that discrimination based on race is a thing of the past and institutional racism is a myth, they promote an opportunistic reading of reality that many white voters are anxious to believe. By asserting that "color blind" policies represent a just distribution of social goods, the right steals a goal of the civil rights movement, pretends it has now been reached, and provides a comforting message for many white voters. These right-wing tactics have been politically successful. Unless progressives and liberals are more effective in exposing the right's misrepresentations and devious strategies, the defeat of affirmative action may even be perceived as a victory for universal fairness. Nothing could be farther from the truth.

Chapter 6

LIBERTARIANISM AND CIVIL SOCIETY:
THE ROMANCE OF FREE-MARKET
CAPITALISM

A t the age of sixteen, I read Ayn Rand's novels and became a rugged individualist who saw each person as the "master of his own fate," in the narrowly gendered language of 1961. I bought a copy of Barry Goldwater's definitive statement of conservative principles, *The Conscience of a Conservative* ($3 in hardback) and was thrilled when Goldwater autographed it for me at a public speaking event. I attended church services around the corner from my urban boarding school several times a week—another manifestation, in that setting, of my independent thinking and nonconformist individualism. Though I didn't know it at the time, I was a libertarian.

Although I fairly quickly renounced my romance with libertarianism, it left me with an understanding of its appeal. It is easy to write off government as an arbiter of social problems because government has not proved reliable in delivering social justice. It is easy to forget that there are cases, such as ending Jim Crow segregation, in which no other institution but the federal government could have effectively defied segregationist practices in the South.

Today, I often meet people who consider themselves liberals, but more accurately should describe themselves as a type of libertarian. They are not liberals because they don't trust "government" and don't look to state institutions for answers to social problems. But they think people's personal beliefs and behaviors are their own business, they believe in liberal immigration policies, and they are inclined to oppose militarism. They are not right-wing, and would resent being associated with right-wing libertarians, who oppose *all* government activity except national defense and believe that not succeeding in the free market is evidence of an individual's lack of hard work, not bad luck or the result of race, class, gender, and other inequities.

Many libertarians are just disillusioned liberals with nowhere to turn. But partly because these people don't call themselves libertarians and, therefore, don't see themselves as part of the libertarian movement, their voice in it is very small. The movement is run and controlled by the "other" libertarians—those who hate government and hate liberals.

Libertarianism is not prominent in U.S. public debate. Popular magazines and journals contain few articles on the subject, and many of those are short, snappy opinion pieces that imply that libertarianism is an ideological oddity. Even well-informed people usually know little about libertarianism. Few know, for instance, that the Libertarian Party has been the longest-running and largest third-party presence in U.S. politics ever since the mid-1970s. Its lack of a public profile masks the important contribution that libertarianism has made to the right's resurgence.

Libertarians approach the state without ambivalence and without nuance. Because they see the freedom of the individual as the greatest good, they believe the state, which possesses the power to coerce and thus to limit individual freedom, should be minimal. The state's only legitimate role, in their view, is to provide an adequate military defense and secure a reasonable level of social order. *Caveat emptor*—let the buyer beware—might be said to be the libertarian motto in all realms, not just in the economic sphere. Antitrust laws, social safety net programs, redistribution of wealth schemes (e.g., a graduated income tax), involvement in foreign affairs, and regulation of environmental pollution are just some of the government roles that libertarians oppose.

Libertarians are often asked: How would a society remain orderly if individuals were allowed complete freedom? What would hold chaos at bay if the state were to become minimalist? For many libertarians, a "Nightwatchman" state is needed to preserve order and a modicum of justice.[1] For right-wing libertarians, however, freedom is the paramount issue, order is a distant second, and justice an even more distant third.

Fortunately for their ideology, right-wing libertarians have identified a mechanism that provides freedom and as much order and justice as necessary. The mechanism is, of course, free-market capitalism, with its "invisible hand" that regulates and allocates with a precision surpassing that of any other political, economic, or social system ever tried. The invisible hand is the concept developed by Adam Smith and popularized by F. A. Hayek and Milton Friedman, the economic gurus of libertarianism. Functions traditionally associated with state power—distributing resources, punishing criminals, educating children, building highways and bridges and other physical infrastructure—libertarians assign to the free market.

Because libertarians believe in radical individualism in relation to the state, they also maintain that individuals should be free to follow their own preferences in the conduct of their personal lives. Thus, ideologically consistent libertarians favor gay rights, choice on reproductive issues (including abortion, birth control, and forced sterilization), complete artistic freedom, free trade, legalization of drugs, and the right of individuals to immigrate/emigrate freely across borders. Holding so many positions that are clearly *not* those promoted by the contemporary right, libertarians are often at odds with it. However, in the 1980s and 1990s there has been a convergence between libertarians and the right, especially the secular right, on the primacy of the free market in economic policy and the need for privatizing many government roles. Libertarians have provided much of the ideological guidance for the right's agenda in these areas.

WHY IS LIBERTARIANISM SO CONFUSING?

People often confuse libertarianism with anarchism, and sometimes with liberalism, because it shares ideological aspects with each. This ideological eclecticism allows libertarians to claim to be "neither right nor left." To add to the confusion, there is a distinct difference between right-wing libertarianism and leftist libertarianism, and right-wing libertarianism itself has two distinct ideological sectors.

Libertarianism is often confused with anarchism because both are opposed to government control over the individual. In some cases, it's a toss-up whether a person or an organization deserves the label "anarchist" or "libertarian." Europeans often use the words interchangeably. However, whereas anarchists seldom relate to the state at all, except to oppose it or unmask its abuses, libertarians are much involved in changing government to meet their criteria. The Cato Institute, the largest and most prolific libertarian think tank, is prominent in creating and advocating for legislation to promote its political principles. It works hand in glove with the right, often providing valuable research to bolster and tailor its policy proposals.

Both libertarianism and anarchism are broad enough to accommodate a rightist wing and a leftist wing. The greatest confusion between anarchism and libertarianism derives from the overlap between right-wing anarchism and right-wing libertarianism. The clearest contrast between anarchism and libertarianism is between left-wing anarchism and right-wing libertarianism. Anarchism of the social revolutionary (leftist) kind, advocated by nineteenth-century Russian-born philosophers Michael Bakunin and Peter Kropotkin, is a reaction to government abuses of individual rights, and especially government's role in protecting private property. Benjamin R. Tucker (1854–1939), an important but now forgotten U.S. journalist and proponent of left libertarianism, promoted the notion of a just capitalism that was anti-monopoly. According to researcher Ulrike Heider, Tucker saw the ideal society "within the spirit of early socialism, as a form of virtuous harmony." She goes on to say, "The protection of private property and of the person by means of voluntary associations and cooperation is, according to him, only a temporary necessity, because with the realization of his utopia, poverty and with it crime will disappear from the world."[2] However, right-wing libertarians oppose the state because the state *interferes* with the possession and accumulation of private property.[3] Currently, right-wing libertarianism is so dominant that most people in the United States are unaware of left libertarianism. The closest contemporary manifestation of left libertarianism is the American Civil Liberties Union, though it has historically eschewed the label "libertarian," perhaps because the label is so closely associated with the right.

Many people today also confuse libertarianism with liberalism.[4] Both are rooted in respect for individual rights, and oppose government attempts to limit those rights, including the right to take unpopular stands and commit unpopular acts, such as burning the flag or smoking marijuana, being a "practicing homosexual," or immigrating across borders. In policy debates, libertarians and liberals are both defending these rights (though, for both, instances of straying from these philosophical positions for political expediency are common). Voting records indicate that it is not uncommon for libertarian and liberal politicians to vote together on many of the social issues. Libertarians and liberals often appear on the same platform to support freedom for a marginalized group or practice.

For liberals, however, libertarianism is too attached to the marketplace to serve as an arbiter of social conflicts and injustices. Liberals recognize that the self-correcting mechanisms which libertarians claim are built into the free-market system are inadequate to assure security for the more vulnerable members of society, especially those who have little or no private property.

The confusion of liberalism and libertarianism paves the way for libertarians to present themselves as "neither right not left," but rather as a third political option that draws from across the political spectrum. This was the lifelong dream of the late Murray N. Rothbard, known as "Mr. Libertarian," who believed that by attracting followers from a broad political spectrum, libertarianism might become a viable alternative for liberals and conservatives. The success of the Libertarian Party in the past has, at times, encouraged libertarians to believe in the possibility of such a coalescing of various political allegiances.

THE ROOTS OF LIBERTARIANISM

Libertarians often call themselves "classical liberals." The same claim to be "the real liberals" is often made by other conservatives. The claim to the mantle of liberalism refers to the writings of two English philosophers who are the "founding fathers" of American political thought, John Locke and John Stuart Mill. In *The Second Treatise of Government* (1690), Locke argued for representative government by the people. Mill refined this founding principle in *On Liberty* (1859) by adding the concept of individual rights and individual freedoms. Since these principles continue to resonate with most Americans, many contemporary politicians lay claim to them.

Libertarians also claim two other icons as the progenitors of their political ideas—Thomas Jefferson and Thomas Paine. Paine's pamphlet *Common Sense* (1776) was widely circulated at the time of the American Revolution and remains a popular statement of the superiority of "society" over "government." In his denunciation of monarchy, Paine provides libertarians the concept of a "civil society" that has become the basis of their alternative to government as the arbiter of people's needs and the protector of their freedoms.

In 1776 Thomas Jefferson drafted the Declaration of Independence, which libertarians adopt as their manifesto for freedom from government interference in citizens' lives. In his later years, Jefferson became even more suspicious of government power, to the delight of libertarians, who rely on his writings to boost the legitimacy of their ideas.

In asserting their belief that they are the true repositories of American values, libertarians can be as rigid and self-righteous as any member of the Christian Right. In contrast with the Christian Right, however, libertarians are also sometimes accused of being *libertine*. That is, when they oppose any restriction on individual behavior that does not harm others, they are often defending behaviors that other sectors of the right consider self-indulgent, sinful, or even Satanic. And it is not just the Christian Right that ridicules libertarians. The secular right, with its traditional support for an aggressive foreign policy and its authoritarian tendencies in the name of social stability, finds coexistence with libertarians difficult.

Imagine, for instance, the average middle-aged, traditional-values rightist encountering the centerpiece of the libertarian canon, Ayn Rand's *The Fountainhead*. Written in 1943, it is the story of a misunderstood but brilliant architect, Howard Roark (played in the Hollywood movie version by Gary Cooper), who struggles against the forces of conformity and mediocrity, but ultimately is beaten by these enemies of all genius. Along the way, he "takes" the beautiful young heroine Dominique Francon by force. She ultimately submits to his power, brilliance, and superiority. The novel, a favorite of college students in the 1960s, is selling briskly again at the end of the century. It is Nietzschean in its glorification of power and its exaltation of an idealized Aryan male super-hero.[5]

To libertarians, Ayn Rand is the "founder" of contemporary libertar-ianism. From her position at the libertarian Nathaniel Brandon Institute in New York City in the 1950s and early 1960s, she ruled the "move-ment" with an iron hand. During the same period, Austrian economist Ludwig von Mises, who in 1922 had published an influential critique of socialism simply titled *Socialism*, taught libertarian economics at the Graduate School of Business Administration at New York University. Von Mises came to the United States after fleeing the Nazis and became the "father" of the Austrian School of Economics and an intellectual giant of libertarian economics. His students included Friedrich Hayek, who was trained by von Mises to be an uncompromising supporter of the free market and became an extremely influential libertarian economist in his own right.

Von Mises and Hayek rested much of their argument for free-market capitalism on the concept of the "invisible hand," originally developed by Scottish economist Adam Smith in his influential book, *The Wealth of Nations* (1776). Smith argued that, through the voluntary cooperation promoted by the free-market system, individuals pursue their own ob-jectives and at the same time produce what is needed for their survival. The balance between needs and the goods produced to meet those needs is maintained by the "invisible hand" of market forces. Von Mises and Hayek built on Smith's defense of the free market to argue against collec-tivism in any form, especially in Hayek's most influential book, his 1944 critique of socialism, *The Road to Serfdom*. In 1974, Hayek won a Nobel Prize, though at that time Keynesian economics, which called for a strong government role in stabilizing the economy, still dominated the thinking of economists.[6]

Another free-market economist, Milton Friedman, has spent his long career as an advocate for free-market capitalism at the University of Chicago. But Friedman, who won a Nobel Prize in 1976 for his work in monetary economics, has been no ivory tower economist. His many opinion pieces on the op-ed pages of mainstream newspapers and his long-running column in the popular magazine *Newsweek* has made him an important opinion maker for the last thirty years.

Friedman's influence extended far beyond his own writing through a cadre of his students known as "The Chicago Boys." It was these students who delivered the major stain on Friedman's career when they put themselves in the service of the Chilean military junta under General Augusto Pinochet. In the 1970s, Pinochet's military dictatorship carried out a brutal terror campaign to destroy "communism" in Chile. He imported a number of "Chicago Boys" to advise him on the establishment of a free-market system. The result was a laboratory in which they conducted a clinical trial of libertarian economics. It was a cruel and bitter experience of political repression and economic exploitation for Chile's poor.[7] Libertarians have never accepted responsibility for the fact that this hero of libertarian economics lent his name and reputation to this project and did so not reluctantly but enthusiastically.

While the country focused its attention on the "red menace" and the civil rights movement in the 1950s and 1960s, Ayn Rand, Ludwig von Mises, Friedrich Hayek, and Milton Friedman mentored a generation of libertarians. Perhaps it was this early training by powerful ideologues that resulted in a movement characterized by intellectualism and ideological rigor. Libertarians often rigidly maintain their intellectual integrity, with the arrogance that is a usual part of the libertarian culture, and therefore have difficulty collaborating with other conservatives. This adherence to principle caused them to split with Young Americans for Freedom in 1969 over YAF's support for the Vietnam War. Those who split from YAF ultimately became the core group that launched the Libertarian Party in 1972.[8] Similarly, libertarians did not join in William F. Buckley's "fusionism," the political compromise arrived at in the 1960s that united the traditional conservative economic agenda with the right-wing social issues agenda by merging two formerly distinct branches of conservatism. Fusionism created a politically appealing ideological package that provided the grounding vision for the rise of the New Right in the later 1970s.

Libertarianism does not blend well with other ideologies, in part because libertarians tend to be dogmatic and combative, rather than pragmatic and compromising. They are ill-suited to be team players within the larger right. As a result, they cling to a vision of a libertarian future in which their ideology has carried the day and they prevail in all spheres—

political, social, and economic. Unwilling to collaborate in ways that threaten their central political tenets, their movement remains rigid and somewhat shadowy.

RIGHT-WING LIBERTARIANISM

Right-wing libertarians combine anti-government fervor with an almost mystical belief in the free-market system of unfettered capitalism. The association of these ideas with conservatism leads most people to see libertarianism as just a variation of traditional conservatism. However, when we compare right-wing libertarians' ideas of a good society with those political philosophers who articulated a more traditional conservatism, such as the English philosophers Thomas Hobbes in the seventeenth century, Edmund Burke in the eighteenth century, and more recently, English political theorist Michael Oakeshott and University of Chicago-based Leo Strauss, the contrast demonstrates that traditional conservatism supports "establishment" power, which resides in societal institutions such as the church, the state, and the family. Traditional conservatives, as exemplified by the *mainstream* of the Republican Party, therefore, most fear the chaos they associate with too much democracy and too few institutions of authority.

Right-wing libertarianism, in contrast, is revolutionary in its desire to eliminate the state and restore men to their rightful place as masters of their own fate. And let there be no mistake that it is *men* (specifically white men) who are captivated by the libertarian vision, with the occasional exception of an icon like Ayn Rand or a token woman like sociologist Anne Wortham or Virginia Postrel, editor of the prominent libertarian magazine, *Reason*. Right-wing libertarians are reactionaries who are vicious in their condemnation of liberal programs for social justice, sharing with the larger right its abhorrence of liberalism. Like the right, they justify their antiliberalism as "getting government off the backs of the poor," and point to complete freedom to own private property and compete in the marketplace as the true road to prosperity for all. The similarity to the Reagan Administration's bogus scheme to cut taxes in order to generate more revenue and "lift all boats" shows the parallel between economic libertarianism and the right's economic agenda.

To right-wing libertarians, government is an evil conspiracy to rob the individual of his money, his freedom, and his soul. This hostility extends to any government endeavor—from schools to foreign aid. Liberals are "dictators." The rhetoric of right-wing libertarians rivals (and sometimes surpasses) that of the New Right. While avoiding the Christian Right's language of morality and setting aside the social issues as the centerpiece of their agenda, rightist libertarians condemn liberal programs with all the fervor of the most reactionary members of the New Right.

Among the many factions of right-wing libertarianism, two ideological schools stand out: "paleo" libertarianism and "rightist" libertarianism. Paleo-libertarians retain the Old Right's ideological principles, complete with explicit racism, anti-Semitism, and sexism. Their titular leader was the late Murray N. Rothbard. Two publications that either represent this hard right libertarianism or live in close harmony with it are *Triple R* (formerly the *Rothbard-Rockwell Report*), the newsletter of the Center for Libertarian Studies in Burlingame, California, and *Chronicles* (formerly *Chronicles of Culture*), published by the Rockford Institute of Rockford, Illinois.

Rightist libertarianism is a more moderate, Washington, D.C.–oriented variety that promotes a softer face for libertarianism, including the claim that it supports the rights of women, people of color, lesbians and gays, immigrants, and other unpopular groups. It is best represented by the Cato Institute and *Reason* magazine, which have exerted impressive influence within the right's policy initiatives, especially efforts to downsize government and privatize public services.

In 1995 Murray Rothbard and his colleague Llewellyn H. Rockwell, Jr. hosted a meeting intended to promote unity among paleo-libertarians. Rothbard and Rockwell were proud of their paleo-libertarian credentials. At their unity meeting, they invited representatives from the Ludwig von Mises Institute and the Center for Libertarian Studies to discuss their shared political values. They made the case that all those in attendance were united as "paleos" in opposing the right's elites—whom they called "welfare-warfare" elites because they supported welfare reform rather than promoted its elimination, and also supported the Gulf War. Particularly hated were the "neoconservatives"—by which the "paleos" seemed to mean the entire New Right, the Christian Right, and members of the neoconservative movement, such as Irving Kristol, Norman Podhoretz, and Midge Decter—and the Cato Institute, which they ludicrously labeled left-libertarian. Rockwell claimed that the most telling evidence of the triumph of paleo-conservative libertarian ideology was the election in 1994 of a class of Congressional "new Republicans" —right-wing Representatives and Senators who were isolationist, conspiracy-minded, and radically reactionary in their opposition to all government programs.[9]

Within the paleo wing, there is no "pandering" to the poor. In the words of Llewellyn Rockwell, Jr.: "The term "poor" is not a designation of material status; it is a political term designating a political status. It has become a synonym for the parasitical class that the middle class is supposed to support at increased levels until the entire stock of the national wealth is gone. The poor are not the victims of the present system, unless you think that criminals are the victims of the people they rob."[10] Right-wing libertarians often and passionately debate points of ideological distinction, both between the two sectors of libertarianism and within each sector. *Triple R*, for example, devotes most of its pages to vicious and snide attacks on rightist libertarians, accusing them of various forms of perfidy, including the extreme "crime" of being neoconservative. Libertarian in-fighting (usually in the form of personal attacks) occurs over the "correct" vision of a future libertarian society. The vision of this future society is so drastically different from contemporary reality that the entire discussion is speculative, though never acknowledged as such. The result is a sense of the debate as a game, in which each ideologue argues for his or her own version of a fantasy future, bitterly trumping the opponent's version. These exchanges generate great heat among the debaters, their differences often looming so large that libertarians are unable to coordinate their actions and create a unified, effective movement that could address pressing policy issues.[11]

LIBERTARIANISM'S DIRTY SECRET

ibertarians view all government programs as coercive and prefer existing inequality to government programs designed to decrease it. They hold social programs in disdain, based on their philosophical objections to any limitations on individual freedom. To them, the individual who is free to sink or swim is freer than the individual who is subjected to government sanctions and victim-producing government "help." The antigovernment rhetoric of paleo-libertarians reaches a fevered expression in right-wing citizens' militias—militant (and usually armed) bands of rugged individualists who see themselves threatened by the "occupying" government, "Blacks," or "Jewish bankers." High-profile paleo-libertarians have embraced the most bald-faced racism and anti-Semitism, basing their theories of the superiority of whites over Blacks and of Christians over Jews on "real" evidence, as opposed to the "myths" they claim are promoted by liberals.

This Old Right racist ideology is evident when paleo-libertarians talk about social justice programs that address racism. They do not argue, as Black conservatives do, that Blacks will fare better if they are "set free" of government assistance. They argue instead that whites are superior to people of color. For example, Samuel Francis, notorious racial nationalist, writing in the *Rothbard-Rockwell Report* in 1993 about the policy implications of "white superiority," says,

> In the first place, the natural differentiation of the races in intellectual capacities implies that of the two major races in the United States today, only one possesses the inherent capacity to create and sustain the level of civilization that has historically characterized its homelands in Europe and America. . . . And secondly, the recognition of racial realities implies that most of the efforts now deployed to combat racism . . . are misplaced, based on a profound misconception of racial capacities. . . . Those policies and laws are the fruit of a discredited egalitarian mythology that animates the federal leviathan's perpetual war against civil society and debilitates white resistance to the gathering storm of racial revolution that the enemies, white and non-white, of the white race and its civilization now openly preach and prepare.[12]

Another example of paleo-libertarian racism is the writing of Charles Murray, right-wing sociologist and coauthor of *The Bell Curve: Intelligence and Class Structure in American Life*, which argues that Blacks are genetically inferior to whites. Murray has recently gone public with his libertarian identity by publishing a book titled *What It Means to Be a Libertarian*.[13] In praise of the publication of *The Bell Curve*, Murray Rothbard wrote:

> Until literally mid-October, 1994, it was shameful and taboo for anyone to talk publicly or write about home truths which everyone, and I mean *everyone* [italics in origi-

nal] knew in their hearts and in private: that is, almost self-evident truths about race, intelligence, and heritability. . . . Essentially, I mean the almost self-evident fact that individuals, ethnic groups, and races differ among themselves in intelligence and in many other traits, and that intelligence, as well as less controversial traits of temperament, are in large part hereditary.[14]

To be sure, any political sector can have a few bad apples who give it a bad name. This is particularly true in the case of libertarianism, where the individual is seen as an independent actor, and even such media creations as New York City shock radio host Howard Stern can declare themselves libertarians and run for governor on a libertarian ticket. In fairness, the label "racist" can only stick when racism is part of a movement's ideology, or when members of a movement's leadership exhibit racism and the movement as a whole does nothing to challenge and remove them.

By these standards, libertarianism has a significant problem with racism as well as anti-Semitism. The late Murray Rothbard, who was ideologically aligned with the Old Right, never renounced the Old Right's racist attitudes during the decades he occupied center stage in the emergence of libertarianism. In his own publication, the *Rothbard-Rockwell Report*, Rothbard is described posthumously as "Dean of the Austrian School of economics, founder of modern libertarianism, and restorer of the Old Right."

Anti-Semitism also is prominent in Rothbard's circles. Rothbard described himself as "a pro-Christian Jew who thinks that everything good in Western Civilization is traceable to Christianity."[15] Rothbard's colleague Llewellyn Rockwell served as a senior advisor to Pat Buchanan's presidential campaign in 1992. Buchanan has repeatedly been accused of anti-Semitism. When the accusation was made by William F. Buckley, who also leveled it against another Rothbard ally, Joseph Sobran (who was serving at the time as one of only two contributing editors at the *Rothbard-Rockwell Report*), the *Report* ran an article by David Gordon attacking Buckley, calling him a hypocrite and "hypersensitive."[16] *Triple R* has repeatedly run articles that not only praise Buchanan, but vehemently align with his Old Right views. Rothbard so admired Buchanan that he once compared Buchanan with two of the right's Hollywood heroes, John Wayne and Gary Cooper.[17]

After Rothbard's death in 1994, the *Rothbard-Rockwell Report* ran a lengthy article by Paul Gottfried titled "Why must Christians routinely grovel and apologize for crimes against Jews which they never committed?" Gottfried not only makes his own case for the superiority of Christian behavior over Jewish behavior, but he describes the difference between his reasoning on this subject and Rothbard's. Gottfried says of accusations of anti-Semitism against Buchanan:

> It is not Christian anti-Semitism but, as Murray Rothbard used to note, Jewish goy-bashing which has become the characteristic act of tastelessness in our time. On the reasons, however, Murray and I disagreed. He attributed this "blatant wrong" to Christian niceness combined with Jewish antipathy (toward Christians). My own reading of the dominant culture is more critical. If Christians want to be punching-bags, others will take advantage of their masochism.[18]

Rothbard may have been an embarrassment to the libertarian movement, as a "pro-Christian Jew" who held Jews in disdain for their liberalism and what he called their "antipathy" toward Christians, a supporter of high-profile racists like Charles Murray, and a reactionary who bragged of his Old Right beliefs. It is telling that, when he died, his death was not mentioned in *Reason* magazine. He was not, however, dethroned or disowned by the movement. In fact, he presided for several decades over the far right wing of the movement, and is quoted and listed with the most famous libertarian thinkers in Cato Institute Vice President David Boaz's 1997 book, *Libertarianism*.[19]

LIBERTARIANISM AND THE RIGHT

ibertarianism is a sort of stepchild of the right. For three decades it has been consigned to the sidelines of the right's resurgence. But that doesn't mean that it has exerted no influence over the right. In fact, it has played a vital role in providing the rationale and policy recommendations that benefit big business, while it is sidelined when its ideology is anti-business or pro–individual freedoms. The right uses libertarian ideas and policies as they suit the movement's goals. Many libertarians could be called "closet" or "pseudo" libertarians because they publicly distance themselves from the label in order to maintain a less complicated membership in the New Right or among the "new Republicans." Among them are Senator Phil Gramm (R-TX) and House Majority

Leader Dick Armey (R-TX).[20] It is hard to name one prominent libertarian politician who will identify as such, and, of libertarian think tanks, only the Cato Institute has a national profile outside the right. Libertarian organizations, including the Cato Institute, are just a small part of the right's infrastructure. The weight and influence of the Heritage Foundation in development of the policies promoted by the Reagan and Bush Administrations dwarfs the role of the Cato Institute.

So, is libertarianism a significant part of the right? The answer to that question has changed since the November 1994 elections, when many "new Republicans" came to Congress to implement the Contract with America—a document laced with libertarian influence. The "new Republicans" are not necessarily aligned with right-wing libertarianism. They also are not necessarily aligned with the Christian Right. But there is enormous political compatibility among the three groups. Right-wing libertarianism, especially the thinking of those at the Cato Institute, is ideologically compatible with many "new Republican" ideas.

In 1977, Edward H. Crane, with money from right-wing industrialist and philanthropist Charles Koch, founded the Cato Institute as an outgrowth of the Libertarian Party. It describes itself as a public policy research organization with the goal of expanding "civil society" and minimizing the role of "political society," the current system which it sees as based on "rigid rules and mandated relationships." Cato's influence has blossomed since 1994, so that by 1999, Cato operated with a budget of $12 million.[21]

Michael Lind describes Cato's role this way in his book *Up from Conservatism: Why the Right Is Wrong for America*:

> The economic program of Newt Gingrich's Republicans, when it has not been written by business lobbyists, has been drafted by experts from the libertarian network, such as Stephen Moore of the Cato Institute. . . . Whether they admit it or not, the libertarians play an assigned, and subordinate, role in the conservative Republican coalition. Their support for the decriminalization of marijuana and gay marriage is tolerated and indulged by the Republican elite because the libertarian policy analysts are so useful in providing the business community with what it wants.[22]

While Cato often seems to accept this subordinate role and panders to the right to gain national influence, other libertarians look down on the right as a political second string. In the eyes of many right-wing libertarians, it is *they* who are the grandfathers of the Reagan revolution and the ideology of minimal government. They maintain that *libertarian* ideas underlie the right's success, implying that, if the right were to examine its own ideology, it would see the superiority of libertarianism's ideological package.

Libertarians certainly have played an important role in the success of the New Right, and, more recently, in formulating the even more extreme antigovernment policies of the "new Republicans." In the words of Robert W. Poole, Jr., publisher of *Reason* and president of the Reason Foundation, "*Reason* was the first magazine to write about privatization of public services." And "it was articles in *Reason* that foresaw the breakup of the Bell monopoly, and made the case for airline deregulation and energy price decontrol long before these actions were taken."[23] In its 1997 Annual Report, the Cato Institute brags that libertarians originated the ideas of school choice and privatizing Social Security, and exerted influence in promoting telecommunications deregulation and fundamental tax reform. More recently, its proposals to privatize the national and state parks and the interstate highways exemplify the right-wing libertarian policy proposals that appeal to the "new Republicans."

Perhaps the greatest source of tension between New Rightists and libertarians is that libertarians are not necessarily anti-modern. Libertarianism appeals to the "me" generation that wants to express itself freely—through choices such as to use drugs, to be publicly lesbian, gay, bisexual, or transgender, or to live an unconventional lifestyle—and enjoy a pattern of material consumption made possible by success in the free-market system. Researcher Stephen L. Newman, analyzing data collected by the Cato Institute, points to evidence that yuppies—young urban professionals who are white, economically successful, well educated, and socially individualistic—make up the bulk of libertarians.[24] While Newman is careful to say that Cato's data do not meet social science standards, they do conform to his and my own sense of who libertarians are.

Another major source of tension is that libertarians ironically resurrect isolationism, an Old Right theme that is a contested issue within the New Right. A recent manifestation of libertarians' isolationism was their opposition to the Gulf War. Seen by the right as a necessary and noble exercise in "drawing a line in the sand" against bullies and authoritarians such as Saddam Hussein, libertarians saw it as adventurism for the sake of the profits derived from Middle East oil. Paleo-libertarians agreed

with Pat Buchanan (an honorary paleo-libertarian himself) when he denounced George Bush as an "internationalist." These are strong words
indeed, because to both the Old Right and libertarians, being an internationalist is by definition putting the "real interests" of the United States
second to those of the "new international order." True, the United States
may dominate in this new world order, but only an isolationist foreign
policy agenda will first and foremost provide protection for U.S. interests. Libertarians and Old Rightists found themselves allied with the political left in their opposition to the Gulf War, though leftists' reasons for
that opposition differed markedly. Is it any wonder that libertarians claim
to be pursuing an agenda that is "neither left nor right"?

There is no better illustration of the differences between libertarians
and the larger right than the 1997 conflict over the nomination by President Bill Clinton of William Weld, former Republican governor of
Massachusetts, to serve as ambassador to Mexico. Weld's nomination
required the assent of Senator Jesse Helms (R-NC), chair of the Senate
Foreign Relations Committee, who is simultaneously a standard-bearer
of the Old Right and an influential leader of the New Right. Helms rejected Weld's nomination, refusing even to hold hearings on it, ostensibly
on the grounds that Weld was not sufficiently tough in his stand on drugs
to be ambassador to a drug-sensitive post like Mexico.

Jesse Helms is a scion of Old Right racism and authoritarianism, but,
more important for this battle, a rabid proponent of the New Right's social issues. William Weld is a rightist libertarian whose libertarianism
makes him a leader on right-wing economic issues, such as privatization
of government services, elimination of welfare, and elimination of government regulation in the private sector. In all these respects, he and
Jesse Helms are comrades in the Republication Party. But as a rightist
libertarian, Weld is pro-choice, pro-gay, and has supported the medical
use of marijuana—all positions that are abhorrent to the "paleo" politics
of Jesse Helms.

Some analysts interpreted the standoff between Weld and Helms
(won easily by Helms) as a personal feud between two men who don't like
each other. Whatever its motivation, it starkly illustrates the split within
the right posed by libertarians, especially rightist libertarians. Should
the Republican Party be forced to choose between Jesse Helms and William Weld, it would no doubt choose Helms. However, Weld did find

some support among Republicans, and it is possible that he was ahead of his time in attempting to split the Republican Party and assert a new role for rightist libertarians.

CATO'S "CIVIL SOCIETY"

ibertarians are often criticized for a heartless indifference to the social contract, or any other civic-minded concern for the larger social good. Even prominent libertarian funder Richard Dennis has complained that libertarians lack sufficient "points of light" and show too little interest in promoting values that lead to moral social outcomes.[25] Libertarians respond with their notion of "civil society," which they claim is nurtured by libertarianism more successfully than by any other political ideology.

The term "civil society" is used in many different ways, making its definition unclear. For some, it is simply the presence of civility among society's members; its breakdown is reflected in "road rage" on freeways, locked doors, and unchivalrous men who sit while a pregnant woman stands on the bus. For others, civil society is the voluntary sector praised by Alexis de Tocqueville in his observations on early American society, published in his 1835 book *Democracy in America*. In this definition, civil society is the key to the long-standing dilemma of Western democracy— how to harmonize the conflict between individual rights and the need of the larger society to promote peace and prosperity for all its citizens.[26]

For libertarians, civil society is the alternative to the current "political society," in which, they charge, government controls (i.e., coerces) citizens' decisions about how to pursue their lives and happiness. To them, civil society involves the voluntary interaction of individuals and associations. A strong civil society is the libertarian answer to the "welfare state." Libertarians believe it provides the same level of security for the individual, while leaving the individual's liberty intact. Civil society would, therefore, fill the holes left when the business sector takes no responsibility for the social good and government no longer plays a role in assuring it. Civil society would become society's social glue, acting to moderate the chaotic competition of radical individualism. As described by Edward Crane, founder and president of the Cato Institute, "Civil society . . . is based on volunteerism and predicated on giving the widest possible latitude to the individual so that he has sovereignty over his own life, so long as he respects the equal rights of others in society."[27]

Here again, libertarians claim they are promoting a plan that is "neither right nor left." But in reality, libertarianism's civil society is simply the private sector, and the assertion that it is superior is based on an unquestioning faith in the free market, and a belief that people will collaborate and create needed social services when they are freed from government restraints and dependence. But why would they? And even giving libertarians the benefit of the doubt, haven't we learned that social services do not assure social justice?

In the free-for-all competitive private sector they call civil society, libertarians show no concern for a level playing field. Further, they attack those who do show such concern as "redistributionists" and claim that "redistributionists" (liberals) advocate a world in which everyone is *the same*, when in reality the actual liberal argument is that everyone is entitled to have the same opportunities. For example, P. J. O'Rourke, well-known author and Fellow at the Cato Institute, delivered a speech at Cato's twentieth anniversary celebration in May 1997 that defined egalitarianism as "worse than stupid, it's immoral."[28]

This complete indifference to people's very different opportunities to access the "bounty" of the free-market system points to the blatant elitism in libertarian ideology, for which libertarian ideologues take no responsibility. Embedded in this elitism is libertarians' arrogant neglect of the coercion that is an integral—though rarely acknowledged—part of the free market. Listen to Steven Forbes, editor-in-chief of *Forbes* magazine and 1996 Republican presidential primary candidate, speaking at the twentieth anniversary celebration of the Cato Institute:

> Just think about what we take for granted. We don't think about the extraordinary web of trust and cooperation that exists in a country like the United States. There is no coercive agent that says that the cooks must cook the food tonight and the waiters must serve it in a timely manner. They do it because of our free system. They have an interest in it and we have an interest in it, but no coercion is involved. No rack is outside the room if they don't do it. This extraordinary web is a tribute to what our Founding Fathers launched over 220 years ago.[29]

The obliviousness to social realities and elitism in this description of the free market is stunning. First, note that the cooks and waiters are not the "we" in this account. "We" are those consuming the food. "They" work because they are exercising their individual freedom, not because they are forced to do so by the need to compete for low wages in a brutal environment that provides no security, except perhaps a job if "they" are lucky enough to have one.

Libertarians' faith in radical individualism makes it impossible for them to support any of the traditional methods of promoting a "glue" to hold society together. They abhor traditional values and state-mandated support for religious beliefs because these limit freedom. Liberalism's notions of "brotherhood," "the people," or "positive" freedom—the freedom to pursue a fulfilling and meaningful life by being assured of basic necessities, such as shelter, food, and a livelihood—are not only laughable to libertarians; they are dangerous ideas that underpin support for state-sponsored programs.[30]

For libertarians, the free market, if only it is left unfettered, will deliver more justice and more prosperity than any configuration of government programs. But, in response to the common-sense assertion that society needs a shared purpose, a shared vision, a guarantee of fairness to its members, or a set of institutions that exercise control and define boundaries, libertarians have no answer but their infatuation with the magic of the free market and their thinly justified expectation that "civil society" will prove stronger and more just than liberalism's mixed economy tempered with government programs.

LIBERTARIAN ENVIRONMENTALISM

ibertarians oppose environmentalism, although the two sectors of right-wing libertarianism hold two distinct positions on the environment. Paleo-libertarians are characteristically rabid in their denunciation of environmentalism, calling it "Marxist" and "statist." In the words of Llewellyn Rockwell:

> Chicken or chicory, elephant or endive, the natural order is valuable only in so far as it serves human needs and purposes. Our very existence is based on our dominion over nature; it was created for that end, and it is to that end that it must be used—through a private property, free-market order. The environmental movement is openly anti-human and virulently statist. Is it any coincidence that the Nazis exalted animals, nature, and vegetarianism above humans, civilization, and civilized eating, or that our environmentalists have an air of green goose step about them?[31]

There are parallels in tone and content between such paleo-libertarian rhetoric and that of the "wise use" anti-environmental movement based in the western states. The murderous rage and self-righteousness of both paleo-libertarians and wise-use activists justify nearly any action taken against "tree huggers" and federal employees enforcing national environmental regulations regarding land use, logging, or mining.[32]

More moderate "rightist" libertarians use less violent language. In describing federal wetland regulations, for instance, the Libertarian Party of California calls these regulations "vicious governmental idiocy," and labels them irrational and absurd.[33] The alternative proposed by rightist libertarians is what they call "free-market environmentalism." In the late 1980s, the Competitive Enterprise Institute, a libertarian think tank in Washington, D.C., published a bellwether collection of articles and newspaper clippings that delineates the rightist libertarian approach to environmentalism, titled "Readings in Free Market Environmentalism."[34]

As these readings make clear, free-market environmentalism rests on two fundamental principles: Resources are not fixed, and free market capitalism is the best manager of environmental health. The first principle refers to the libertarian belief that there is a safety net built into the environment—the ability of humans to find a *substitute* for whatever the environment no longer provides. According to this principle, resources are the products of science and technology. Human imagination and free action can always replace, replenish, or substitute depleted or endangered resources.[35] This faith in technology and creative thinking runs throughout rightist libertarianism. In promoting it as a libertarian value, Virginia Postrel calls it "dynamism" and contrasts it with utopian liberal visions that require massive social change, but then result in "stasis," a stable, motionless state.[36] The second principle—that the free market is the best environmental manager—promotes the conversion of all property that is now publicly owned to private ownership. Property owners would then exercise "creative stewardship" over their property. As always in libertarian policy, the advantages accrue to *individuals*. Creative stewardship would allow "greater scope for minority tastes, independent of political consensus." Individual tastes often would be superior to government regulation and controls, as there would be "minorities or those with vested interests [who] have the will to protect individual species or resources." Air and water rights would be handled by the same property-rights approach.[37]

Within their paradigm, called "New Resource Economics," also known as the "property rights approach," libertarians endlessly debate complex and arcane schemes to maintain the environment through the free-market system. Cost-benefit analyses, efficiency criteria, cost sharing, "polluter pays" plans, "end-state criteria," and self-interest calculations are just a few examples.

In the end, however, the logic of libertarian environmentalism rests on the same total faith in the marketplace that we've seen in their other policy recommendations. Sometimes a libertarian author simply cannot avoid admitting it. In "How Capitalism Saved the Whales," James S. Robbins, an editor at *Liberty* magazine, tells the story, now well known in libertarian circles, of how the distilling of kerosene from petroleum made obsolete the use of whale oil. Robbins brags that "stopping technology in its tracks in the 1850s would have doomed the whales." Robbins concedes that this benefit and others like it were unintended consequences of technological change, but goes on to argue that "the fact that technological development under capitalism manages to produce such consequences consistently argues in favor of the system."[38] Such illogical and naive faith that the free market will control the greed and hostility of "man" contrasts bizarrely with libertarianism's rigid devotion to logical reasoning.

FREE MEN

It is obvious to even a casual student of libertarianism that it is a white, male movement. Rarely do women appear in a libertarian organization or publication. The 1997 Annual Report of the Cato Institute, for example, features page after page of photographs of white men. Only toward the back of the report, when the organization's administrative staff is pictured, do women appear in any numbers. The sixteen-member Board of Directors includes only one woman. People of color also appear in the report in small numbers.

True, *Reason* magazine's long-term editor is Virginia I. Postrel. She works, however, under Reason Foundation President Robert W. Poole, Jr. and presides over an editorial staff of ten people, eight of whom are men. Cathy Young, a contributing editor to *Reason*, is listed with the sixteen "Fellows" at the Cato Institute, though she alone is given the qualifying description "Research Associate." Year-by-year, more women are appearing in the pages of libertarian publications and at libertarian conferences. Nevertheless, the racial homogeneity of the movement and the absence of women in positions of leadership are striking.

In 1987, Marsha Hoffman, a libertarian writer and artist, wrote what remains the most impressive critique of the male culture pervading libertarianism. Her "Women and the Libertarian Movement—Will They Ever Get Along?" was published in *Nomos*, a modest libertarian publication whose editor and managing editor at the time were women. Hoffman thinks that a more libertarian society would benefit women because it would reduce "authoritarian-ness." So why, she asks, are there so few women in the movement? She answers her own question with a convincing account of the movement's "Good Ol' Boys' Club" image, its infatuation with high-tech innovation, its affluent male identity, and a cult-like culture whose secret terminology is open only to those with a demonstrated ability to "reason." Hoffman complains that libertarians neglect both education and child care because they consider these public policy issues to be "women's issues." Much of the culture, Hoffman suggests, has its roots in Ayn Rand's worldview, with its emphasis on physical power and a male-identified definition of logical reasoning.

Hoffman admits, with regret, that such a movement puts off most women. No doubt, most people of color are put off for similar reasons. However, she fails, perhaps because she is so committed to libertarianism, to identify another crucial turn-off for women—the toxic combination of sexism and *elitism* that characterizes both sectors of libertarianism. She doesn't acknowledge that libertarianism rewards successful men with an ideology that sees the aggressive free-market competitiveness that led to their success as evidence of their superiority. It associates virtue with the ability to master the game of playing the free market. It is little wonder that nearly all the members of the Board of Directors of the Cato Institute are successful businessmen. Even the one woman is a corporate "Chairman."

Despite the male culture of the libertarian movement, many successful professional women and businesswomen are attracted to libertarian ideology. Unsupported within the male-dominated libertarian movement, they find a more hospitable outlet in the small but influential submovement known as "equality feminism." Its two flagship organizations—the Women's Freedom Network and the Independent Women's

Forum—are difficult to "fix" on the ideological spectrum. There is confusion over their ideological identity much like that which often attaches to libertarianism.

Equality feminists support the free market and hate feminists, but don't identify with Christian antifeminist women's groups. As we saw in chapter 3, they are economically conservative, professionally oriented, media savvy, chic, and male-friendly. They reject any notion that men and women are not equal, or that women are victimized by sex-role stereotyping or patriarchal oppression. They reject what they call the "women-go-home" antifeminism of Phyllis Schlafly's Eagle Forum or Beverly LaHaye's Concerned Women for America, as well as "radical" feminism's "male-bashing" and "rhetoric of victimhood." The equality feminist-libertarian connection is particularly striking in the case of the Women's Freedom Network, which has attracted the libertarian movement's two most prominent women—Virginia Postrel, editor of *Reason* magazine and member of WFN's board of directors, and Cathy Young, a WFN vice president.

Before the founding of either the Women's Freedom Network or the Independent Women's Forum, Cathy Young published an important 1992 article in *Reason* attacking feminists and right-wing antifeminists alike for depicting women as victims.[39] Her formulation of the attack on feminism and the research that has flowed from it have not been a prominent theme in the white, male libertarian movement. The many successful and conservative women who are ripe for recruitment by libertarianism are more likely to be attracted by the "equality feminism" organizations that take them seriously than by the larger libertarian movement that seems organizationally and intellectually stuck in its male culture.

WHY IS LIBERTARIANISM IMPORTANT?

There is some truth to libertarians' claim that they are the intellectual grandfathers of the current right-wing resurgence. Their influence within the right stretches from moderate Republicans to far-right members of citizens' militia groups. Nevertheless, in the near future, libertarianism will remain in the shadows, failing to gain the power, recognition, and credit libertarians feel it deserves for producing many of the right's ideas. It will remain an *intellectual* movement, with a following largely made up of yuppies and quirky ideologues, making forays into the policy sphere only under cover of the right's electoral success.

But, as the right moves beyond its initial wave of victories and its agenda becomes increasingly disputed, libertarianism may very well again play the spoiler role. Its free-market extremism will continue to parallel the right's economic agenda, but its laissez-faire social agenda will increasingly challenge the Christian Right's narrow social agenda. Libertarianism offers a loyal opposition within the Republican Party that could act as a monkey wrench in the gears of the right. Increasing numbers of libertarian-minded voters could make it harder for the Christian Right to move its social agenda forward. However, there is more to libertarianism than just its potential to cause a split within the right. Its "rightist" wing could, by itself, gain popularity as an ideology that is "neither right nor left," and that supports secular self-indulgence and materialism while preserving the right's antigovernment, antitax agenda.

There are several specific ways that rightist libertarianism could come into its own. First, rightist libertarianism could gain strength through its platform of social tolerance by seducing people who see themselves as liberals. Libertarianism could win the allegiance of those who are economic conservatives and socially attuned with libertarianism's indulgent attitude toward personal freedom, such as lesbians and gays, middle-class drug users, feminists whose principal concern is protecting abortion rights, or those concerned with immigrant rights. Just such a coalition of conservative businessmen, professionals, white middle-class lesbians and gays, and some feminists supported William Weld's tenure as a popular Republican governor in Democratic Massachusetts. Because a large sector of the U.S. public is now convinced that the free market delivers prosperity, especially if it is "left alone" by government, libertarians will find their economic message easier to sell to these constituencies. Without a strong progressive movement to counter the right's seductive message, rightist libertarianism could achieve tremendous popularity among middle-class, and some working-class, voters. It could offer an alternative to the values of the Christian Right for those who agree with the right on economic matters, but cannot accept its Christian content.

A second path to success for rightist libertarians would be to gain influence within the "Rockefeller wing" of the Republican Party, the moderate Republicans who were once a vital sector of the Party and commanded large numbers of Republican votes. Should that sector make a comeback, as appears possible in the elections of 2000, it will fly a more conservative ideological flag than it flew when the Party's right wing soundly defeated it. Rightist libertarianism may be attractive to this constituency. The Cato Institute would like to lead just such a comeback of moderate Republicans heavily influenced by libertarian ideas.

Though the rightist sector of libertarianism is the most obvious candidate for future success in U.S. politics, paleo-libertarianism also might catch on in the near future. "Angry white men"—both conservative Republicans and far-right independents—may be brought to libertarianism, if paleo-libertarians reach out to them by giving a nod to traditional values. Two influential rightists, Pat Buchanan and Charles Murray, represent a "bridge" between Old Right conservatism, with its appreciation of traditional values enforced by strong social sanctions, and libertarianism's antigovernment rhetoric and commitment to individual freedom. There is precedent for this bridge. After all, both John Locke and Thomas Jefferson, two "fathers" of libertarianism who promoted representative government with a hefty component of populism, theorized within the boundaries of a "Christian" consensus. Much more recently, we may have seen a glimpse of the future in the popular support for Pat Buchanan's 1996 presidential primary bid and the lower-profile 1999 presidential primary candidacy of Senator Bob Smith (R-NH).

There are two strategies for winning power in the U.S. system of representative democracy—by extensive grassroots organizing to create a groundswell of political sentiment or by influencing elite opinion makers and decision makers. Because libertarianism is in many ways two movements, it has a chance for success using either strategy. Paleo-libertarianism attracts grassroots voters who are resentful of change and avidly antigovernment, especially working people who bear a dramatically disproportionate burden when jobs disappear and wages stagnate. Rightist libertarianism attracts conservative elites and some special interest groups. In either case, there's a brand of libertarianism in place at the turn of the millennium to catch the political fallout.

Even if libertarian ideologues do not capture political power, support for libertarianism's ethic of rugged individualism will likely continue to grow. Libertarianism appeals to the increasing number of people who are hostile to government and who feel that they are safer and stronger when government is minimal. By promoting that view, libertarians exert a disorganizing influence within the larger society by discouraging mutual collective action and asserting that rugged individualism's "Each man for himself" is a legitimate path to safety and security.[40] But an organized "establishment" made up of political elites and economic barons dominates our free-market society. Without collective action to hold that establishment in some check, those who control power and resources are free to dominate weaker, unorganized individuals. Libertarianism produces a weakened public sector and an ever-greater resistance to any notion of a collective good. It is an ideology that fits alarmingly well with the spirit of the New World Order.

Chapter 7

WHAT NOW? STRATEGIC THINKING ABOUT THE PROGRESSIVE MOVEMENT AND THE RIGHT

do "opposition research." As a field of study it has gotten a bad name. Many people now associate opposition research with the work done by political campaign operatives who dig up dirt to smear their candidate's opponent. But opposition research has a noble history that has little to do with exposing personal dirt. Those who do good opposition research ferret out the substantial points in an opponent's arguments in order to refute them better or, where appropriate, to recognize their validity. Unions used it in the 1960s to defend themselves against attacks by owners and anti-union legislators. Civil rights workers used it to disclose the secret misconduct of the FBI and collaborations between local police and white supremacists. Antiwar activists used it to uncover government-sanctioned lies told to the American people during the Vietnam War. At Political Research Associates we use opposition research to deepen the public's understanding of the right and to provide liberals and progressives with an accurate and reliable account of their adversaries' thinking and agenda.

A thorough understanding of the right also provides the opportunity to learn whatever lessons it may have to teach us. To learn from those who are attacking you helps you move beyond a defensive position. Many of the right's tactics, especially stereotyping, scapegoating, demonizing, stealth campaigning, and outright lying are opportunistic and unprincipled and should be abhorrent to progressives. Also, the hierarchical nature of the right's structures and leadership style runs counter to progressive principles. Even if progressives chose to mimic the right, they would not have the same success. The right is sustained and supported by the economic and political power structure, though not always visibly. The pro-capitalist, pro-church, and pro-defense views of the political "establishment" support the status quo and those who prosper as a result—not the progressive movement.

As liberals and progressives live in the shadow of the right's current resurgence, a body of literature has emerged that addresses the future of the progressive movement.[1] In addition to publishing books and articles, various sectors of the progressive movement hold conferences every year.[2] These discussions address a number of questions: Why has the right been so successful? What vision unites the progressive movement at this historical moment? Are there fatal contradictions within the existing vision? Should progressives question the basic principles of social justice, such as equality, impartial justice, respect for diversity, self-determination, and the redistribution of power and resources to marginalized and excluded people? What strategies and tactics are most appropriate for the come-from-behind position of progressives at this moment? To whom should we look for leadership in these matters?

A theme common to nearly all those who discuss the state of the progressive movement and its future is our lack of agreement on a vision around which the movement's different groups can coalesce. Progressive analysts blame the absence of such an overarching vision on fragmentation caused by identity politics, or distraction from economic issues caused by cultural studies, or overreaching by the left, or the white, male leadership's inflexibility and closed-mindedness to power-sharing, or on the right's successful exploitation of political differences and resentments between groups by race, class, religion, gender, sexual orientation, or age.

There is, most likely, a certain truth in each argument. Whatever the reason, I believe it is unlikely that in the near future a shared vision will unite progressives, as it did at times in the past. It is also unlikely that progressives will experience major victories, a dramatic turnaround of the right's dominance, or a substantial change in the globalization of the economy and the hegemony of free-market capitalism. Current conditions dictate a period of small victories, achieved as the progressive movement gradually rebuilds.

The work of rebuilding will involve incremental progress toward a long-term goal of radical social change. This step-by-step process first and foremost responds to the reality of the moment. One leader or one party or one cause won't turn this situation around. Rather, all the small victories, all the person-by-person recruiting, all the media campaigns that succeed issue by issue in delivering a progressive message will force complexity into the public debate. Progressives must scale down our expectations and must focus on movement rebuilding and practical experimentation—defiant toward, but aware of, the limitations imposed by current historical conditions.[3]

LESSONS FROM THE RIGHT

The progressive movement can learn important lessons from the right's success. First, dramatic social change *can* be achieved through the electoral system. It is not necessarily true, as many progressives have believed, that the electoral system can only deliver minor changes in the status quo. Second, moving into political dominance means recruiting new constituencies or winning to your side opposing and undecided constituencies. Third, movement-building institutionalizes a social movement and prevents the movement from collapsing during periods of electoral setback. Fourth, multiple strategies—both a national *and* a state/local focus, both religious *and* secular organizing, both an electoral *and* a movement-building focus, both single-issue *and* broadly ideological public education—protect the movement from electoral vicissitudes. And fifth, a movement must resonate with the public mood, so that its messages can "hitchhike" on it. While an effective movement helps *create* that mood, it is difficult to swing completely against the tide of dominant public fears and aspirations.

Ironically, many of the techniques the right has used so successfully have characterized the liberal/left protest movements of the 1960s and

1970s. As social and economic conditions changed, the right adapted these techniques to support its own reactionary agenda. Phyllis Schlafly, for instance, borrowed from the feminist women's movement many of the techniques she used to organize right-wing women. Such cooptation, like the use of the title "Civil Rights Initiative" for California's anti–affirmative action proposition, is a form of political compliment.

But the right has not only successfully appropriated much of the language and many of the organizing techniques of social change activism, it has courted liberalism's base, debunked liberal solutions, and caricatured liberal ideology. Much of the public now sees a "liberal" as a big-spending, high-taxing, socialist-leaning, government-supporting, bleeding heart. Policy discussions do not even consider socialist solutions. And the right's spokespersons now appear in the mainstream media as just another centrist voice.

In response, the progressive defense of social programs has been sincere, even impassioned, but ultimately ineffective. As the right has used stereotyping and scapegoating to attack low-income people, progressives have been unable to mount an effective counterattack. As a result, the right has picked off programs like public housing, welfare, and legal aid, one by one. Progressives have been unable to convince the country that it is losing the only recourse to social justice now available.

A center/left coalition that had defended and expanded New Deal social programs was split apart in the 1980s by the right's promotion of "traditional values" as a wedge to divide those with common economic interests, especially in the South. Now the right has caricatured members of that coalition as obsessed with "political correctness" and derided feminists as "femi-nazis." Further, many (though not all) of the sectors that make up the broad base now known as the progressive movement have diminished in both numbers and left activism since the early 1980s.[4]

Widespread acceptance of the right's caricatures, and the use of their language even by some progressives, illustrates how far the progressive movement has fallen. Liberalism has become a scapegoat for an economic reordering in which the average person has less and the wealthy and the corporate sector have more. Liberalism's constituents—low-income people, workers, immigrants, welfare recipients, women—have become scattered and confused, at times seemingly unsure of their own interests.[5] For many people, politics has become a matter of "cutting an individual deal," rather than identifying with a movement.[6]

Progressives have lacked a ready response. Using a marginalized group as a scapegoat is not an option for us. For progressives, the villains are racism and anti-Semitism, an unjust economic system, sexism, homophobia, and foot-dragging, miserly federal programs—an analysis obvious to us, but not to the general public. Without the cooperation of the media and a public receptive to this message, we could not effectively rebut the right. The result was the spread of the right's disinformation, loss of popular support for liberalism, and electoral defeat.

Progressives must face head-on this bleak picture of our current political context. In order to craft an effective response, we need an accurate understanding of existing conditions. Although the situation is not hopeless, only clearheaded thinking based on reality, not denial, is a firm grounding for political recovery. We must examine the vision—the goals and principles—on which we have based our movements, identify the weaknesses exposed by the right's success, and identify strategies to move forward.

Some are tempted to believe that progressives could simply emulate the right's strategies and enjoy similar political success. But even if we could or would, the country has moved deliberately and cruelly to the right, creating an environment in which progressive messages are nearly shut out. As we continue to sort out what went wrong, we must press forward with the search for *new* solutions to the social problems we face. This search must include a wide spectrum of progressives: frontline activists, researchers, theorists, the spiritually motivated, the electorally inclined, and especially those whose voices have too often been marginalized within the progressive movement—such as low-income women or gay Black men—and who live with double and triple forms of oppression.

CONTRADICTIONS IN THE CURRENT VISION

In the growing body of literature critiquing our past mistakes and recommending steps for the future, progressives have examined mistakes in communicating and promoting our vision. They have identified mistakes of strategy and tactics as the reasons for the dramatic drop in acceptance of the movement's vision. The vision itself usually remains unexamined. They put only its execution (and movement leaders and activists) under the microscope.

I too see the long-standing progressive principles of social justice as basically sound. A vision that seeks a high level of equality, an end to discrimination, freedom from government repression, and shared public responsibility for those left behind by a rapacious free market leads to policies like a progressive income tax, government housing programs, and guaranteed health care for all.[7] Although progressives differ as to whether this vision is best achieved under socialism, reformed capitalism, or a mixed economy, in all cases the vision relies on a powerful central government.

Like many progressives, I tend to see government as responsible for assuring a critical level of social justice. If I trusted government agencies and agents more, I would argue for a government program for every social ill. But in the context of U.S. capitalism, government is only able to deliver social justice when the needs of the market allow it. Government programs often serve as tools of the rich and powerful. Government security agencies are the principal agents of the repression of left forces, both in the United States and internationally.

So, we have to watch government programs constantly and with unblinking suspicion. They are quite likely to conceal boondoggles for the wealthy. They are often underfunded, coopted, looted, or stolen from. They sometimes serve as agents to punish or humiliate people. But, nonetheless, they also can act as a moderating force on the gross injustices of unfettered capitalism.

One important strength of federal programs as a delivery system for social welfare is that they are not locally based. They can, therefore, override local power structures—in which racial, ethnic, and class prejudices and discrimination so often thrive—with federally mandated principles of fairness. Correctly conceived, federal social welfare programs do have the potential to increase both equality and the public welfare. But because they are so often ill conceived, progressives have often taken antigovernment stands, even though ideologically we look to government as a vital part of our political platform.

The right is antigovernment for very different reasons. In its pursuit of radical individualism and free market capitalism, it opposes any government role in ameliorating the effects of the free market system. Its pro-business, anticommunist, and conservative Christian roots justify a government role in only three areas: support for individual and corporate capitalists, defense against external and internal enemies, and defense of conservative Christian values and practices.[8] Both progressives and the right have saturated the public with antigovernment messages. As a result, the public is alienated from government, though it largely lacks a political analysis of that alienation.

Progressives need to maintain a careful balance in our attitude toward government. We must, of course, oppose uncompromisingly government that practices corruption and abuses power, and/or becomes a vehicle for the interests of the rich or of authoritarian forces. But we should not confuse the need to scrutinize and control government with delegitimizing it altogether. Under the capitalist economic system that, for the near future, has a lock on the American economy, democratically conducted government is still the greatest hope for serving the needs of the vast majority of people, and, especially, for protecting the interests of the least powerful.[9]

Unfortunately, a truly responsive and democratic government now seems so distant a possibility in the United States that reliance on it as the central progressive solution has become nearly untenable. In the long run, we will have to identify a new vision that incorporates progressive principles of equality and fairness with new thinking about the means for assuring the implementation of those principles.

THE ROLE OF IDENTITY GROUPS AND SINGLE-ISSUE GROUPS

An equally important challenge for the progressive movement is to reach consensus over the political significance of "identity" groups, distinctive groups of activists and group members who organize to address the special nature of their shared oppression. In the 1960s, for example, the Civil Rights Movement both reflected and affected the consciousness of African Americans with its demands for the end of their distinct oppression—especially the *de jure* and *de facto* segregation maintained by a racist system. Building on the model of the civil rights movement, other groups soon mobilized around the profound nature of their shared oppression, and began to see themselves as distinct groups with distinct grievances. The Native American movement, the women's movement, the lesbian and gay movement (now known as the lesbian/gay/bisexual/transgender movement), the disability rights movement, the Latino rights movement, and the Asian rights movement "identified" themselves and grew in political effectiveness. Movements also formed around issue areas, such as environmentalism, housing, jobs, welfare rights, and children's rights, and are sometimes referred to as single-issue groups because they focus exclusively on achieving reforms in one specific area of public policy.[10]

Identity groups are a favorite target of some critics who bemoan the current state of the progressive movement and accuse them of promoting fragmentation and betraying the movement's larger goals. Three white male writers who are representative of these critics—Todd Gitlin (1995), Michael Tomasky (1996), and Michael Lind (1996)—argue that the fragmentation of the progressive movement into various "identity groups" has reduced progressive politics to a simple aggregation of the specific concerns of each group. They attack identity politics for abandoning the movement's long-standing focus on class. All three see identity politics as a source of elitism within the current progressive movement. They trace that elitism to the tendency for identity groups' agendas to be middle-class—pursuing goals that benefit middle-class members of the group, often by advocating for individual rights. From this perspective, members and activists are not necessarily committed to the struggles of those outside their own group, or even to poor and working-class members of their own group. In this political fragmentation, these critics argue, the broader progressive agenda of social justice for all is lost.[11]

I too worry about the narrowness of identity politics. Like many other middle-aged progressive activists, I was first radicalized by the class-conscious, anticapitalist, anti-imperialist politics of the Old Left, and only later found a more personal connection to those political principles through the New Left and identity politics. I am dismayed that so many identity group activists never talk about the exploitative nature of capitalism, the role of U.S. imperialism, or the existence of a class-based power structure.

But I don't blame identity politics for this change. First, it is simplistic to assume that identity politics has somehow acted as a temptress, drawing attention away from larger, "more profound" and universal forms of oppression. In fact, work done by identity groups has often moved us forward by deepening our understanding of how oppression functions and has enlarged and widened the movement's consciousness of various oppressions. This is the nature of the radicalizing power of identity politics. For instance, Black feminist intellectuals—ostensibly a narrow fragment of one specific identity group—have not only raised the issues and themes specific to Black women, but have contributed the best broad analysis of how race, class, and gender interact in this society. This analysis is of vital use to *all* progressives.

Nevertheless, it is clear that the progressive movement has become a "movement of movements." Not only do different visions drive different groups, but the groups often have different and conflicting goals. For instance, in seeking to preserve old forest and clean air, the single-issue environmental movement is often at odds with the labor movement, whose primary concern is jobs, including those in lumbering and heavy industry. When class issues are obscured or ignored, there is no means to mediate the two groups' conflicting goals and to enable both to work within a larger vision of social and economic justice.

Though the result may be a fragmentation of the progressive movement, to blame "identity politics" for the decline of the larger movement fails to look at the reason identity groups arose in the first place—the neglect of their input and their issues. To the heterosexual, white, male leadership of the Old Left, class oppression (and hence the demands of the labor movement) was the movement's principal concern. The neglect of "other" oppressions stemmed in large part from their lack of relevance to that leadership. Identity constituencies forced their issues onto the progressive agenda by demanding that attention be paid to race, ethnicity, poverty (as opposed to class), gender, sexual orientation, and disability. In this context, labor became just another sub-movement, in part because it missed its opportunity to reach out to the identity groups and actively address the issues they raised.

Critics of identity politics say that a focus on identity groups has led the progressive movement to abandon its long-time constituency, the white working class (including southern whites and northern ethnic workers). They argue that it is seductively comfortable inside an identity group, and that it is not surprising that, while each group organizes its constituency to become politically active, it far too often confines that activism to the concerns of its particular movement.

Again, there is truth to this critique. But the idea that identity groups are narrow, self-absorbed, and indifferent to larger progressive goals reflects a reading of identity politics that is itself narrow and uninformed. Identity politics has striking political virtues, as well as costs. Within an identity group, activists link up with others who share the same type of oppression. There they find strength, celebrate a shared culture, discover skills, and have a better chance to emerge as leaders. Learning about the lives of those who share their own identity, they gain new, invaluable insights into their own lives. For those belonging to multiple identity groups, each affiliation is an opportunity to raise consciousness about a separate aspect of their oppression (and can painfully highlight the insensitivity of one group to another's oppression). And others within the group raise neglected issues that are particularly relevant to them as group members.

For groups that were virtually invisible within the left, identity politics has not simply been a place for self-promotion. It has been a place for the exploration of liberation. When author bell hooks talks about "the most urgent need" to "write our way into freedom, publishing articles and books that do more than inform, that testify, bearing witness to the primacy of struggle, to our collective effort to transform," she is talking about work that is at the heart of identity politics. It is often within identity groups that a crucial, bottom-line understanding of the history of struggle against oppression occurs. When such revelations are specific to a group's experience, it can be especially meaningful and eye-opening to group members.[12]

Obviously, there is a danger that identity group organizing creates a political cocoon, in which group members do not develop a larger vision. Plenty of examples illustrate this danger—gay conservatives, promilitary lesbians, racist cancer activists, and homophobic civil rights activists, to name just a few. We know very well that a person who advocates the liberation of his or her own group does not necessarily extend that advocacy to other groups. Although identity politics has transformative and radicalizing potential, it can also allow political retreat into an inward-looking, "me-first" individualism.

It is also possible for identity groups to place themselves in relation to other identity groups, by comparing oppressions or drawing parallels between oppressions, in ways that are damaging to their collaboration. Urvashi Vaid, in her book *Virtual Equality*, discusses the hard feelings aroused when the lesbian and gay movement compares its work to that of the Black Civil Rights Movement. She points out that "our use of analogies is suspect, coming as it does from a movement deeply splintered over the relevance of racism to the fight against homophobia. Interestingly, even those who believe that the racial justice movement should be completely distinct from the gay rights movement often draw analogies in order to defend gay rights. This dichotomy—between our actions and our rhetoric—leads a largely white gay movement to sound hollow and opportunistic and fuels tremendous resentment."[13]

However, because there is a great deal of overlap among different identity groups, being politicized about one issue of injustice often makes a person more sensitive to other issues. Thus, in many cases, those who are politically active in an identity group acquire a broadened political vision. Rather than blame identity politics for the decline of the progressive movement, we should instead address the need for all activists to "make the connections" among identity issues. It is quite possible to work within one identity group while simultaneously working to promote the social justice goals of the broader progressive movement.[14]

At the moment, the validity and role of separate identity groups is a matter of debate within the progressive movement. Both the white male progressive critics cited previously, who are harshly critical of identity politics, and the identity politics activists who believe that identity groups should seek a shared ideological commitment to certain progressive principles, share the goal of uniting the movement and defeating the right. Therefore, in discussing the future of the movement, we must explore what vision or set of ideas might be powerful enough to play that unifying role, by drawing the political allegiance of members of each identity group into coalition and common purpose.

SEEKING A VISION TO CREATE A UNIFIED MOVEMENT

Four "new" visions are currently being discussed among progressives: human rights, the politics of meaning, prophetic political morality, and economic populism. Each attempts to transcend the fragmentation of the movement and unite the separate identity groups. Interestingly, each ducks the question of the role of government in a postindustrial, globalized capitalist system. To varying degrees, each vision has the capacity to fuel future attempts at creating a unifying ideological umbrella.

HUMAN RIGHTS

In the United States we associate "human rights" with government repression in other countries—specifically arbitrary imprisonment, murder, and torture. President Jimmy Carter used a foreign country's human rights record as a factor in considering foreign aid, military aid, and trade relations. Even when applying an uneven yardstick, Carter's policy on human rights clearly advanced the conduct of U.S. international relations.

In other countries, the concept of human rights is more broadly defined than it is in the United States. In addition to the right to be free of brutal government repression, human rights in many countries is the umbrella concept for all the rights we classify as civil, economic, political, social, and cultural. Internationally, many include under the umbrella of human rights a wide range of progressive principles—from democratic elections to an end to economic exploitation of children to free artistic expression to the right to different sexual orientations.

A number of U.S. activists of different races, including some deeply affected by exposure to the human rights paradigm at the 1995 United Nations Fourth World Women's Conference in Beijing, would place a human rights agenda at the center of progressive politics.[15] Human rights encompasses resistance to the oppressions identified by the identity groups, as well as incorporating the economic analysis that has long characterized the left. A progressive movement that used the internationally accepted definition of human rights would advocate a broad range of individual freedoms and class/group rights. It would, presumably, have a harmonizing effect on the competition and resentments among various groups that can interfere with the success of the progressive movement as a whole. It would create a point of entry into the movement for anyone whose rights have been violated.[16]

Presumably, no particular cause would reside at the center of such a movement. The bottom line would not be race, gender, class, or sexual orientation, but our common humanity and the individual and group rights (including religious rights) that properly belong to each human being. The human rights concept is, in short, a plea for a return to the humanism of the Enlightenment, when, in theory, the individual was elevated to full humanity, complete with rights, powers of individual choice, and the dignity of full consciousness. Although in practice, the Enlightenment's humanism was limited to privileged white men, the powerful idea that a person could be, in some respects, elevated to a status formerly allowed only to God, was a profoundly liberatory political principle.[17]

Such Enlightenment ideas are anathema to the right, especially to the ultra-conservative Christian Right. To this sector, the secular humanism associated with the Enlightenment is the ultimate evil, because it replaces the rule of God with human rule. A correct society, in their view, is biblically based and led by those whom God has chosen.[18] The result is an authoritarian theocracy, the opposite of the society envisioned by the promoters of human rights.

Despite its enormous appeal, I see two major weaknesses in the human rights paradigm. First, its vague scope does not provide clear guidelines when two rights conflict. A classic example is the conflict between the right to free speech, even when it is aggressive and frightening, and the right to freedom from violence. The U.S. standard for free speech protection—that crying "Fire!" in a movie theater is not protected speech—often is not adequate to distinguish which of the two freedoms should prevail. Second, the term "human rights" has been applied very narrowly in the United States. Were it to become the central progressive organizing concept here, progressives would have to initiate a massive public education process regarding the use of the concept internationally by pro-democracy activists. Given the difficulty progressives are experiencing in gaining access to mass media, such a huge public education project would be daunting.

These weaknesses do not, however, detract from the sheer appeal of human rights as a possible "new vision" for the progressive movement. Speaking a universal truth about the rights of people, this concept could conceivably touch a deep chord in the American public.

THE POLITICS OF MEANING

In response to the New Right's "family values" agenda, Michael Lerner was perhaps the first to argue that liberals and leftists should take seriously the relationships and attachments (both religious and secular) that the right's rhetoric had both addressed and captured. Writing in a magazine he founded, *Tikkun: A Bi-monthly Jewish Critique of Politics, Culture and Society*, Lerner spoke with persistence to a skeptical progressive audience about the importance of family values. As the New Right scored victory after victory in the 1980s by using the family values theme to attack liberals and identity groups, progressives' reaction to Lerner's recommendations ranged from caution to hostility.

Lerner envisions a public "awakened" to a reality different from the current one of individualism and selfishness. He imagines a transformation of people through a change of consciousness and changes in the way people live. Lerner sees those who undergo (or have undergone) these changes as the base for the successful progressive movement in the twenty-first century. He argues that a "politics of meaning" is the only hope of breaking through a "meaning-deadening society."[19]

Lerner's awakening has parallels with that experienced by members of the Christian Right. Clearly, born-again Christian evangelicalism appeals to spiritual yearnings and to idealistic values of community and selflessness. It excludes, however, those outside the community, and draws the boundaries of the community by demonizing them. Lerner proposes a *progressive* version of this awakening. Much as the Christian Right was led to its awakening by the exhortations of its leaders—Jerry Falwell, D. James Kennedy, Pat Robertson, and many others—Lerner sees himself as the guide for progressives toward a similar awakening and a more fulfilling life.

In April 1996, Lerner's new organization, the Foundation for Ethics and Meaning, held an inaugural conference in Washington, D.C. The conveners were surprised when approximately 1,500 people attended. The conference, however, reflected many of the shortcomings of Lerner himself. Conference attendees were overwhelmingly white, reflecting a lack of multiracial base-building. The skills and experience of those at the conference were not mobilized. In fact, for many, the conference confirmed a deep-seated suspicion of Lerner, who does not solicit or incorporate feedback from colleagues and supporters and fails to examine the implications of his position as a white man who is the sole leader of "his" organization.

More important, Lerner's "politics of meaning" is not truly progressive in either its values or the programs that might emerge from them. A general humanitarian consciousness and renewed spiritual connectedness are not solutions to the problems created by unregulated free-market capitalism. It is a particularly anemic program for all those who fall outside the economically secure white male model that pervades this vision.

PROPHETIC POLITICAL MORALITY

"We can find common ground only by moving to higher ground." These words, written by Jim Wallis, founder of Sojourners, a Washington, D.C.–based Christian evangelical community, represent the message of many Christian progressives and appeal as well to many who are not religiously affiliated.[20] Much of Wallis's "higher ground" has to do with building community and with emphasizing our connectedness as a society.

Wallis bases his recommendations on a sweeping and perceptive critique of contemporary society. Out of that critique he rejects both liberal and conservative politics, saying, somewhat simplistically, that "the critical link between personal responsibility and social change is missing on the left."[21] Wallis speaks from a position of solidarity with the poor. Closely related to that of liberation theology, his perspective is simultaneously radical and compassionate.

Wallis doesn't claim to propose a new vision. Indeed, he says we do not yet have the new vision we need, nor should we look for any.[22] He accurately points out that new visions emerge from movements rather than from political parties. Most importantly, he advocates a renewed consciousness of the priority of the poor in a spiritual revolution, which, in turn, could lead to a new vision.

Wallis shares with Lerner certain shortcomings in his political consciousness. First, like Lerner, he comes out of a specific identity group base. In Lerner's case it is his identity as a Jew; in Wallis's case, as a white evangelical Christian. Although both are, of course, valid bases, broadening them to the full breadth of the progressive movement requires scrupulously inclusive organizing—not only reaching out to women, people of color, lesbians and gays, and other oppressed groups, but placing them at the center of decision making. There is scant evidence that Wallis is committed to that broadening process, though his work with low-income people in Washington's inner city puts him in close contact with people who are excluded from power. It is particularly troubling that he shows little consciousness of women's issues or the impressive and brave work of Catholic and Protestant feminists to challenge institutional sexism within the churches. He is at best patronizing toward lesbians and gays, who are struggling to gain equal rights and especially need support from heterosexuals as they are increasingly targeted by the right. Nor has he reached out systematically to Jewish or Muslim communities. In these respects, he has failed to transcend important pitfalls within progressive Christian social justice activism.

ECONOMIC POPULISM

Progressives have always understood that capitalism guarantees inequality. Within the progressive movement, there is a wide range of responses to capitalism: from the left's conviction that it must be overthrown, to liberalism's reform-minded regulations and anti-poverty programs.

The right has been remarkably effective in its campaign to free capitalism of the constraints of regulations, taxation, and unionization. This implementation of an unfettered free-market capitalism has given new urgency to the progressive anticapitalist critique. However, the likelihood that the U.S. public will adopt socialism as an alternative to capitalism is now slight, to say the least. Socialism has so little popular support in this country that, for practical, if not theoretical, reasons it is difficult to promote it as a realistic alternative to capitalism.

Progressives are now discussing less ambitious anticapitalist critiques that might be called "economic populism," though its activists may not use that title. It advocates breaking up the concentration of economic power in megacorporations, reversing the growing inequality of wealth, and punishing public and private greed, corruption, and exploitation.[23] Rev. Jesse Jackson has always been the most prominent spokesperson for this anticapitalist critique. Jackson's economic populism—demonstrated by his frequent support of striking workers—is interwoven with his consistent antiracism. This ideological combination has led him to call attention to the plight of white farmers during the (ongoing) crisis in the farm belt, as well as to maintain a constant focus on the neglect and decapitalization of inner-city Black and Latino neighborhoods.

An example of a broad coalition formed in the 1990s around issues of economic populism was that against the ratification of the General Agreement on Tariffs and Trade (GATT) and, especially, the North American Free Trade Agreement (NAFTA). Although labor took the lead, individuals and groups from across the progressive spectrum joined together in that struggle. Such activism draws on a growing documentation of the current redistribution of wealth upward and the globalization of corporate power.

Progressive economic analyst Holly Sklar, in her book *Chaos or Community?*, presents a hard-hitting analysis of the dramatic increase in income inequality under government deregulation, globalization, and an increasingly regressive tax structure.[24] She proposes a sixteen-point plan to "foster fair and sustainable development" for what she calls "economics for everyone."[25] This is an action guide for economic populism. While it depends on an active role for government, the last recommendation—several steps to create a more participatory democracy—demonstrates her understanding that government, as now constituted, cannot deliver the previous fifteen recommendations.

Progressives closer to the Democratic Party, who believe in economic reform through government programs, advocate a return to the notion of a social contract that tried to apply "standards of human decency to the amoral marketplace."[26] Recognizing the importance of government's role in creating a fair society, they look to the Democrats to return to the principles of the New Deal and to take the country toward economic populism with a program of public-private collaboration. Unlike the Reagan/Bush version of public-private collaboration, in this vision the interests of private profit would not trump the public interest.

Unfortunately, Jesse Jackson's once-large following has shrunk, through his neglect of political base-building. Although still a major progressive spokesperson, Jackson is not building a movement around economic populism's themes. However, organizations are emerging that are refining the themes of economic populism and polishing the organizing techniques needed to build a movement around them. Later in this chapter I discuss two such organizations, Just Economics and the Labor Party.

INCREMENTAL STRATEGIES TO REBUILD THE MOVEMENT

Although the visions discussed above hold varying degrees of promise in the long term, each most likely will fail to provide the progressive movement with a common ideological and programmatic agenda on the short term. Instead, it is far more likely that, despite its fragmentation, the movement will rebuild incrementally, step by step. Our continuing long-term search for a unifying vision should not overshadow the important work being done right now to rebuild the progressive movement. That work is visible everywhere in the day-to-day work of the progressive movement—in all the discussions of strategy, organizing of defensive campaigns, mounting of strikes, and building of educational programs. A critical review of some of that work paints a profile of how the progressive movement is indeed rebuilding.

STABILIZING THE MOVEMENT'S INFRASTRUCTURE

Though the progressive movement may lack a unifying vision, it does have its own movement infrastructure, made up of political organizations that cover the broad spectrum of progressive issues and are experienced at promoting and defending those issues. These organizations are, in activist Jeff Faux's words, "institutions with a longer-term perspective for whom the goals of politics go beyond the next election."[27] They are the stable, usually larger organizations that make a movement viable by consistently providing the basic resources needed for the movement to survive and prosper, including research, publications, training, funding, legal work, media work, strategic planning, and analysis. Examples include the NAACP Legal Defense Fund, Oakland's Center for Third World Organizing, the National Council of La Raza, the National Gay and Lesbian Task Force, the National Network of Women's Funds, or my own organization, Political Research Associates. Rebuilding the progressive movement should start with an assessment of its infrastructure. If it is not stable, well funded, and internally coordinated, it cannot serve its role as the movement's support structure.

Many of the organizations that make up the progressive movement's infrastructure were in serious financial crisis in the late 1980s and early 1990s. The crisis eased slightly after the 1994 elections and the resulting Republican Congressional takeover. At that time, many people who oppose the right, including foundation staff and individual funders, became alarmed at this show of "new Republican" strength and paid greater attention to the weakened state of the progressive movement. As a result, they now appreciate the importance of strong infrastructure organizations, as well as of increased financial support for them.

Though we need a thoughtful assessment of the strengths and weaknesses of the progressive movement's infrastructure, several things make that difficult. Because the movement is fragmented, infrastructure organizations exist for each of the identity movements, as well as those that function across identity movements and across single-issue movements. Of the organizations cited above, the National Network of Women's Funds serves the women's movement, and the Center for Third World Organizing focuses on communities of color, while Political Research Associates is a backup center for a range of identity groups and issue areas. These organizations need to be assessed within the context of the work they do, rather than by abstract standards that do not reflect their actual role. Further, we must honestly confront the ways that infrastructure organizations are often weakened by turf wars, internal power struggles, and rifts over competition for funding—not surprising during a time of political defeat and scarce resources.

Nevertheless, the movement rebuilding process has begun.[28] An important ingredient in that process is an increased emphasis on coalition building among infrastructure organizations. Rebuilding a movement infrastructure will do little to advance progressive goals without strong internal coordination and cooperation—the great benefits of coalition work.[29] Innumerable conferences, "alliances," and coalitions have sprung up to facilitate better coordination among activists. In many cases, these provide an opportunity for very diverse sorts of progressive organizations, from smaller, local fight-the-right groups to multimillion-dollar think tanks, to meet and get a better understanding of each other's work. Even mainstream social service, religious, and humanitarian aid organizations seem more aware of the role their "movement" colleagues play in their mutual defense from attack by the right.

But every infrastructure organization doesn't deserve our support as we engage in the process of rebuilding the movement. Some signs of organizational ill health deserve our negative assessment. Certainly ideological groping and a lack of programmatic clarity are understandable at a time when, as a movement, we are working through honest political differences. But if an organization has no internal power-sharing, is known to have problems with racism, sexism or homophobia, or spends a lot of time posturing, nurturing its leaders' egos, or pursuing opportunistic projects, it should address these problems or support for it should be withdrawn.

GRASSROOTS ORGANIZING

Many progressives agree that we need to rebuild the movement from the bottom up. This is an enormous task, and one rife with difficulties. Among the problems that have hindered progressive grassroots organizing are: 1) the project or coalition collapses when outside support (funding or personnel) is withdrawn; 2) the agenda of the organizers takes precedence over the needs and desires of the community; or 3) at the end of a campaign organized to address a specific goal, there is neither a standing coalition left behind nor an increased consciousness of progressive principles and values among participants.

Grassroots organizers in the 1990s are confronting these shortcomings, debating the best ways to avoid them, and searching for new approaches and strategies for more effective organizing. Much of this debate is over how best to conduct grassroots organizing that is responsive to the needs of communities, while recruiting community members to the progressive movement. Organizers also are turning their attention to constituencies not traditionally targeted by progressives, especially religious people and youth.

The Debate over Organizing Strategies. For the sake of simplicity, imagine that there are two approaches to a particular organizing challenge (say, to defeat a toxic dump permit, or to expose a right-wing "stealth" school board member): one that focuses exclusively on winning, or one that aspires to win, but is equally interested in movement-building. The former style is usually more effective in the short run. Often, a local electoral race, a media campaign, or a campaign that targets an issue or a piece of legislation uses shrewd political strategies—clever and catchy political ads or well-crafted opinion pieces strategically placed to reach opinion makers—that may carry the day, but leave behind no coalition, no momentum toward other issues or causes, and no raised consciousness or expectations. This task-oriented approach could be called "instrumental" organizing. It focuses on strategies that will assure victory. But a short-term victory may be gained at the expense of a missed opportunity to bid for the long-term political "transformation" of those organized.

Transformative organizing avoids working strictly according to the laws of expediency—that is, basing organizing on shifting power from one group to another or on winning a single individual fight. Rather, it redefines "winning" as achieving a shift in consciousness among those who have been mobilized.[30] Ideally, this transformation is the first step in a strategic recruitment process designed to achieve the twin goals of increasing real community power and building the member base of the progressive movement.[31]

During the 1980s and 1990s, the right has demonstrated the effectiveness of transformative organizing for movement-building. Many of its campaigns targeted issues that were long shots. If they were not doomed to failure, they were at least unlikely to succeed. The multi-city protest against the photographic exhibit of Robert Mapplethorpe's work titled "A Perfect Moment" is a good example. Although it was unlikely that local right-wing organizations would be able to close the exhibit in cities where it was already booked, mobilizing a coalition to protest it was an effective movement-building exercise. It brought like-minded people together, not for a short-term victory, but to allow them to identify each other. It built bridges among Catholic conservatives, Protestant fundamentalists, and secular rightists, and activists got experience with media and with public protest. This in-your-face political move demonstrated that it was politically possible for cultural conservatives to take forceful action against cultural expressions that offended them.

Confronting Prejudice in Community Organizing. Progressives are also debating the role of "identity" concerns in community organizing. Many who believe that organizing must incorporate consciousness-raising about racism, sexism, homophobia, anti-Semitism, and other fault lines of bigotry, see themselves as practicing a "new" form of community organizing. The term "new" is misleading in this context, because this organizing style has been used in various settings in the past, including organizing by socialist feminists, many women of color, and rainbow coalition activists. While it is not new, it does stand in contrast to a number of the practices of the more traditional community-organizing style developed by Saul Alinsky in the 1960s and most often used by the labor movement.

In their influential pamphlet "Square Pegs Find Their Groove," Francis Calpotura (Co-Director of the Center for Third World Organizing) and Kim Fellner (Director of the National Organizers Alliance) argue that if *all* the people who are marginalized and excluded from power are to achieve real self-determination, progressive organizers must address not only class inequities, but also related forms of oppression, such as racism, sexism, homophobia, and anti-Semitism—even if these are not directly germane to a specific organizing goal. People from marginalized groups, the "square pegs" of the pamphlet's title, are sources of strength who bring to progressive organizing a wide range of experiences, talents, and resources.[32] An uncompromising solidarity with marginalized groups is the bottom line of this model of grassroots organizing.

Potentially, however, narrowly conceived identity concerns and agendas may themselves be suffused with classism, racism, sexism, or just plain arrogance. Organizing by the women's movement in support of abortion rights, and by the lesbian/gay/bisexual/transgender community to promote AIDS education has often suffered from these problems. Further, identity concerns will very often impose "outside" values on a community, rather than relying exclusively on supporting the values and concerns indigenous to that community. An organizing style true to progressive principles, one that values multiculturalism, for instance, may very well be an *imposed* organizing style.

But these very considerations separate liberal and mainstream organizing from progressive organizing. A movement cannot build its base with integrity if it fudges its values and doesn't challenge the antidemocratic prejudices of its potential recruits. Discussing the concept of "empowerment," political scientist Adolph Reed, Jr., says, "As any decent organizer knows . . . people can sense that they're being sold a bill of goods, and the result is further discrediting of the left. Our only hope is to hold firmly and self-confidently to our politics, approach others as equal citizens, and stand or fall on the strength of our analysis and practice."[33] While organizing must be sensitive to the cultural norms of a community and respectful toward community members, to be transformative it has to be very straightforward in taking unpopular positions when those positions are central to progressive values.

The great danger in these debates is that they will devolve into a battle over whose oppression comes first. Should homophobia be overlooked if it is of less pressing consequence when compared with some gross injustice currently agitating the community? Another danger is that these debates might well break progressives into "idealistic" and "practical" camps. The more "practical" organizer might adjust her position on choice in deference to the community's religious norms. Although both dangers are real, the debate between those who support "instrumental" and "transformative" organizing must continue as a means of clarifying the goals of progressive organizing. Though I am biased in favor of the transformative goals that I think distinguish progressive organizing from more mainstream forms of organizing, I know that progressives are far from unanimous on what form of organizing is best. It may be that this debate cannot be resolved, but will persist as a permanent difference among progressive grassroots organizers.[34] In her thoughtful 1997 *Nation* article on progressive organizing, JoAnn Wypijewski talks about the *value* of this period when there is no one way to fight, when the door is open to risk, experimentation, flexibility, and creativity. She insists, I think correctly, that "radicals outside organizing always hanker for the new paradigm, the secret formula. Now, as before, there isn't one; just people trying and trying to do some things differently so that people can start to move again."[35]

Religious Organizing. Many evangelical or fundamentalist Christians are not ideologically aligned with the Christian Right. Nevertheless, organizations like the Christian Coalition claim to represent the Christian perspective on all political and social issues. The Christian Right's narrow reading of Christian tenets and its aggressive organizing style, within both the religious and political spheres, exclude Jews, Muslims, Hindus, and others and have left mainstream and liberal Christian denominations on the defensive. The conservative takeover of the Southern Baptist Convention, the attacks mounted on the National Council of Churches by the Institute for Religion and Democracy and other right-wing groups, and the demonization of feminist and New Age spirituality—all signal the Christian Right's intention to dominate religious practice.[36]

Until recently, mainstream and progressive religious groups seemed unwilling to confront the Christian Right head on. Although Jews are one of the groups most threatened by its rhetoric, the leaders of the largest Jewish organizations have been cautious and accommodating in their critique of the Christian Right's intolerance. But the dramatic success of the right in the 1994 Congressional elections awakened even the most complacent liberal religious groups to an understanding of just how serious the religious right is about implementing its agenda. At the same time, the agenda itself has become subtler, as religious right organizations reach out to recruit new constituencies towards whom they have expressed hostility in the past. For example, the 1996 Southern Baptist Convention approved a resolution calling for Baptists to direct their "energies and resources toward the proclamation of the Gospel to the Jewish people."[37] Both the Christian Coalition and Promise Keepers— two huge Christian Right organizations—launched campaigns to promote "racial reconciliation," though the Christian Coalition's Samaritan Project quickly folded. At the end of the 1990s, religious progressives are now confronting the Christian Right's aggressive (and even predatory) style more forcefully.

The work of Jim Wallis and Michael Lerner, discussed previously, provides examples of religious organizing that explicitly address the Christian Right, although that is not their central mission. The Washington, D.C.–based Interfaith Alliance, however, was formed by mainstream Christian and Jewish activists after the 1994 elections specifically to defend mainstream religion from attacks by the right, and to promote a more tolerant, less exclusionary reading of Christianity. It provides an alternative voice to the literal reading of the Bible promoted by the Christian Right. Through its national office and local chapters across the country, the Interfaith Alliance is becoming a strong voice that is able to denounce the intolerance and stealth political ambitions of the Christian Right.[38] Another progressive faith-based voice is Equal Partners in Faith (EPF), a Washington, D.C.–based group that "opposes the manipulation of religion to promote exclusion and inequality." EPF has conducted campaigns challenging the Promise Keepers and the Christian Right's promotion of the ex-gay movement.

A handful of Jewish organizations also have taken up the challenge of the Christian Right. For a number of years, the most outspoken was the explicitly progressive New Jewish Agenda (NJA), which opposed the right vigorously but was unable to survive at the national level and closed its national office in 1992. Several local NJA chapters still exist. Currently, Jews for Racial and Economic Justice, a local organization based in New York City, incorporates a fight-the-right agenda. Within mainstream Jewish organizations, the American Jewish Congress is more progressive on domestic issues than is the Anti-Defamation League of B'nai B'rith or the American Jewish Committee, though in all three organizations there are progressive individuals. For the most part, however, the mainstream Jewish leadership has not aggressively confronted the Christian Right, in part because the right has been (for its own political and theological reasons) extremely supportive of the state of Israel.[39] There are also other areas of agreement between the two groups, especially on opposition to affirmative action and support for a strong military.

There is a pressing need for mainstream and progressive religious communities to show political backbone in confronting the right's appropriation and perversion of religious values. Sitting on the political sidelines is not an option. We need a forceful, self-confident, and defiant voice from religious communities—in defense of lesbians and gay men, immigrants, welfare recipients, women who wish to have abortions, and all the others slandered regularly by the Christian Right. While the right's vituperative Institute for Religion and Democracy attacks nearly all mainstream Christian groups, especially those it labels "liberal," no correspondingly clear voice is coming from the religious defenders of inclusivity and justice who are best able to trump that message and play a crucial role in rebuilding the progressive movement.

Youth Organizing. The right has long understood the importance of winning over young people. Its systematic recruitment and grooming of conservative campus activists could accurately be described as a courtship. The right's infrastructure of movement organizations has funded both campus organizing and the subsequent careers of conservative students who want to become movement professionals. Right-wing youth activists are nurtured and cultivated like rare flowers, though they are, in fact, no longer rare.

The success of the right in recruiting young people is a buffer against the aging of its movement leadership. It is also a buffer against any future waning of the right's dominance. The right has always understood that investing in youth is their movement's Social Security plan.

For more than fifteen years, since the mid-1980s, right-wing campus newspapers (with funding and articles supplied by the larger, off-campus movement) and right-wing student groups have put progressive campus youth on the defensive time and time again. Using words and images designed to shock, and sometimes using physical violence, right-wing students are applauded by their movement elders, published by movement presses, and assured of movement jobs. This activism finds an increasingly hospitable environment on campus, as the country moves to the right and students grow up experiencing liberalism as a discredited, out-of-favor ideology. Also, faced with a tightening job market and the pressures of an unpredictable economy, fewer young people are drawn to social justice work.

Despite these barriers, students and other young people have organized around progressive issues, most notably in their opposition to apartheid in South Africa and, in the late 1990s, their protests against California's anti-immigrant Proposition 187. Many terrific progressive projects and organizations are driven by youth or target them. Young lesbian/gay/bisexual/transgender people of color are particularly active, taking the lead in much of the thinking on gender and mixed race identities. Queer youth have blazed the trail in youth organizing throughout the 1990s.

Although many liberal funders understand the importance of support for young people, most of that support presently is targeted toward keeping teens off the streets, preventing teenage pregnancy, or saving teens from drugs and gangs. These projects are seen not as "political," but as an extension of the social safety net. Much of the more political work done by and with young people remains underfunded. A progressive teenage girls' magazine like *Teen Voices* constantly struggles to meet its budgets. Nonetheless, it has developed a mentoring program for teenage girls throughout Boston. The Minority Activist Apprenticeship Program (MAAP) of Oakland's Center for Third World Organizing, the War Resisters League's YouthPeace program (a national program with local chapters that promotes nonviolence and social justice among youth), and the New York–based Third Wave Foundation (young women who pool their money to support grassroots projects initiated and led by young women) are just three examples of youth groups that deserve support and recognition. A few youth organizations, such as the Center for Campus Organizing, and a number of individual projects mounted by larger organizations (such as the AFL-CIO's "Union Summer" programs) have been able to gain an adequate level of support for their important progressive youth work.

It is crucial that the progressive movement allocate more of its scarce resources to develop its future leaders and activists. Young women of all races and male students of color are being harmed by attacks on affirmative action; low-income students and immigrant students are losing access to scholarship money to attend college; and increasing living costs make it more difficult for students to work as volunteers in movement organizations. These material conditions are more daunting than those faced by the campus activists of the 1960s and 1970s. There is no Vietnam War to catalyze students and no impassioned Civil Rights or Black Power Movement to provide a focus for their idealism. Further, the social programs created by the Johnson Administration's Great Society initiative have been defunded, so there is far less opportunity to earn a living after graduation working for social reform and social change.

Only a commitment of resources by every progressive organization will make it possible for large numbers of young people to explore their political ideas, start their own organizations, and get the experience they need to move into leadership positions within the progressive movement. We cannot expect young people to buck the conservative tide without encouragement and concrete assistance from the movement that needs them—and would like to claim them.

MEDIA WORK

One of the right's most successful strategies has been to target mainstream media outlets while simultaneously creating alternative media of its own, with particular attention to building Christian TV and radio networks. Increased access to the public, coupled with a style of simple, short, media-friendly messages, has been crucial to the right's recruitment and in spreading its message.[40]

Until 1980, centrist and liberal positions were well represented on TV and radio. The right has exaggerated that presence by labeling it "leftist domination" of the airwaves, a distortion that progressives have not successfully debunked, despite the important work of Fairness and Accuracy in Media (FAIR), which exposes the exclusion of liberal and progressive voices from mainstream media.[41] The right's accusations of media bias—often coupled with boycotts of corporations that advertise on programs deemed "too liberal" or make films deemed "immoral"— have intimidated programmers and narrowed the current spectrum of opinion in mainstream TV, radio, film, and newspapers. That spectrum now ranges from centrist to right-wing.

The right also has benefited from a wave of right-wing talk shows, primarily aired on A.M. radio stations. Angry venting of antigovernment themes on these shows attracts a wide audience and provides a forum for right-wing populist ideology. Talk show rhetoric is often laced with ill-disguised racism, women-hating sexism, and undisguised homophobia. Even when not affiliated with right-wing organizations, these talk shows do the recruitment work of the right.

Progressives are now scrambling to strengthen our media organizing in order to access the mainstream media. In the late 1980s, progressive media work was so slight that even alternative publishing outlets were neglected, and some were unable to survive financially. The closing of the *Guardian, Gay Community News* (a weekly now reopened and published quarterly) and *New Directions for Women*, as well as many progressive and women's bookstores, indicated the serious erosion of the influence of alternative news sources and the decline in support for them.

Effective use of the media has now become a central strategy of progressive organizing. Alternative newspapers and magazines seem slightly stronger, as readers and funders increasingly appreciate the important role they play. Larger single- and multi-issue organizations within the movement are giving more time and attention to packaging their messages for easy access by journalists. Smaller organizations are being trained in media access and learning to refine their message for easier media consumption. The annual "Media and Democracy Congress," an in-gathering of small and large progressive organizations to focus on media issues, makes an important contribution to that effort. Newer organizations and projects, such as the Wisconsin-based Progressive Media Project, which distributes progressive opinion pieces through Reuters and other news services, San Francisco's We Interrupt This Message, and the SPIN Project (Strategic Progressive Information Network), which offers guidance and advice on effective media strategies, are now increasing the effectiveness and impact of progressive media work. Although the infrastructure of progressive media organizations is still relatively weak and underfunded, the process of claiming a voice in the mainstream media is well underway.

BUILDING COMMUNITY/CIVIL SOCIETY

Some liberal, white, middle-class academics, journalists, and philanthropists refer to the punitive mean-spiritedness of the right's policies and rhetoric (in its ugliest forms, the use of hate language, intolerance, bullying, self-righteousness, stereotyping, scapegoating, and intimidation) as "the current breakdown of civility" or "a crisis of democratic values." In response to that crisis, they have generated a great deal of discussion about building a more civil society and finding common ground among those who think of themselves as on opposite sides of the fence. These efforts often seek a mode of interacting that will allow us to move beyond political standoff, and in general restore the sense of community that, according to the nostalgic myth promoted by the right, characterized the post–World War II period. Proposals include "community building" (bringing together the members of a community so that they know, understand, and support each other) and "building civil society" (encouraging adherence to norms of common courtesy in public discourse).

"Civil society" is defined in two ways, which are sometimes confused and sometimes used interchangeably. In its more popular usage, a *civil* society would be one in which debate over important political and social issues occurs without resorting to demonization and disinformation. In its second definition, "civil society" refers to the self-organized parts of society that are not connected to the state—associations that are organized from the bottom up, rather than from the top down. Examples are independent labor unions or self-organized subsistence farmers. "Civil society" used in this way can also refer to independent organizing that is political. The left in Latin America bases much of its political thinking on this concept of civil society, and it is beginning to appear in the writing of U.S. progressives, who use it to refer to public-spirited voluntary associations that act as intermediaries between the private sector and government, collaborating with both while representing the people. The resulting mix is a new political approach that is "neither right nor left," but instead represents a fresh, less ideological view of social policy.

Many commentators discuss a "crisis of democratic values," implying that in the recent past democratic values were widely accepted. They seldom lay the blame for the nastiness they see in contemporary society at the feet of the right—where it belongs—even though most of their suggestions and programs to restore democratic values address the damage wrought by the right.

Programs to oppose the hatred and division promoted by the right are proliferating.[42] Anti-hate advertisements on television and billboards appeal to the spirit of more civil interactions among racially and ethnically diverse citizens. Elementary and high school curricula, designed to build more tolerance and a greater understanding of democracy among young people, include the "Teaching Tolerance" curriculum of the Southern Poverty Law Center, the "World of Difference" curriculum of the Anti-Defamation League of B'nai B'rith, and *The Holocaust and Human Behavior*, the primary resource book of Facing History and Ourselves, as well as its study guides, such as "Participating in Democracy."

Another answer to the "crisis of democratic values" is the communitarian movement. Begun and still largely led by sociologist Amitai Etzioni, it aims to lead the way from individualism and isolation toward community and connection. Communitarians emphasize that responsibility, traditional values, and tough anticrime legislation can legitimately trump individual rights. It is, at best, a centrist movement that attracts both liberals and conservatives. Perhaps for this reason, communitarianism has received attention from Senators, Representatives, and President Bill Clinton.[43]

"Community building" is a more local response to the rancor of the current "crisis." It refers to the need for members of a community to circumvent the forces that divide them by knowing each other better. Community building as a political strategy is based on the belief that knowing your neighbors makes it less possible to demonize or scapegoat them because those neighbors become individuals rather than members of an identity group. Community building is not a prominent progressive theme. More often, progressives talk about grassroots movement building, which is usually done by organizers. But lesbian civil rights activist Suzanne Pharr, a member of the Women's Project in Little Rock, Arkansas, writes eloquently about community building as a progressive goal:

> The difficult part is learning how to honor the needs of the individual as well as those of the group, without denying the importance of either. It requires a balance between identity and freedom on the one hand and the collective good and public responsibility on the other. It requires ritual and celebration and collective ways to grieve and show anger; it requires a commitment to resolve conflict. Most of all, it requires authenticity in relationships between and among whole people.[44]

Progressives have largely rejected communitarianism, seeing it as compromised by its anticrime and pro–traditional values positions. Those promoting civil society have also come under fire. Benjamin DeMott, writing in *The Nation* magazine, argues that the very phrase "civil society" blames those whose civility has broken down for good reason. Seeing the public's current cynicism as the justifiable result of political and economic scandals revealed by both left and right, DeMott views the "fad" of civil society as a cover-up for the abuses of power that have led people to incivility.[45]

DeMott is right. Civil society is not the answer to social injustice and the right's drive to restore white, male hegemony. Nevertheless, in the current political climate, defending democracy and pluralism are important to fight-the-right work. We must defend those political bottom lines. However, if progressives are drawn too far into finding common ground and building civil society, we will have compromised everything that makes us politically progressive. The political "center" sought by promoters of consensus and civility is now far to the right of its location twenty years ago. Because the right has done its job so well, progressives will have to fight their way back into the debate, rather than seeking acceptance within an increasingly conservative political center.

GAINING ELECTORAL STRENGTH

Progressive analysis of the right's resurgence often views electoral gains as essential to a comeback for both the Democrats and the larger liberal/ progressive coalition. Long shut out of electoral politics, even leftists now pay attention to electoral races. The right has vividly demonstrated that the mainstream route of electoral politics can be the vehicle for radical political change.

Identifying effective and appropriate strategies is critical for those specifically concerned with the loss of progressive electoral power. The central questions are: What is possible in the current political climate? What practical and workable electoral plan can reinvigorate the progressive movement, and move it from its current weakened position to a dynamic political force that shrewdly and effectively competes for real political power?

In the Institute for Effective Action's 1995 report, "American Progressives at the Crossroads: A Challenge to Lead and Govern the Nation," Donald Cohen, Paul Milne, and Glen Schneider propose just such a plan. Their strategy for the progressive movement's return to power focuses on both movement-building and capturing electoral power. They call for "determined action" to uncompromisingly promote a progressive message, without camouflaging the message as centrist or liberal. This strategy mirrors the boldness of the plans proposed in the 1970s by the New Right's young leadership.[46]

Other progressive strategists focus on the Democratic Party. Jeff Faux, for example, approaches the challenge faced by the Democrats from the perspective of a party loyalist in his widely-read book, *The Party's Not Over*. He argues that the Democratic Party should return to its historical advocacy of active government—one that intervenes in the marketplace when the free-market system violates standards of morality and decency. This intervention, he says, represents the *real* values question. Implicitly rejecting identity politics, Faux argues that the Democratic Party can return to its roots only if Democrats are willing to return to "majority" themes of economic security and rising living standards, create a new political "story" that captures the ideal of an activist government working for the common good, and reform government to free it from the corruption of big money.[47]

Calls of this sort are pleas for the stiffening of the political will of a party moving rapidly from left of center to political center. Despite the existence of a caucus of Congressional Democrats known as the Progressive Caucus, and the generally left-of-center politics of the Congressional Black Caucus, the Democratic Party's leadership has chosen to compete with the right by embracing the right's ideas.

Third Parties. For many progressives, the Democratic Party has drifted too far to the right for it to legitimately carry the progressive banner. So, much of the progressive electoral strategizing of the 1990s focuses not on the Democratic Party but on developing third parties. Although there are no structural barriers against independent or third party candidates in nonpartisan elections, for the most part, only local-level elections are nonpartisan. At the state and national levels, the winner-take-all nature of the U.S. electoral system has made the success of third parties unlikely.

Nevertheless, third parties do form as an expression of voter dissatisfaction with the two major parties. The most successful recent third party has been Ross Perot's Reform Party, which is tinged with right-wing populism and, if led by a more skillful leader, could have represented a serious threat to democracy. Also gaining prominence is the Libertarian Party, which has grown largely as a spinoff of the right's political success. Progressives have mounted several third parties: the New Party, the Labor Party, the Green Party, and, sporadically, a Women's Party. The Communist Party, the Workers' World Party, Democratic Socialists of America (DSA), and others still run candidates in some venues.

The most successful progressive third party has been the New Party, whose candidates have done surprisingly well at the local level, serving as an alternative to conservative Democrats. In the past, the New Party was a predominantly white, middle-class effort in which women were under-represented. In the late 1990s, it has now become more representative of the diverse base of the progressive movement.

The New Party focused on a structural reform known as "fusion politics," long practiced in New York State by the Liberal, and later the Conservative, Parties. Fusion voting allows a minor party to ally with one of the major parties behind a joint candidate, so that people can support the third party without "wasting" their vote.[48] Unfortunately the New Party lost its attempt to sue for the legality of fusion voting in the 1996–1997 session of the U.S. Supreme Court. Though fusion politics does not abolish the larger structural barriers to third party emergence, it could have enabled a third party to gain strength and eventually become an electoral contender.

Another notable development in third party politics is the Labor Party's broadening of the definition of its labor base from the traditional one—working-class workers—to include all people who have to, or are expected to, work for a living. According to political scientist Adolph Reed, Jr., "This is an explicit attempt to project a collective identity that can help to break down the ultimately artificial distinction between 'economic' and 'social' issues; it's an attempt to establish a broad and inclusive definition of the working class."[49] If this broader definition sticks, it will provide labor with a larger constituency for its recruiting and organizing. The Labor Party has already shown the potential of this new broader agenda by reaching out to organize former welfare recipients who are now in the labor force.

Proportional Representation. Many progressives think that the only guarantee of real competitive status for third parties would be to change the electoral system from a single-party, simple-majority system to a proportional representation system, similar to that of most European countries. A multiparty electoral system would be a radical institutional reform that could mean a more democratic form of government. In contrast to the current system of winner-take-all plurality voting (which makes it difficult, or impossible, for a third party to win seats), proportional representation divides the seats according to the percentage of votes received by any one party. Those not on the winning side are still represented. Because it is unlikely that any one party would capture a plurality, coalitions become necessary. No one's voice is silenced in a system of proportional representation, with the exception of those who do not win an adequate number of votes to gain even a single seat in the representative body.[50]

A national organization pursuing this option, the Center for Voting and Democracy in Washington, D.C., supported a narrowly defeated 1996 San Francisco ballot initiative that would have changed the system of electing the Board of Supervisors to one of proportional representation. This system has long been used to elect the City Council and the School Committee in Cambridge, Massachusetts.

Many progressives cling to the compromised politics of the Democratic Party because they assume that victory through third party politics is too distant a possibility and prefer to practice "reality-based" politics. Others view the uphill struggle of third party work as the only viable, long-term solution now available. I think it is likely that, were proportional representation better understood, it would hold enormous appeal for large numbers of progressives and other voters. It would, of course, require a huge public education campaign to overcome the bitter opposition that would be mounted by the entrenched interests of the two-party system. Nevertheless, in the current populist electoral mood, the inherently more democratic nature of a proportional representation system just might prove compelling.[51]

Campaign Finance Reform. The 1996 and 1998 elections, which set new spending records in local, state, and national races, were a crash course for the public on the need for campaign finance reform. The power of money in politics is now clear to all, and people widely acknowledge that it represents a threat to democracy. Without genuine campaign finance reform, the corrupting influence of campaign fund-raising will continue to dominate U.S. politics.[52] Every European democracy imposes curbs on campaign fund-raising, understanding that it represents the reality, not just the appearance, of influence peddling.

The political power of money is a stable feature of U.S. politics, not a new problem. For many progressives working in electoral politics, it is *the* single most important systemic reform, holding the promise of wrenching control of elections away from corporations and wealthy individuals. The 1974 Electoral Reform Act set limits on campaign donations and set caps on the expenditures of candidates in their campaigns. Unfortunately, that second provision was overturned by the Supreme Court (*Buckley v. Valeo*) as a violation of individual free speech, and the first provision has proved no match for those willing to use loopholes and third parties to exceed allowable limits.

The right opposes campaign finance reform, arguing that the reforms would be more damaging to "freedom" than campaign finance abuse. Another factor hindering reform is the self-interest of sitting Congressional legislators, who are unwilling to legislate reforms that would damage their own fundraising efforts.

However, some state-level efforts have been effective. California mounted two initiatives in 1996, one (Proposition 212) more far-reaching than the other. The milder initiative passed. In 1996, Maine Voters for Clean Elections also managed to get on the state ballot a campaign finance reform proposal that was approved by the voters. It provides a public financing option for candidates, as well as setting restrictions on those who opt for private campaign financing. The initiative resulted from a coalition effort by state and national organizations, and a base-building process that recruited people from various sectors throughout the state. It is designed both to level the playing field within politics and to address people's cynicism about the corrupting influence of money in politics.[53]

After campaign financing abuses received widespread media coverage during the 1996 elections, public support developed for campaign finance reform. In the 1998 elections, Massachusetts passed a campaign finance reform initiative known as the Clean Elections initiative by a margin of 2 to 1. Unfortunately, its sponsor, Massachusetts Voters for Clean Elections, was required to mount a new campaign in 1999 to get the initiative funded by the Massachusetts Legislature and a reluctant Republican governor, Paul Cellucci.

Campaign finance reform is an instance of a progressive reform that is popular with the public. Perhaps more important, a public debate over campaign finance reform represents an opportunity for public education about the corruption of democracy when public servants are "bought," and the need for the average person to organize in order to begin a cleanup of electoral politics.

ATTACKING ECONOMIC INEQUALITY

Many progressives consider the dramatic and alarming growth of economic inequality since the early 1980s as the single most absorbing challenge to progressives. As political scientist Sheldon Wolin argues, "Strategies that look to third parties or proportional representation to provide the momentum for regaining control over the federal government are hopelessly inadequate. The power of wealth is too highly organized and the morale of the citizenry too low to enable reformers to compete for control of the centers of power. . . . Corporate power has managed to tailor representative government to its needs."[54]

The standard progressive response to growing inequality is a program of aggressive redistribution—including high employment policies, progressive (rather than regressive) federal and state tax structures, industrial policies to promote economic activities that result in lessened inequalities, higher minimum wages, strengthened unions, improved public services, and direct cash subsidies.[55] Unfortunately, the support for income equality has so eroded in the United States that there is virtually no political support for policy responses of this sort. In the current political context, such policies would have little chance of being enacted.

Before a progressive program can succeed, the public must be reeducated. Despite the dramatic growth of economic inequality during the Reagan, Bush, and Clinton Administrations, the right's campaign to convince people that liberalism is responsible for people's economic insecurity has been remarkably successful. Fortunately, progressives have been doing public education on the injustices and inequities inherent in capitalism for decades. However, much of that work assumes a public that is open to government regulation and other liberal policies as antidotes to capitalism's unchecked profit motive.

Since the election of Ronald Reagan to the presidency in 1980, anticapitalist militancy has been muted. Many progressives have been forced by the right to fall back to a position less explicitly critical of capitalism

and less aligned with powerful government intervention in the economy. This results in somewhat anemic themes, such as the message that
domination of the economy by large private corporations is creating an
alarmingly unfair distribution of wealth. Opposing unfettered free-
market capitalism on the basis of its lack of "fairness" is one of several
messages that have a chance of slipping under the public's current anti-
liberal screen. Other messages include: large corporations do not deserve
government "welfare" in the form of subsidies, tax breaks, and deregulation; and GATT and NAFTA agreements are U.S. capitalism's grab
for low-cost labor and international domination.

So far, these themes have not been successful in blunting the right's
drive to eliminate all constraints on free-market capitalism. The trim-
ming of the progressive income tax, the campaign to eliminate the long-
term capital gains tax, and the attack on corporate taxes, federal regulations, and unions—all rely on a public that identifies with free-market
forces. The right has created just such a public.

Nevertheless, the unfairness of an unchecked free market remains the
single most powerful message in the progressive ideological arsenal. It
has practical common-sense appeal, as well as tapping powerful populist
instincts that, for better or worse, run throughout U.S. culture. Organizations such as Just Economics, a Berkeley-based collective of women
who link economic education with grassroots organizing, or Share the
Wealth, a project of Massachusetts-based United for a Fair Economy, are
developing public education programs that unmask the rapacious nature
of free-market capitalism and appeal to *fairness*, an unthreatening, all-
American concept. Both organizations stress the concentration of 70
percent of U.S. wealth in the hands of the top 10 percent of the population.

MOVING BEYOND INCLUSION AND TOLERANCE

Progressives like to think that our leadership style (egalitarian, more or
less) is morally superior to the right's pattern of hierarchical leadership. Further, because progressive principles include explicit opposition to racism, sexism, anti-Semitism, and to oppression based on class,
sexual orientation, or age, progressives are more likely to demand that
their leaders adhere to egalitarian principles. In fact, attention to preju-

dice has earned the movement a reputation for "political correctness"—a pejorative label used by the right to simultaneously make fun of progressives and pander to the resentments of those white people who feel left behind by social justice programs or resent being called on their intolerance. [56]

However, for the progressive movement truly to reflect the principles it promotes, it will have to address several disturbing patterns within it that require self-criticism and struggle. For instance, in innumerable instances, progressive leaders have been criticized for racist, sexist, homophobic, or anti-Semitic behavior and still have failed to learn from those experiences. Another troubling pattern within predominantly white organizations is the tendency for the race, class, and gender of the movement's leadership to look much like that of any mainstream apolitical, or even rightist, movement. White, middle- and upper-class men and women disproportionately occupy positions of power, and people of color, especially women of color, are underrepresented. Another pattern is that many organizations whose membership is predominantly made up of people of color find themselves marginalized within the larger, predominantly white movement. And finally, progressives who are privileged by the dominant culture—white people, middle- and upper-class people, and heterosexuals—all too often feel qualified to speak for those who are underrepresented or absent within the movement.

Many predominantly white progressive organizations have attempted to grapple with such contradictions, often by adopting an agenda of "outreach" and "inclusion" to achieve various forms of diversity. Outreach and inclusion, however, are insidious goals. They often result in superficial changes in style, rather than changes in substantive content or in the organization's culture. If individual organizational power structures remain unchanged, outreach and inclusion at that level will not necessarily lead to power-sharing or to a change of culture within the progressive movement as a whole.

When the right uses the label "political correctness" to ridicule such concerns, it attacks both the progressive movement and the struggle against racism and other forms of oppression. Arguing that "tolerance" of difference is important in a pluralistic society in order to temper the urge of the majority to dominate and exploit minorities, white progressives often fall back on the concept of tolerance in demanding full political rights for people of color, lesbians and gay men, immigrants, welfare recipients, women who seek abortions, and others under attack from the right. But "tolerance" is a liberal concept that does not question the standard against which it is applied—traditional white American society. "We" are tolerating "them." Tolerance does not necessarily lead to real equality, just as inclusion does not guarantee power-sharing. These approaches may sound progressive, but fall far short of the movement's stated principles. Real equality does not occur when one group allows another to have a bit of power or when the powerful tolerate the presence of the less powerful. Power-sharing cannot be an afterthought. Those with less power know this, but those with more often have trouble seeing it.

A number of progressive organizations have met the challenge of building truly multiracial, pro-gay, pro-women programs and membership. In *Beyond Identity Politics*, editor John Anner of the Center for Third World Organizing collects and expands stories of successful organizing in communities of color previously told in the Center's magazine, *Third Force*. The story of Providence, Rhode Island–based Direct Action for Rights and Equality (DARE) is typical of the success stories in Anner's collection. Realizing that DARE was not attracting Latino members with flyers in Spanish translations, the organization created *Comité Latino*, a membership committee that conducted monthly meetings (in Spanish) and developed its own organizing campaign to galvanize the Latino community. Only when DARE's membership was one-third Latino and two Latino representatives served on the Board of Directors did *Comité Latino* disband.[57]

It is worth noting that DARE spent five years and over $100,000, including the cost of a multi-channel translating machine that allows simultaneous translation from English into several other languages. Many predominantly white organizations struggle to be truly multiracial, but must do so with limited resources. Smaller organizations often exist in an almost permanent crisis mode, stretched so thin that there is little room for organizational strategizing or planning. Many organizations of color that have the potential to be models of truly inclusive organizing are small, underfunded, and understaffed. They do not attract media attention and remain "off the screen" of the larger organizations that could learn from them.

WORKING FOR RACIAL JUSTICE

The right, while claiming to have cleansed itself of Old Right racism, has attacked nearly every area in which civil rights advancements were made during the 1960s and 1970s. Activists working for racial justice at the turn of the twentieth century spend the bulk of their time fighting defensive battles simply to retain past gains. In most cases, the right has succeeded depressingly well in mobilizing popular opinion against a range of reforms that benefited people of color, including affirmative action, bilingual education, and multicultural curriculum, and in promoting reactionary steps that disproportionately affect people of color, such as restoration of the death penalty, mandatory prison sentences, and increased police powers.[58] In 1999, two decades after the emergence of the New Right, there is no widespread public outrage at the revelation that Senate Majority Leader Trent Lott (R-MS) and Representative Bob Barr (R-GA) have ties to an explicitly racist organization called the Council of Conservative Citizens.

Nonetheless, progressive people of all races continue to organize for racial justice. Some belong to organizations that are large, national in scope, and specialize in legal challenges and legislative initiatives. These include the Lawyers' Committee for Civil Rights under the Law, the Leadership Conference on Civil Rights, the Center for Constitutional Rights, the Mexican American Legal Defense and Education Fund, the Asian Pacific Legal Defense Fund, and the Indian Law Resource Center. Some progressives are active in medium-sized groups that focus on education, advocacy, and organizing, such as Atlanta's Center for Democratic Renewal, which monitors far right white supremacist activities; Minneapolis-based Rethinking Schools, which publishes research on the right's attack on public education; or Oakland's Applied Research Center, which researches institutional racism. Other activists work in small grassroots organizations that are flexible and can mobilize a demonstration in response to a particular outrage, such as Southerners on

New Ground (SONG) or the North Carolina Lambda Youth Network. The work of all three sectors is crucial to holding the line against further attacks on racial justice.

Unfortunately, there is often poor communication, or even hostility, among the three "levels" of antiracist organizing. By frequently not listening to or respecting the grassroots organizations, the larger organizations miss the valuable input and guidance the smaller groups could provide. The smaller organizations often don't appreciate that the institutional change pursued by the larger organizations is crucial to long-term gains in racial justice. Mid-level groups, well placed to serve as a communications conduit between the larger and grassroots organizations, are often financially strapped and overworked, and unable to prioritize that work.

In working for racial justice, the progressive movement might well take a lesson from the right, which has skillfully coordinated the work of its different organizational "levels." Large civil rights organizations should be closely attuned to the demands and complaints of grassroots organizations. With large staffs of lawyers and deep pockets, the national organizations can bring suits, such as the 1999 suit brought by five civil rights organizations against the University of California at Berkeley for "discriminatory policies that deny admission to disadvantaged members of minorities with excellent academic records."[59] They should be in contact with the small, community-based groups that can respond with "people power" to specific racial incidents, such as the 1997 torture of Haitian immigrant Abner Louima by four white police officers, or the 1998 killing of Tyisha Miller in a hail of twenty-four bullets fired by Riverside, California, police while she sat in her car. The mid-sized groups deserve appreciation for their invaluable expertise on specific issues, and should not have their contributions overlooked or their work duplicated by the larger, national organizations.

Progressives also should work to improve coordination between organizations working at all three levels and campus racial justice work. On college campuses, African, African American, Latino/a, Asian, Asian Pacific, and Native American programs are educating students about cultures other than the Western European culture that has traditionally dominated the curriculum. "Multiculturalism," the concept used to represent a commitment to privileging all cultures equally, often also includes women's studies and lesbian and gay studies.[60] Multiculturalism is under increasing attack from right-wing students, faculty and alumni, supported and organized by secular right and Christian Right groups. Student organizations need the advice, training, and financial resources of off-campus organizations, and national organizations need to stay in touch with—and learn from—student initiatives and perspectives. Faculty research, often extremely helpful to racial justice organizations, also must be more accountable to their needs.[61]

An important part of racial justice work is educational work with individuals to address the racism that every white person has internalized as the result of living in a racist culture. White journalists and commentators often talk about this work, which is known as "diversity training," as if it were the principal focus of antiracism work. Although individual prejudice reduction is important, diversity training can focus too little on the progressive goal of justice for people of color and too much on the less progressive goals of bringing harmony to race relations and increasing the efficiency of a multiracial workplace.

Good individual antiracism work incorporates an understanding of the variety of bases for systemic inequality, such as class, gender, ethnicity, sexual orientation, disability, or age. It makes connections and common cause among groups marginalized and oppressed by mainstream society and analyzes racism within a context of institutions, cultural norms, and history. It moves white people to see beyond tolerance and inclusion, to envision actual power-sharing, and to learn to *take leadership* from people of color who are fighting for racial justice. It moves white people to see people of color as multifaceted individuals with rich, sustaining, and diverse cultures and histories, not just as members of an "oppressed" group.

But when all this must be accomplished in a brief training session or a workshop, the results can be disastrous. I have attended nearly a dozen such workshops, some lasting only three hours and others three days. In each case, the starting point was the individual racist feelings of white people. Some trainers have people of color meet separately so they can freely discuss their experiences of racist oppression. From that point forward, the trainers frame white racism as a problem of individual attitudes that can be solved through individual enlightenment. Along the way, the trainers often identify history, economic and political institutions, and cultural norms as important contributing factors. Often I can see that they passionately appreciate the role of these factors and have a thorough understanding of institutional racism. But time constraints make it difficult for them adequately to explore and discuss these issues. When they use a model that is psychological and inward-looking, they cannot give the necessary time and attention to a discussion of institutional racism and oppression that can lead white participants to a deeper understanding of the social causes and effects of racism and to ways to confront it.[62]

While engaging in continuous self-education and self-reflection, white progressives need to avoid individualistic models of antiracism work. Separating antiracism work from the progressive vision of social justice for *all* people ignores the history of U.S. racism and the persistence of institutional racism. White progressives need to promote a model of antiracism that values the leadership of people of color and holds white people accountable to them—an important step away from models that demand that white people change their consciousness, but leave their dominance intact.[63] Effective racial justice organizing also connects those who are vulnerable to attack from the right by highlighting the parallel, though unique, roles of racism, anti-Semitism, homophobia, sexism, class oppression, and other forms of bigotry in maintaining justice for some, but not for all.

LISTENING FOR LEADERSHIP

Progressives have often dismissed messages that sound racist or sexist or homophobic because those who utter them seem "hopelessly reactionary." But other messages have also been dismissed—from constituencies progressives claim as their own—because they were at odds with a particular progressive analysis. For instance, in the 1970s and 1980s, when women of color demanded that the largely white feminist pro-choice movement pay attention to how abortion is understood in communities of color, and asked that the pro-choice agenda expand to include sterilization abuse, they often went unheard. For many white women, especially those in the larger, mainstream reproductive rights organizations, staying the narrower course seemed the more practical way to save women's right to abortion. Too little dialogue went into this decision. The progressive movement has lost many potential members because of its neglect of their agendas and an unwillingness to thoroughly debate their criticism.

In fact, people who have had trouble being heard may be the very people who hold the key to new visions, new ways of formulating solutions, or new views of equality in post-industrial capitalism. Leaders usually emerge when their voices are loud and their programs touch a sympathetic chord in a large following. But sometimes they emerge when, though their voices are not loud, people look to them for leadership. The current leadership of the progressive movement won't hear those ideas if it thinks the movement already has the answers or it doesn't recognize the value and legitimacy of those promoting them. Only a full understanding that the movement must look for new leadership and new ideas (or old, unrecognized leaders and unheard ideas) will open us to hearing ideas that challenge dominant movement thinking.

Take the voice of women, for instance. Women of all races and ethnicities, but especially women of color and working-class women of all races, have complained about being unnoticed in the progressive movement and of having to struggle to make their voices heard, often to no avail. Yet women have an enormous amount to bring to any movement. As a group that has been subjected to sexism, often compounded by racism, poverty, and homophobia, our history is full of the experience of organizing, of developing coping strategies, of hidden patterns of strength, courage, and resistance. Women's political work is often characterized by a collaborative leadership style, a problem-solving orientation, and a talent for making connections among individuals and groups. These resources are not the exclusive preserve of women; they can also be found in men. But because they are so closely associated with women, they are often ignored or dismissed, especially within progressive groups dominated by male leadership.

The resources found within low-income communities often are similarly unrecognized. Middle-class and/or white progressive leaders sometimes fail to appreciate that low-income communities—whether white, of color, or racially mixed—are the sites of greatest struggle and the places where people devise strategies for survival on a daily basis. Many of the progressive activists within these communities are women who have the sharpest view of the realities of the community's problems. We have no better example than the environmental justice movement, a multiracial movement that grew out of low-income communities of color and represents a direct challenge both to the corporations that pollute them and the "Big Ten" environmental organizations that seldom speak for them.

After decades of claiming to speak for oppressed people of all races and ethnicities, the progressive movement must now learn to look to the same people for leadership, in the form of individual leaders within those communities and/or ideas that come out of them. Many poor and working-class people are also women, and a progressive consciousness should have a third ear for the special double or triple nature of poor women's oppression.

This means that we don't just follow the leadership that climbs to the top and captures the megaphone. As John Anner says in *Beyond Identity Politics*, "The strategies and struggles that will drive future political movements are being incubated in the places where direct experience of oppression and injustice is fresh and raw, among people without political turf to defend, who are willing to try new ideas and experiment with new strategies."[64] Sadly, it is far from clear that the current progressive leadership, with long-standing habits of power, will take the necessary action to recognize Anner's other sources of leadership, and step aside to allow that leadership to emerge. It is even less certain that they would then follow it.

MOVING FORWARD

As we work to rebuild the progressive movement, we must value that work for itself. To focus on rebuilding does not mean we have given up the goal of radical social change. It is a response to the reality of the moment. We are living in a time when the U.S. government will no longer take responsibility for the welfare of low-income people or for incorporating marginalized people into the larger society. It is probably a mistake to chase the notion of a single political strategy—a sort of magic bullet—that will turn the political tide. Understanding this, Pete Seeger has said, "It won't be one leader or one party or one cause that turns this situation around. It will be all the small little victories."[65]

We can rebuild the progressive movement only within an accurate reading of reality, one that acknowledges the current grim picture of right-wing dominance. Bold, brash responses to that dominance are entirely appropriate. In-your-face organizing and larger-than-life political plans are all part of movement-building. But we must understand bold, brash actions, or "magic bullet" thinking in the context of a realistic assessment of current conditions. They cannot substitute for the small-scale, everyday work of careful, thoughtful movement-building.

This movement-building may involve a process of "falling back," engaging in self-examination that results in confronting the movement's problems. For example, women's organizations dominated by white women will have to confront their own racism, homophobia, and anti-Semitism. Middle- and upper-class lesbian and gay activists will have to confront their class biases. Male-dominated labor organizations will have to examine their sexism and homophobia. Achieving a deep understanding of these biases must be a central political concern. Leadership that proposes to skip this step should be rejected. Indeed, "Step by step" might be an appropriate motto for the progressive movement as we enter the twenty-first century.

NOTES

1. THE RESURGENT RIGHT: WHY NOW?

1. There is no rigorous and universally agreed upon definition of a "movement." In the case of religious and social movements, often something as specific as a campaign mounted by a group of like-minded citizens is labeled a movement. In this discussion I am reserving the term "movement" for umbrella movements rather than their sub-movements. Thus, "social movement" will refer to the collectivity of active campaigns mobilized by the right around the social issues. "Economic," "political," and "religious" movements will refer to the collectivity of active campaigns mobilized by the right around economic, political, and religious issues. All these movements unite under the rubric of the contemporary U.S. "right."

2. See David H. Bennett, *The Party of Fear: The American Far Right from Nativism to the Militia Movement* (New York: Random House, 1988); and Leo P. Ribuffo, *The Old Christian Right: The Protestant Hard Right from the Great Depression to the Cold War* (Philadelphia: Temple University Press, 1983).

3. Adele Stan, "Power Preying," *Mother Jones* (November/December 1995), p. 45.

4. For an excellent short account of the history of the rise of the right, see Chip Berlet, "Following the Threads," in Amy Ansell, ed., *Unraveling the Right:*

The New Conservatism in American Thought and Politics (Boulder, CO: Westview Press, 1998), pp. 17–40.

5. I will address the sectors of the right that operate within the electoral sphere, and right-wing movements that operate in tandem with the Republican Party. Variously called the New Right, the "new" Republicans, the Christian Right, or the hard right, this sector does not include the extremist, paramilitary right, such as the Ku Klux Klan, neo-Nazi groups, the Aryan Nations, and other violent white supremacist groups. Violent members of the anti-abortion movement, Christian Reconstructionists, and certain individuals, such as David Duke and Pat Buchanan, represent "bridges" that link the electorally oriented right and the paramilitary right (sometimes called the far right). Though I am not addressing the paramilitary right here, much of what I say applies to that sector as well.

6. William B. Hixson, Jr., *Search for the American Right Wing: An Analysis of the Social Science Record, 1955–1987* (Princeton: Princeton University Press, 1992).

7. Right-wing campaigns also can bubble up from the right's base; individual grassroots activists might provide the catalyst for a campaign by taking the lead themselves. Most often, however, the campaign target has been identified by the leadership, the justification for the attack has been conceptualized, and the grass-roots "leader" then seizes a moment to build on that. Examples include Ward Connerly in the case of Proposition 209 against affirmative action in California, and Tony Marco in the case of the anti-gay initiative Amendment Two in Colorado.

8. From the 1950s into the 1960s, rightist intellectuals attempted to smooth over the differences among various sectors of the right—especially libertarians and traditionalists. The effort was given the name "fusionism." Though never entirely successful, this pre–New Right integration of different types of right-wing ideology laid the path for the internal movement collaboration from the 1970s onward. See Jerome J. Himmelstein, *To the Right: The Transformation of American Conservatism* (Berkeley: University of California Press, 1990), pp. 55–60.

9. Tanya Melich, *The Republican War Against Women: An Insider's Report from Behind the Lines* (New York: Bantam Books, 1996).

10. The strategy of capturing votes for the Republican Party from disaffected conservative Democrats (especially those who voted for George Wallace in 1968) was proposed in Kevin Phillips, *The Emerging Republican Majority* (Garden City, NY: Doubleday, 1970). For excellent discussions of the outcome of "the southern strategy," see Thomas Ferguson and Joel Rogers, *Right Turn: The Decline of the Democrats and the Future of American Politics* (New York: Hill and Wang, 1986).

11. I use the term "Christian Right" to refer to the explicitly religious sector

of the right, rather than the term "Religious Right," because, though there are many conservative Jews and Muslims and adherents within other religions, they are not, for the most part, active within the contemporary U.S. right. There are exceptions, of course, but the religious sector of the movement I refer to as the "right" is overwhelmingly conservative Christian. I agree with John Green when he rejects the term "religious right," which is meant to encompass conservative Catholics, Jews, Muslims, and mainline Protestants as well as evangelical Protestants. Green notes that "to date, most of the political action has been limited to one segment of this unrealized alliance, evangelical Protestants. While far from perfect, the term Christian Right best describes the phenomenon in question: a movement that seeks to restore 'traditional values' in public policy by means of mobilizing evangelical Protestants, many of whom self-consciously identify as 'Christians' in the sectarian usage of the term." John C. Green, "The Christian Right and the 1994 Elections: An Overview," in Mark J. Rozell and Clyde Wilcox, eds., *God at the Grassroots: The Christian Right in the 1994 Elections* (Lanham, MD: Rowman & Littlefield Publishers, 1995), p. 2.

12. Bert Klandermans researches the social psychology of protest movement activists within social movement organizations (SMOs). He explores activists' individual motivations, their collective goals and identity (which becomes the basis for a "collective action frame"), and their subsequent collective actions. See Bert Klandermans, *The Social Psychology of Protest* (Cambridge, MA: Blackwell Publishers, 1997), pp. 1–63. Also see William A. Gamson, "Constructing Social Protest," in Hank Johnston and Bert Klandermans, eds., *Social Movements and Culture* (Minneapolis: University of Minnesota Press, 1995), pp. 85–106.

13. Sara Diamond, *Roads to Dominion: Right-Wing Movements and Political Power in the United States* (New York: The Guilford Press, 1995), pp. 128–31.

14. Clarence Y. H. Lo, "Counter-movements and Conservative Movements in the Contemporary U.S.," *Annual Review of Sociology* 8 (1982): 107–34.

15. This is the case when the Bureau of Alcohol, Tobacco, and Firearms (BATF) has attacked right-wing enclaves that have stockpiled weapons, right-wing tax protesters who have defied the IRS, or far right movement activists who have engaged in illegal activity.

16. Beth Schulman, "LOOK THIS UP," *Extra!*, newsletter of Fairness and Accuracy in Reporting (March 1995); Joel Bleifuss, "Building Plans," *In These Times* (July 10, 1995).

17. The role of this sort of strategic funding by right-wing funders was detailed by researcher Sally Covington in her 1997 report on the funding patterns of the twelve largest right-wing foundations. Sally Covington, *Moving A Public Policy Agenda: The Strategic Philanthropy of Conservative Foundations* (Washington, DC: National Committee for Responsive Philanthropy, 1997). Also see Jean Stefancic, "Funding the Nativist Agenda," in Juan F. Perea, ed., *Immigrants Out!: The New Nativism and the Anti-Immigrant Impulse in the United States* (New York: New York University Press, 1997), pp. 119–35.

18. The definitions of "evangelical" and "fundamentalist" are murky because they describe theological views rather than institutions. George Marsden attempts a definition: Christian evangelicalism includes any Christian who is traditional enough to affirm the basic beliefs of: 1) the final authority of the Bible, 2) the reality of Scripture, 3) redemption through Christ, 4) the importance of missionary work, and 5) the importance of a spiritually transformed life. A Christian fundamentalist is an evangelical who is militant in opposition to liberal theology or to changes in cultural values or mores. Pentecostalism, which dates to the 1920s, is associated with faith healing and speaking in tongues, signifying dramatic intervention of the supernatural. A slightly different and more modern form of supernatural religious practice is practiced by Christian "charismatics." To be born-again refers to a conversion experience in which one surrenders his or her life to Jesus Christ, thus making Jesus your personal Lord and savior. See George M. Marsden, *Understanding Fundamentalism and Evangelicalism* (Grand Rapids, MI: William B. Eerdmans, 1991), pp. 1–6; and Sara Diamond, *Spiritual Warfare: The Politics of the Christian Right* (Boston: South End Press, 1989), p. 237.

19. Rev. Billy Graham was one of the rare high-profile conservative Christians who was willing to locate his ministry very close to political power. He gave spiritual counsel to every president from Eisenhower to Clinton, but his friendship with President Richard Nixon was especially public. Also, a number of explicitly political groups within the Old Right, such as the Christian Anti-Communism League, Summit Ministries, the Church League of America, and the John Birch Society were Christian-based organizations.

20. President Jimmy Carter, an evangelical "born-again" Christian, has attracted the votes of previously nonvoting, Democratic Party-leaning evangelical Christians, providing an important lesson to the New Right's strategists. See William Martin, *With God on Our Side: The Rise of the Religious Right in America* (New York: Broadway Books, 1996), pp. 149–59.

21. William Fore, "Religion and Television: Report on the Research," *Christian Century* (July 18–25, 1984), p. 711. Fore is reporting on research conducted by the Annenberg School of Communication at the University of Pennsylvania, which estimates that the *entire* viewing public for religious TV is approximately 13.3 million.

22. Gallup Opinion Organization, "Religion in America, 1981," *Gallup Opinion Index* 184 (1991): 1–77.

23. "Approximately 5 million Muslims live in the United States. Islam will probably be the largest non-Christian religion in the United States in the next century." Sam Husseini, "Islam: Fundamental Misunderstandings about a Growing Faith," in Don Hazen and Julie Winokur, eds., *We the Media: A Citizens' Guide to Fighting for Media Democracy* (New York: The New Press, 1997), p. 113.

24. Anthony F. C. Wallace, "Revitalization Movements," *American Anthropologist* 58 (April 1956): 264–81.

25. Diamond, *Roads to Dominion*, pp. 161–77.

26. Corwin Smidt, Lyman Kellstedt, John Green, and James Guth, "The Characteristics of Christian Political Activists: An Interest Group Analysis," in William Stevenson, ed., *Christian Political Activism at the Crossroads* (Lanham, MD: University Press of America, 1994).

27. See Chip Berlet, "Dances with Devils: How Apocalyptic and Millennialist Themes Influence Right-Wing Scapegoating and Conspiracism," *Public Eye* XII: 2/3 (Fall 1998): 1–22. Also see Robert Fuller, *Naming the Antichrist* (New York: Oxford University Press, 1995).

28. Jessicqa Wadkins, "Y2K: 'End of the World?' or 'No Big Deal'?" *Family Voice* 20: 11 (November/December 1998): 4–12.

29. Lynn Vincent, "Backward Christian Soldiers?" *World* 13: 32 (August 22, 1998): 16–17.

30. In the late 1950s and the 1960s, JBS founder Robert Welch developed the organization's signature conspiracy theory—the desire by secret elites, through the United Nations, to promote a one-world government. While the JBS membership fell off after Welch's death in 1985, the Bush Administration's "New World Order" resonated with its old conspiracy theory and breathed new life into the organization. Membership has increased since 1985, and JBS not only survives, but occasionally exerts influence in policy matters. See Michael O'Keeffe and Kevin Daley, "Checking the Right: Rightist Backlash against the Environmental Movement," *Buzzworm* (May 1993): 39–44.

31. A number of Jews have been central players in the larger secular right, especially within neoconservative intellectual circles, and through the Committee on the Present Danger, the Coalition for a Democratic Majority, and the magazines *The Public Interest* and *Commentary*. Important right-wing strategies were mapped by neoconservatives, including the attack on welfare recipients and affirmative action. Most recently, William Kristol, son of neoconservative Irving Kristol, updates his father's neoconservatism with an emphasis on morality in the magazine he edits, the *Weekly Standard*. See Andrew Sullivan, "Going Down Screaming," *New York Times Magazine*, Oct. 11, 1998, pp. 46–51, 88–91.

32. See Daniel Lapin, *America's Real War: An Orthodox Rabbi Insists Judeo Christian Values Are Vital for Our Nation's Survival* (Sisters, OR: Multinomah Press, 1998). Also see Hillel Kuttler, "U.S. Jewish Conservatives Find a Scapegoat," *Jerusalem Post*, October 14, 1994, 4B.

33. See Ruth W. Mouly, *The Religious Right and Israel* (Somerville, MA: Political Research Associates, 1985); and Grace Halsell, *Prophecy and Politics: Militant Evangelists on the Road to Nuclear War* (Westport, CT: Lawrence Hill, 1985).

34. Berlet, "Dances with Devils." Also see Michael Lind, "Rev. Robertson's Grand International Conspiracy Theory," *The New York Review of Books*, February 2, 1995, pp. 21–25.

35. David Cantor, *The Religious Right: The Assault on Tolerance and Pluralism in America* (New York: ADL, 1994).

36. Holly Sklar, *Chaos or Community? Seeking Solutions, not Scapegoats for Bad Economics* (Boston: South End Press, 1995), pp. 31–34, 53–60. Also see John J. Sweeney, *America Needs a Raise: Fighting for Economic Security and Social Justice* (Boston: Houghton Mifflin, 1996), pp. 29–54; and Marina v.N. Whitman, *New World, New Rules: The Changing Role of the American Corporation* (Boston: Harvard Business School Press, 1999).

37. I have generalized in drawing a "map" of the sectors for the sake of brevity. New Right organizations have received financial support from sources within the multinational sector, and many aspects of the political and economic agendas of the two sectors overlap.

38. See Martin J. Levitt, *Confessions of a Union Buster* (New York: Crown Publishers, 1993); Kim Phillips-Fein, "A More Perfect Union Buster," *Mother Jones,* September 1, 1998, pp. 62–65; and Patricia Cayo Sexton, *The War on Labor and the Left: Understanding America's Unique Conservatism* (Boulder, CO: Westview Press, 1991), pp. 224–26.

39. Matthew N. Lyons, "Business Conflict and Right-Wing Movements," in Ansell, ed., *Unraveling the Right,* pp. 80–102.

40. Edward N. Wolff, *Top Heavy: A Study of the Increasing Inequality of Wealth in America* (New York: Twentieth Century Fund Press, 1995), pp. 7–13; Jerry Kloby, "The Growing Divide: Class Polarization in the 1980s," *Monthly Review* 39 (September 1987): 1–8. Also see Chuck Collins, Betsy Leonard-Wright, and Holly Sklar, *Shifting Fortunes: The Perils of the Growing American Wealth Gap* (Boston: United for a Fair Economy, 1999).

41. Lester C. Thurow, "The Boom That Wasn't," *New York Times,* January 18, 1999, p. A19.

42. Stephen Steinberg, *Turning Back: The Retreat from Racial Justice in American Thought and Policy* (Boston: Beacon Press, 1995), esp. pp. 180–85.

43. Alan Brinkley, "Reagan's Revenge as Invented by Howard Jarvis," *New York Times Magazine,* June 19, 1994, p. 36. Also see Daniel A. Smith, *Tax Crusaders and the Politics of Direct Democracy* (New York: Routledge, 1998).

44. Examples include Sidney Blumenthal, Michael Lind, Kevin Phillips, and Andrew Sullivan.

45. Examples include Salim Muwakkil, Derrick Jackson, Clarence Page, Julianne Malveaux, and Adolph Reed, Jr.

46. The term "white" is used here to refer to Americans of European descent who are non-Jews. Needless to say, skin color and racial identification are far more complex than allowed by schemes of racial classification. Such classifications in reality are social constructions. See Michael Omni and Howard Winant, *Racial Formation in the United States: From the 1960s to the 1990s* (New York: Routledge, 1994).

47. Deborah Toler, "Black Conservatives, Part One," *Public Eye* VII, 3 (September 1993): 1–7.

48. Stereotyping is assigning characteristics (usually negative) not to individuals but to entire groups of people. Scapegoating is fixing blame for social stress, economic loss, or loss of political power on a target group whose constructed guilt provides a simplistic explanation. Scapegoating usually relies on stereotyping.

49. See Ward Churchill and Jim Vander Wall, *Agents of Repression: The FBI's Secret Wars Against the Black Panther Party and the American Indian Movement* (Boston: South End Press, 1988); and Bud Schultz and Ruth Schultz, *It Did Happen Here: Recollections of Political Repression in America* (Berkeley: University of California Press, 1989).

50. See Eleanor Clift and Mark Miller, "Rev. Moon's Political Moves," *Newsweek*, February 15, 1988, p. 31; "Lyndon LaRouche: Cat Among the Pigeons," *Economist*, April 26, 1986, p. 32.

51. In the world of the far right, of course, white supremacism is endemic; far right white supremacists feel no obligation to obscure it. The far right is more extremist and ideologically alienated than the sector of the right that works within the political power structure. While there is important political cross-pollination between the far right and the electoral right, my discussion here does not address the racism and anti-Semitism of the paramilitary far right.

52. Friedrich A. Hayek, *The Road to Serfdom* (Chicago: University of Chicago Press, 1944); Barry Goldwater, *Conscience of a Conservative* (Sheperdsville, KY: Victor Publishing Co., 1960).

53. Daniel Bell, ed., *The Radical Right* (Garden City, NY: Doubleday, 1963); Richard Hofstadter, *The Paranoid Style in American Politics and Other Essays* (New York: Alfred A. Knopf, 1965).

54. Susan Faludi reports a 1988 interview with Connaught (Connie) Marshner (who, in the 1980s, was one of the New Right's most influential "profamily" strategists), in which Marshner takes credit for identifying the importance of the social issues to the movement. She refers to a talk she gave in 1979, titled "Why social issues are going to be important in the 1980s" as "prophetic." Susan Faludi, *Backlash: The Undeclared War Against American Women* (New York: Crown Publishers, 1991), pp. 243–44.

55. The specific strategies and tactics used by the right to carry out its attacks on liberal values and policies have been documented in a number of cases, perhaps most impressively by Ellen Messer-Davidow and Lucy A. Williams. See Ellen Messer-Davidow, "Manufacturing the Attack on Liberal Higher Education," *Social Text* 36 (Fall 1993): 40–80; "Dollars for Scholars: The Real Politics of Humanities Scholarship and Programs," in George Levine and E. Ann Kaplan, eds., *The Politics of Research* (New Brunswick: Rutgers University Press, 1997), pp. 193–233; Lucy Williams, *Decades of Distortion: The Right's Thirty-Year Assault on Welfare* (Somerville, MA: Political Research Associates, 1997).

56. In a 1980 speech, Paul Weyrich said, "We are different from previous

generations of conservatives. We are no longer working to preserve the status quo. We are radicals, working to overturn the present power structure of the country." Faludi, *Backlash*, p. 237.

57. See Alan Crawford, *Thunder on the Right* (New York: Pantheon Books, 1980); Joseph R. Gusfield, *Symbolic Crusade: Status Politics and the American Temperance Movement* (Urbana, IL: University of Illinois Press, 1963), pp. 111–12.

58. Thomas Byrne Edsall and Mary D. Edsall, *Chain Reaction: The Impact of Race, Rights, and Taxes on American Politics* (New York: W. W. Norton, 1991).

59. Janine R. Wedel, "The Harvard Boys Do Russia," *The Nation*, June 1, 1998, p.11.

60. Nonna Mayer, "The French National Front," in Hans-Georg Betz and Stefan Immerfall, eds., *The New Politics of the Right: Neo-Populist Parties and Movements in Established Democracies* (New York: St. Martin's Press, 1998), pp. 11–25.

61. The period most closely comparable to the right's current resurgence is the "Redeemer counterrevolution" that defeated post–Civil War Reconstruction. See Eric Foner, *Reconstruction: America's Unfinished Revolution, 1863–1877* (New York: Harper & Row, 1988).

2. MOBILIZING RESENTMENT: HOW THE RIGHT ORGANIZED AT THE GRASSROOTS

1. The New Right distanced itself from the Ku Klux Klan and other extremist white supremacist groups. It was ambivalent, however, about the John Birch Society. I attended a number of conferences during the early 1980s where I found the John Birch Society's book table quite literally tucked in a far corner of the room in which movement literature was sold (still in the room but not embraced or showcased).

2. William Buckley, Jr., is most often given credit for leading conservatives to fusionism, but Sara Diamond demonstrates the important roles played by other conservatives, especially Russell Kirk, Frank Meyer, Leo Strauss, and Richard Weaver. Sara Diamond, *Roads to Dominion: Right-Wing Movements and Political Power in the United States* (New York: Guilford Press, 1995), pp. 29–36.

3. See Hans Toch, *The Social Psychology of Social Movements* (Indianapolis: Bobbs-Merrill Co., 1965), pp. 86–90.

4. A useful framework for this exploration is resource mobilization theory, a field of sociology developed in the 1970s to explore the strategies and tactics employed to build a movement and increase its influence and power. The resource mobilization paradigm poses questions such as: Where are the resources available for the movement? How are they organized? How does the state facilitate or impede mobilization? and What are the outcomes?

In the 1990s, sociologists expanded the paradigm to include social, psychological, and cultural factors, such as the value structures of the participants, the grievances they bring to the movement, the ideological commitments they share, and the sector of society they represent. These factors are all relevant to the means and methods used by the movement in its mobilizing efforts.

For a review of the evolution of the resource mobilization paradigm, see Carol McClurg Mueller, "Building Social Movement Theory," in Aldon D. Morris and Carol McClurg Mueller, eds., *Frontiers in Social Movement Theory* (New Haven: Yale University Press, 1992), pp. 3–25.

5. William Lind, "Exercising the Right Kind of Hatred," Next Revolution commentary [online]; available from www.freecongress.org/NextRevolution; accessed April 28, 1997.

6. See: Clyde Wilcox, "Popular Support for the New Christian Right," *Social Science Journal* 26: 1 (1989): 55–63, for the distinction between a "pathological" and "representational" explanation for the beliefs and activities of Christian evangelicals.

7. Ted G. Jelen, *The Political Mobilization of Religious Beliefs* (New York: Praeger, 1991), p. 137.

8. Alan Crawford, *Thunder on the Right: The "New Right" and the Politics of Resentment* (New York: Pantheon Books, 1980), pp. 51–52.

9. Thomas J. McIntyre, *The Fear Brokers* (New York: Pilgrim Press, 1979), p. 88.

10. Richard Viguerie, *The New Right: We're Ready to Lead* (Falls Church, VA: The Viguerie Company, 1980). Crawford, *Thunder on the Right*, p. 50.

11. David Droteau, William Hoynes, and Kevin M. Carragee, "Public Television and the Missing Public: A Study of Sources and Programming," *Extra!*, 6: 6 (September/October 1993).

12. See Laura Flanders, *Real Majority, Media Minority* (Monroe, ME: Common Courage Press, 1997), pp. 157–61.

13. Flanders, *Real Majority, Media Minority*, pp. 135–39.

14. At end of the 1980s, Paul Weyrich called for this strategy at a meeting of the Conservative Leadership Conference in Washington, D.C. After bemoaning the loss of Ronald Reagan's leadership (and castigating himself for being so critical of Reagan toward the end of his tenure), Weyrich called for the movement to change its focus from the national level to the local level. (Author's notes.)

15. *Group Research Report* (Summer 1989), p. 11.

16. Elizabeth Drew, *Whatever It Takes: The Real Struggle for Political Power in America* (New York: Viking, 1997), pp. 1–13.

17. A number of loose-knit organizations were developed by the New Right specifically to coordinate the movement internally, including the Religious Roundtable and the Council for National Policy (CNP).

18. McIntyre, *Fear Brokers*, pp. 84–91.

19. A similar program was developed by the Promise Keepers in the mid-1990s.

20. William H. Marshner and Enrique T. Rueda, "The Morality of Political

Action: Biblical Foundations" (Washington, DC: The Free Congress Research and Education Foundation, 1984), pp. 38, 19–20, 59.

21. For a review of the history of right-wing populism's anti-elite themes, including a brief discussion of H. Ross Perot, see Michael Kazin, *The Populist Persuasion: An American History* (New York: BasicBooks, 1995), pp. 246–84.

22. Raphael S. Ezekiel, *The Racist Mind: Portraits of American Neo-Nazis and Klansmen* (New York: Penguin Books USA, 1995), p. xxxii.

23. James L. Guth and John C. Green, "Salience: The Core Concept?" in David C. Leege and Lyman A. Kellstedt, eds., *Rediscovering the Religious Factor in American Politics* (Armonk, NY: M. E. Sharpe, 1993), pp. 157–76.

24. John C. Green, *Understanding the Christian Right* (New York: The American Jewish Committee, 1996), pp. 28–32.

25. Jerome Himmelstein, *To the Right: The Transformation of American Conservatism* (Berkeley: University of California Press, 1990), p. 117.

26. One reason the New Right leadership knew that Christian evangelicals could become politically mobilized is because they had seen an intense and violent cultural upheaval in Kanawha County, West Virginia, in 1974–1975 over sex education in the schools and the content of school textbooks. The Kanawha County organizing took much of its direction from that of Mel and Norma Gabler of Longview, Texas, accomplished right-wing textbook critics, and brought conservative Christianity and right-wing politics together. See William Martin, *With God on Our Side: The Rise of the Religious Right in America* (New York: Broadway Books, 1996), pp. 117–43.

27. Green, *Understanding the Christian Right*, pp. 31–32.

28. Robert C. Liebman, "The Making of the New Christian Right," in Robert C. Liebman and Robert Wuthnow, eds., *The New Christian Right* (New York: Aldine Publishing Company, 1983), pp. 230–31.

29. Clyde Wilcox, *Onward Christian Soldiers?: The Religious Right in American Politics* (Boulder, CO: Westview Press, 1996), pp. 55–56.

30. Donald Heinz, "The Struggle to Define America," in Liebman and Wuthnow, *The New Christian Right*, pp. 133–48.

31. Bill Berkowitz, "Point of Departure: Ralph Reed Resigns from Christian Coalition to Form Century Strategies," *Culture Watch* 42 (May 1997): 1. Despite his impressive work as the "builder" of the Christian Coalition, Reed is said to have left the organization in debt, an organizational problem which Randy Tate, Reed's successor, was forced to shoulder. See Melinda Henneberger, "Ralph Reed Is His Cross to Bear," *New York Times Magazine*, August 9, 1998, pp. 24–27.

32. For a review of the takeover of the Republican Party by its right wing, see Tanya Melich, *The Republican War Against Women: An Insiders' Report from Behind the Lines* (New York: Bantam Books, 1996).

33. John C. Green, "The Christian Right and the 1994 Elections: An Over-

view," in Mark J. Rozell and Clyde Wilcox, eds., *God at the Grassroots: The Christian Right in the 1994 Elections* (Lanham, MD: Rowman and Littlefield, 1995), p. 16.

34. TCAN's Web site is www.vvm.com/~ctomlin

35. James Ridgeway, "Taking Aim at Campus Commies," *Village Voice*, August 13, 1985, n. p. Also see "Accuracy in Academia," *Washington Inquirer*, July 26, 1985, p. 1.

36. Rosanna Perotti, "Campus Watchdogs Bare Teeth," *In These Times*, November 13–19, 1985, n. p.

37. In 1991, the Collegiate Network was a program of the now-defunct Madison Center for Educational Affairs.

38. See an excellent resource for progressive campus activists: Center for Campus Organizing, *Uncovering the Right on Campus* (Houston, TX: Public Search, Inc., 1997).

39. See Sally Covington, *Moving a Public Policy Agenda: The Strategic Philanthropy of Conservative Foundations* (Washington, DC: Committee for Responsive Philanthropy, 1997). Also, *Buying a Movement: Right-Wing Foundations and American Politics* (Washington, DC: People for the American Way, 1996), and Leon Howell, *Funding the War of Ideas* (Cleveland, OH: United Church Board for Homeland Ministries, 1995).

40. Sally Covington, in *Moving a Public Policy Agenda*, has identified twelve foundations that have been most significant in supporting the right. People for the American Way's *Buying a Movement* identified eleven foundations that fund the right. Leon Howell's *Funding the War of Ideas* discussed eight rightist foundations. The foundations named here appear in all three reports.

41. Richard J. Herrnstein and Charles Murray, *The Bell Curve: Intelligence and Class Structure in American Life* (New York: The Free Press, 1994). For a refutation of *The Bell Curve*'s statistics and conclusions, see Claude S. Fischer, Michael Hout, Martin Sanchez Jankowski, Samuel R. Lucas, Ann Swidler, and Kim Voss, *Inequality by Design: Cracking the Bell Curve Myth* (Princeton: Princeton University Press, 1996).

42. *Buying a Movement*, p. 17.

43. Philip Weiss, "The Clinton Haters; Clinton Crazy," *New York Times Magazine*, February 23, 1997, p. 34.

44. Don Van Natta, Jr., and Jill Abramson, "Quietly, a Team of Lawyers Kept Paula Jones's Case Alive," *New York Times*, January 24, 1999, p. A1.

45. For a discussion of the anti-Clinton campaign as a continuation of an ongoing culture war, see Chip Berlet, "Clinton, Conspiracism, and the Continuing Culture War," *Public Eye* XIII: 1 (Spring 1999).

46. Melinda Henneberger, "Ralph Reed Is His Cross to Bear," *New York Times Magazine*, August 9, 1998, pp. 24–27.

3. KITCHEN TABLE BACKLASH: THE ANTIFEMINIST WOMEN'S MOVEMENT

1. See Connaught Marshner, "The New Traditional Woman" (Washington, DC: Free Congress Research and Education Foundation, 1982). Also see Onalee McGraw, "The Family, Feminism, and the Therapeutic State" (Washington, DC: The Heritage Foundation, 1980). For an excellent discussion of Marshner's career, see Susan Faludi, *Backlash: The Undeclared War Against American Women* (New York: Crown Publishers, Inc., 1991), pp. 241–47; and William Martin, *With God on Our Side: The Rise of the Religious Right in America* (New York: Broadway Books, 1996), pp. 161–67.

2. Carol Felsenthal, *The Biography of Phyllis Schlafly: The Sweetheart of the Silent Majority* (Chicago: Regnery Gateway, 1982).

3. Phyllis Schlafly, *A Choice Not An Echo.* rev. 3d ed. (Alton, IL: Pere Marquette Press, 1964).

4. Tanya Melich, *The Republican War Against Women: An Insider's Report from Behind the Lines* (New York: Bantam Books, 1996).

5. "Star Wars" programs are still funded by the government, despite the end of the Cold War.

6. James Bennet, "Buchanan, Exalted, Pushes Economic Insecurity Theme," *New York Times*, February 22, 1996, p. 1.

7. Phyllis Schlafly, "The Republican Party: Back to the Future." Speech delivered at Eagle Council XXVII, Sept. 12, 1998, Arlington, VA.

8. See Bill Berkowitz, "Who is John Ashcroft? And Why are the Leaders of the Christian Right Saying Such Nice Things About Him?" *CultureWatch*, newsletter of the DataCenter, Oakland, CA (June 1998), p. 1. Also see Thomas B. Edsall, "Christian Right Lifts Ashcroft," *Washington Post*, April 14, 1998, p. A1.

9. Fred Clarkson, "Christian Reconstructionism," in Chip Berlet, ed., *Eyes Right!* (Boston: South End Press, 1995), pp. 59–80; and Frederick Clarkson, *Eternal Hostility: The Struggle Between Theocracy and Democracy* (Monroe, ME: Common Courage Press, 1997).

10. Faludi, *Backlash*, p. 247.

11. Beverly La Haye, *The Spirit-Controlled Woman* (Eugene, OR: Harvest House Publishers, 1995), pp. 11–15.

12. Sara Diamond, *Facing the Wrath: Confronting the Right in Dangerous Times* (Monroe, ME: Common Courage Press, 1996), p. 14.

13. See Jean Hardisty, "Kitchen Table Backlash: The Anti-Feminist Women's Movement," *Public Eye* X: 2 (Summer 1996): 1–11. Also see Susan E. Marshall, "Rattle on the Right: Bridge Labor in Antifeminist Organizations," in Kathleen M. Blee, ed., *No Middle Ground: Women and Radical Protest* (New York: New York University Press, 1998), pp. 155–79; and Jerome Himmelstein, "The Social Basis of Antifeminism: Religious Networks and Culture," *Journal for the Scientific Study of Religion* 25:1 (1986), pp. 1–15.

14. Laura Flanders, "Conservative Women Are Right for Media," *Extra!* 9: 2 (March/April 1996): 6.

15. Daphne Patai and Noretta Koertge, *Professing Feminism: Cautionary Tales from the Strange World of Women's Studies* (New York: Basic Books, 1994).

16. Elizabeth Fox-Genovese, *Feminism Is Not the Story of My Life: How Today's Feminist Elite Has Lost Touch with the Real Concerns of Women* (New York: Nan A. Talese/Doubleday, 1995).

17. Alice Dembner, "Alumni Bring View from Right to Campus," *Boston Globe*, June 24, 1995, p. 1.

18. Rita J. Simon, "Introduction," in Rita J. Simon, ed., *Neither Victim nor Enemy: Women's Freedom Network Looks at Gender in America* (Landham, MD: Women's Freedom Network and University Press of America, 1995), p. vii.

19. WFN encouraged its readers to call WFN for a copy of an Amicus Brief written by Attorney Michael Weiss, submitted in opposition to the Violence Against Women Act. "WFN Update," Women's Freedom Network *Newsletter* 4: 2 (Spring 1997): 3.

20. Kay A. Schwarzberg, "Gender Bias in Sentencing: A Look at Statutory Rape," Women's Freedom Network *Newsletter* 5: 1 (January/February 1998): 1, 3–4.

21. Elizabeth Fox-Genovese, "Rethinking Sexual Harassment: WFN's Third Annual Conference Wrap Up," Women's Freedom Network *Newsletter* 3: 4 (Fall 1996): 4–6. (Quote on p. 6.)

22. Melinda Sidak, "The New Hysteria," *Women's Quarterly* 7 (Spring 1996): 4–7.

23. Sally L. Satel, "It's Always His Fault," *Women's Quarterly* 12 (Summer 1997): 4–10.

24. Kimberly Schuld, "Look Who's Losing," *Women's Quarterly* 14 (Winter 1998): 6.

25. Diana Furchtgott-Roth and Christine Stolba, *Women's Figures: An Illustrated Guide to the Economic Progress of Women in America* (Washington, DC: AEI Press, 1999).

26. Laura Flanders, "The 'Stolen Feminism' Hoax," *Extra!* 7: 5 (September/ October 1994): 6–9.

27. See "You Asked For It," and interview with Laura Schlessinger conducted by Maureen Sirhal. *Women's Quarterly* 9 (Autumn 1996): 8–12.

28. Rebecca Klatch, *Women of the New Right* (Philadelphia: Temple University Press, 1987).

29. Simon, *Neither Victim Nor Enemy*.

30. Phyllis Eckhaus, "Antifeminist and Unhinged," *The Nation*, May 13, 1996, pp. 30–32. Eckhaus notes that she has been "claimed" as a supporter of WFN, though she does not support them.

31. Anita K. Blair, "Sexual Harassment Law: When It's Bad It's Horrid," *Ex*

Femina: The Newsletter of the Independent Women's Forum (July 1998): 11–12. Also see "Rethinking Sexual Harassment: WFN's Third Annual Conference Wrap Up," Women's Freedom Network *Newsletter* 3: 4 (Fall 1996): 4–6; and Daphne Patai, *Heterophobia: Sexual Harassment and the Future of Feminism* (Lanham, MD: Rowman & Littlefield, 1998).

32. George Gilder, *Wealth and Poverty* (New York: Basic Books, 1981).

33. R. Marie Griffith, "The Affinities Between Feminists and Evangelical Women," *Chronicle of Higher Education*, October 17, 1997, p. B6.

34. Brenda E. Brasher, *Godly Women: Fundamentalism and Female Power* (New Brunswick: Rutgers University Press, 1998), p. 4.

35. Brasher, *Godly Women*, p. 149. Quotes from Ephesians taken from the Commemorative Edition *New Testament*, published by American Bible Society and distributed free to men at "Stand in the Gap," Washington, DC, October 4, 1997.

36. Gustav Niebuhr, "Southern Baptists Declare Wife Should 'Submit' To Her Husband," *New York Times*, June 10, 1998, p. A1.

4. CONSTRUCTING HOMOPHOBIA: THE RIGHT'S ATTACK ON GAY RIGHTS

1. Terence Stutz, "Education Board Approves Textbooks, Despite Protests from Some Members," *Dallas Morning News*, November 8, 1997, p. 40A; Kathy Walt, "Board Vote on 'Rain Forest Algebra' Textbook Spurs Member to Protest," *Houston Chronicle*, November 8, 1997, p. A30; Rick Lyman, "Best Little Election-Year Brawl in Texas Is for Control of Schools," *New York Times*, October 12, 1998, p. 1.

2. In his research into middle-class attitudes, Alan Wolfe of Boston University conducted twenty-five interviews in each of eight suburbs of four cities, as part of his Middle Class Morality Project. Despite the widespread notion of a "culture war," he found his middle-class respondents: "Reluctant to pass judgement, they are tolerant to a fault, not about everything—they have not come to accept homosexuality as normal and they intensely dislike bilingualism—but about a surprising number of things. . . ." Alan Wolfe, *One Nation, After All: What Middle-Class Americans Really Think about God, Country, Family, Racism, Welfare, Immigration, Homosexuality, Work, the Right, the Left, and Each Other* (New York: Viking Penguin, 1998), p. 278.

3. I refer here to "lesbians and gay men" rather than the more accurate "lesbian, gay, bisexual, and transgender people" out of no disrespect for bisexuals and transgender people but because the right does not usually include them in its attacks. Most likely, the right simply overlooks bisexuals and does not see the need to reinforce anti-transgender prejudice because, throughout U.S. society, it is still considered acceptable.

4. Although "Stonewall" is often used to mark the beginning of the gay rights

movement, lesbians and gay men had pressed for equal rights for many years before Stonewall. See Andrea Weiss and Greta Schiller, *Before Stonewall: The Making of a Gay and Lesbian Community* (Tallahassee, FL: Naiad Press, 1988), and Martin Bauml Duberman, Martha Vicinus, and George Chauncey, Jr., *Hidden From History: Reclaiming the Gay and Lesbian Past* (New York: Penguin Books, 1989).

5. That same year, David A. Noebel, later to head Summit Ministries of Colorado, published *The Homosexual Revolution*, which he dedicated to Anita Bryant. David A. Noebel, *The Homosexual Revolution* (Tulsa, OK: American Christian College Press, 1977).

6. Enrique T. Rueda, *The Homosexual Network* (Old Greenwich, CT: Devin Adair Co., 1982).

7. Enrique T. Rueda and Michael Schwartz, *Gays, AIDS and You* (Old Greenwich, CT: Devin Adair Company, 1987), p. viii.

8. Tim LaHaye, *The Unhappy Gays* (Wheaton, IL: Tyndale House Publishers, 1978).

9. Alan Crawford, *Thunder on the Right* (New York: Pantheon, 1980), p. 146.

10. "Wisconsin Proves ERA Effects" (January 1983); "The Incredible Wisconsin ERA" (February 1983); "Law Professor Admits ERA-Gay Effect" (June 1986); "Equal Rights Amendment Defeated in Vermont—and Forever" (November 1986). News Updates sent to members by Eagle Forum, Alton, IL.

11. *Notice: Persons dropped from membership in the American Psychological Association* (1984). Internal communication to all APA members.

12. Sara Diamond, *Spiritual Warfare: The Politics of the Christian Right* (Boston: South End Press, 1989), p. 102 and n. 68.

13. For a review of the origins and growth of the anti-abortion movement, see Sara Diamond, *Not By Politics Alone: The Enduring Influence of the Christian Right* (New York: The Guilford Press, 1998), pp. 131–55.

14. Interviewed by Didi Herman; quoted in Didi Herman, *The Antigay Agenda: Orthodox Vision and the Christian Right* (Chicago: University of Chicago Press, 1997), p. 137.

15. Michael Booth, "Legal Defense Dropped by CFV," *Denver Post*, Dec. 10, 1992, p. 3B.

16. "The Religious Right's Anti-Gay Campaign of Hate: A Strategy for the 1990s" (Washington, DC: People for the American Way), n. d., p. 2.

17. Rev. Jerry Sloan, "Sheldon Breeds Hatred," Letter to the Editor, *Sacramento Union*, December 22, 1990.

18. Peggy Lowe, "Ideas Clash in Focus on Family Values," Associated Press, November 15, 1992.

19. Peter H. Stone, "All in the Family," *National Journal* 27: 43 (October 28, 1995): 2641.

20. David A. Noebel, Wayne C. Lutton, and Paul Cameron, *AIDS: Acquired*

Immune Deficiency Syndrome (Manitou Springs, CO: Summit Ministries Research Center, 1986).

21. "Anti-Red Buys Hotel at Manitou," *Denver Post*, May 27, 1962, p. 11A.

22. Beverly LaHaye, "The Hidden Homosexual Agenda" (Washington, DC: Concerned Women for America, 1991), pp. 20, 22.

23. Tony Marco, "The Homosexual Deception: Making Sin a Civil Right" (Washington, DC: Concerned Women for America, 1992).

24. Concerned Women for America, direct-mail letter dated August 1998. On file at Political Research Associates. Also see two policy papers in CWA's *Policy Concerns* Series: "Debunking the Myth of Gay Suicide" (April 1996); and "Born or Bred? The Debate over the Cause of Homosexuality" (March 1997).

25. Phyllis Schlafly, "Why Congress Must Amend the E.R.A.," *Phyllis Schlafly Report* (November 1983), pp. 1–4.

26. Christian Coalition direct mail letter. On file at Political Research Associates, Somerville, MA.

27. Michael Isikoff, "Christian Coalition Steps Boldly Into Politics: Tax Exempt Robertson Group Has Raised $13 Million, Eyes GOP Takeover," *Washington Post*, September 10, 1992, p. A1.

28. Frederick Clarkson, "The Christian Coalition: On the Road to Victory?" *Church and State* (January 1992): 4–7. Quote at 4–5.

29. Booth, "Legal Defense."

30. Urvashi Vaid, *Virtual Equality: The Mainstreaming of Gay and Lesbian Liberation* (New York: Doubleday, 1995), p. 26.

31. "Disney Facts," American Family Association, Tupelo, MS, 1998.

32. Letter to CFV dated June 1991, from Brian McCormick of the National Legal Foundation. On file at Political Research Associates, Somerville, MA.

33. Suzanne Pharr, *In the Time of the Right: Reflections on Liberation* (Berkeley: Chardon Press, 1996), pp. 61–85.

34. Jean Hardisty and Amy Gluckman, "The Hoax of Special Rights: The Right Wing's Attack on Gay Men and Lesbians," in Amy Gluckman and Betsy Reed, eds., *HomoEconomics: Capitalism, Community, and Lesbian and Gay Life* (New York: Routledge, 1997), pp. 209–22.

35. M. V. Lee Badgett, "Beyond Biased Samples: Challenging the Myths on the Economic Status of Lesbians and Gay Men," in Gluckman and Reed, *HomoEconomics*, pp. 65–86; and M. V. Lee Badgett, *Income Inflation: The Myth of Affluence among Gay, Lesbian, and Bisexual Americans* (Washington, DC, and Amherst, MA: The Policy Institute of the National Gay and Lesbian Task Force and The Institute for Gay and Lesbian Strategic Studies, 1998).

36. In several of the cities where he conducted interviews, Alan Wolfe reports that middle-class African Americans, Hispanics, and Jews showed greater tolerance for homosexuals than he had expected, based on other surveys. This greater tolerance stems from their understanding that lesbians and gay men suffer dis-

crimination that resembles that which they have suffered. Wolfe, *One Nation*, pp. 80–81.

37. Roger Magnuson, *Are Gay Rights Right? Making Sense of the Controversy* (Portland, OR: Multnomah Press, 1990); Paul Cameron, Ph.D., William L. Playfair, M.D., and Stephen Wellum, B.A. "The Homosexual Lifespan," paper presented at Eastern Psychological Association, *Family Research Institute*, April 17, 1993.

38. John Gallagher, "Colorado Coach's Anti-gay Comments Spark Dispute," *Advocate*, March 24, 1992, p. 29.

39. Virginia Culver, "Armstrong Credits Religion for Changes," *Denver Post*, February 20, 1992, p. 4B.

40. Transcript of Kevin Tebedo tape on file at Political Research Associates, Somerville, MA.

41. Herman, *Antigay Agenda*, p. 168.

42. For an excellent history and analysis of the ex-gay movement, see Surina Khan, *Calculated Compassion: How the Ex-Gay Movement Serves the Right's Attack on Democracy*, a 1998 report copublished by Political Research Associates, the Policy Institute of the National Gay and Lesbian Task Force, and Equal Partners in Faith. An accompanying publication is titled *Challenging the Ex-Gay Movement: An Information Packet* (1998). Both are available from Political Research Associates, Somerville, MA. Also see Kim I. Mills, "Mission Impossible: Why Reparative Therapy and Ex-Gay Ministries Fail" (Washington, DC: Human Rights Campaign, 1998).

43. Michael J. Gerson, Major Garrett, and Carolyn Kleiner, "A Righteous Indignation," *U.S. News and World Report*, May 4, 1998, pp. 20–29.

44. "Christian Groups Differ on Tactics," *National Journal's Congress Daily*, July 7, 1998.

45. An example is Bauer's opposition to privatization of social security (because it would not provide for stay-at-home mothers, as government social security does) and "immoral" trade agreements, where Bauer's positions often conflict with the Republican Party's business agenda. For instance, most-favored-nation (MFN) trade status for China, a priority for business interests, is vigorously opposed by both Bauer and Dobson on the grounds that China's domestic governmental policies are immoral. Stone, "All in the Family."

46. The new headquarters signaled FRC's growing prosperity and influence in Washington and with the Congress. FRC's major financial angel, the Prince Foundation of Holland, Michigan, established the corporation that owns the building. Space is leased to FRC at below-market rates. Stone, "All in the Family."

47. James Carney, "The G.O.P.'s Troublemaker," *Time*, January 19, 1998, p. 32. Also see David M. Shribman, "One Nation Under God: How the Religious

Right Changed the American Conversation," *Boston Globe*, January 10, 1999, p. 14.

48. Ben Irwin, "The Bible and Homosexuality: Confronting the Challenge to Scriptural Authority" (Washington DC: The Family Research Council, n.d.).

49. For an account of the right's role in blocking a federal response to AIDS, see Vaid, *Virtual Equality*, pp. 320–34.

50. John Weir, "In God's Country," *Details* (May 1994): 120.

51. An example of a coalition effort within the Christian Right is the Alliance Defense Fund, a self-described "servant organization" that provides backup for lawsuits brought by disgruntled Christians and anti-gay activists. Started with money from the late William Pew, the list of founders is a virtual "Who's who" of the Christian Right: Bill Bright of Campus Crusade for Christ, James Dobson of Focus on the Family, D. James Kennedy of Coral Ridge Ministries, and Donald Wildmon of the American Family Association. ADF provides grants to, trains attorneys for, and coordinates lawsuits in the areas of "religious freedom, family values, and the sanctity of life." See its Web site: www.alliancedefense fund.org.

52. For an understanding of how fear of secular humanism serves as the theoretical basis for right-wing organizing, see Chip Berlet and Margaret Quigley, "Theocracy and White Supremacy: Behind the Culture War to Restore Traditional Values," in Chip Berlet, ed., *Eyes Right! Challenging the Right Wing Backlash* (Boston: South End Press, 1995), pp. 15–43, esp. pp. 30–35.

53. "The Pro-Family Movement: An Interview with Paul Weyrich," *Conservative Digest* (May/June 1980): 15.

54. "Quotations of the Day," *New York Times*, October 13, 1998, A2.

55. *FBI Uniform Crime Report, 1997* (Washington, DC: United States Department of Justice, Federal Bureau of Investigation, Criminal Services Division, n.d.).

56. Many progressive activists insist that acts motivated by the gender, age, or disability of the victim are hate crimes, but these categories are not included in the 1990 Hate Crimes Statistics Act. However, by 1997, eleven states had adopted hate crimes statutes that include gender. Feminists successfully lobbied for the 1994 Violence Against Women Act, which explicitly states that "some of the most common forms of violence women suffer, such as rape and domestic violence, are essentially hate crimes . . . which warrant federal civil rights protection." See Valerie Jenness and Kendal Broad, *Hate Crimes: New Social Movements and the Politics of Violence* (New York: Aldine de Gruyter, 1997), p. 147. Activists will continue to fight for an expansion of the definition of a hate crime, not because they crave the status of victims, as the right maintains, but so that the penalty enhancement attached to hate crimes will increase public awareness and, ultimately, deter them. See Leslie R. Wolfe, *Violence Against Women as Bias-*

Motivated Crime: Defining the Issues (Washington, DC: Center for Women Policy Studies, 1991).

57. *FBI Uniform Crime Report, 1997.* Hate crimes based on religious bigotry rank second in frequency and account for 15 percent of reported 1997 hate crimes.

58. Gregory Herek, "The Context of Anti-Gay Violence: Notes on Cultural and Psychological Heterosexism," *Journal of Interpersonal Violence* 5: 3 (1990): 316–33.

59. Helms proposed an Amendment to the Hate Crimes Statistics Act that read, "The homosexual movement threatens the strength and the survival of the American family as the basic unit of society; state sodomy laws should be enforced . . . ; the federal government should not provide discrimination protections on the basis of sexual orientation; school curriculums should not condone homosexuality. . . ." The amendment was rejected by a vote of 77–19 in the Senate after an alternative amendment, brokered by Senator Edward Kennedy (D-MA), was agreed to by gay rights leaders. Senator Trent Lott (R-MS) voted for the Helms amendment. See Urvashi Vaid, *Virtual Equality*, pp. 144–45; Robin Toner, "Senate, 92–4, Wants U.S. Data on Crimes That Spring from Hate," *New York Times*, February 9, 1990, A17; and Deb Price, "As Dole's Likely Successor in Senate, Lott Is a Real Worry for Gay Americans," *Detroit News*, March 22, 1996, 1E. The right as a movement did not mobilize its grassroots base against the Hate Crimes Statistics Act, perhaps because it would not have been a "winnable" issue for its anti-gay campaign.

60. In most hate crimes legislation, the penalty for the crime can be increased by establishing that the victim's race, religion, ethnicity or other characteristic played a role in the crime, and in some cases, penalties can be increased based on "speech" uttered by the perpetrator, because speech is often evidence of the perpetrators' racist, sexist, or homophobic motivation. See Harvard Law Review, "Penalty Enhancement Does Not Punish Free Speech," in Paul A. Winters, ed., *Hate Crimes* (San Diego, CA: Greenhaven Press, 1996), pp. 121–29.

61. Jack Levin and Jack McDevitt, *Hate Crimes: The Rising Tide of Bigotry and Bloodshed* (New York: Plenum Press, 1993), pp. 11–12. Also see a 1996 Florida study that "found that homosexual homicide victims manifest a greater number of fatal injuries from sharp and blunt objects and a greater extent of injuries over the body compared to heterosexual victims. See M. D. Bell and R. I. Vila, "Homicide in Homosexual Victims: A Study of Sixty-Seven Cases from the Broward County, Florida, Medical Examiners Office (1982–1992), with Special Emphasis on 'Overkill,' " *American Journal of Forensic Medicine and Pathology* 17:1: 65–69.

62. "Bias Crimes in NYC, 8/25/98–9/15/98." Available from The New York City Gay and Lesbian Anti-Violence Project, online at www.avp.org; accessed March 2, 1999.

5. AFFIRMING RACIAL INEQUALITY

1. Washington, D.C.–based Americans for a Fair Chance (a consortium of six leading civil rights legal organizations that was formed to defend affirmative action) disagrees. It has published a 1998 report titled "Women's Voices Left Out," which critiques the news media for failing to discuss the impact of affirmative action on women. The report is based on a study done by Fairness and Accuracy in Reporting (FAIR), a progressive New York–based media watchdog group, which also reported the results in its newsletter. See Janine Jackson, "Affirmative Action Coverage Ignores Women—and Discrimination," *Extra!* 12: 1 (January/February 1999): 6–8.

2. From the beginning, it was possible for affirmative action to be expanded to include people of color other than African Americans because the wording was always generic (on the basis of race, religion, etc.) and focused on overcoming "underutilization." Later, women were included when President Lyndon Johnson amended Executive Order 11246 with Executive Order 11375 to include women.

3. The 1964 Civil Rights Act addressed only the most pressing problems of the times: Jim Crow practices of racial exclusion, segregation, and discrimination against people of color, especially Blacks. In fact, it was because it avoided any language of preference that some southern white Congressmen and senators grudgingly voted for it.

4. Martin Luther King, Jr., *Why We Can't Wait* (New York: Signet Books, 1964) p. 134. Another civil rights leader who took a clear stand on preferential treatment when it was unpopular to do so was Whitney Young, then president of the Urban League, who advocated a "domestic Marshall Plan" for the Black community. See Whitney Young, *To Be Equal* (New York: McGraw-Hill, 1964).

5. See Johnson's famous commencement address at Howard University on June 4, 1965, titled "To Fulfill These Rights," reprinted in Francis J. Beckwith and Todd E. Jones, eds., *Affirmative Action: Social Justice or Reverse Discrimination?* (New York: Prometheus Books, 1997), pp. 56–63.

6. John David Skrentny, *The Ironies of Affirmative Action: Politics, Culture, and Justice in America* (Chicago: University of Chicago Press, 1996), pp. 197–221.

7. Stephen Steinberg, *Turning Back: The Retreat from Racial Justice in American Thought and Policy* (Boston: Beacon Press, 1995), pp. 101–2, 166. Also see *Affirmative Action to Open the Doors of Job Opportunity: A Policy of Fairness and Compassion That Has Worked* (Washington, DC: Citizens' Commission on Civil Rights, 1984). I am indebted to Aileen Hernandez, who shared her firsthand knowledge of the history of affirmative action in a letter dated April 27, 1999.

8. Phillip Shabacoff, "U.S. Inaction Seen on Minority Jobs," *New York Times*, December 19, 1972, p. 1.

9. Susan Eisenberg, *We'll Call You If We Need You* (Ithaca: Cornell University Press, 1998), p. 3.

10. Stephen Steinberg states that the first appearance of "institutional racism" in the sociological lexicon was in the book *Black Power: The Politics of Liberation in America*, by Stokely Carmichael and Charles Hamilton (New York: Vintage Books, 1967), pp. 1–4. Steinberg, *Turning Back*, p. 3.

11. Paul Weyrich, "It Would Help If They Really Knew Us," *Conservative Digest* 10: 3 (March 1984): 44.

12. Amy Ansell, *New Right, New Racism* (New York: New York University Press, 1997). Paul M. Sniderman and Thomas Piazza reject the phrase "new racism," but find, based on their own and others' survey research, what they call a "racial double standard." *The Scar of Race* (Cambridge, MA: Harvard University Press, 1993), pp. 66–87.

13. Stephan Thernstrom and Abigail Thernstrom, *America in Black and White: One Nation Indivisible* (New York: Simon and Schuster, 1997). Abigail Thernstrom's earlier book is *Whose Votes Count: Affirmative Action and Minority Voting Rights* (Cambridge, MA: Harvard University Press, 1987). Lani Guinier addresses that book in her book *The Tyranny of the Majority: Fundamental Fairness in Representative Democracy* (New York: The Free Press, 1994), pp. 65–66. Also see Laura Flanders, "The Anti-Feminists Money Can Buy," *In These Times*, April 11, 1999, p. 9; and Michael A. Fletcher, "The Color of Controversy; They Say They're Liberals, So Why Do Conservatives Tout Their Views on Race?" *Washington Post*, October 11, 1997, p. H01.

14. Lawrence D. Bobo, "The Color Line, the Dilemma, and the Dream," in John Higham, ed., *Civil Rights and Social Wrongs: Black–White Relations Since World War II* (University Park, PA: The Pennsylvania State University Press, 1997), p. 35.

15. Lawrence Bobo and Ryan A. Smith, "From Jim Crow Racism to Laissez-Faire Racism: An Essay on the Transformation of Racial Attitudes in America," in Wendy F. Katkin, Ned Landsman, and Andrew Tyree, eds., *Beyond Pluralism: The Conception of Groups and Group Identities in America* (Urbana: University of Illinois Press, 1998) pp. 182–220.

16. Barbara F. Reskin, *The Realities of Affirmative Action in Employment* (Washington, DC: American Sociological Association, 1998), pp. 71–74.

17. Carl Cohen, "Is Affirmative Action on the Way Out? Should It Be? A Symposium," *Commentary* 3: 105 (March 1998): 21. Also see Carl Cohen, *Naked Racial Preference* (New York: Madison Books, 1995).

18. Kathanne Greene discusses affirmative action in the larger context of social justice by reviewing two principles of justice: compensatory justice, in which specific injustices must be rectified to those who suffered them by those who committed them; and distributive justice, which is concerned with an equitable distribution of goods within society. These principles of social justice are the

philosophical basis for Carl Cohen's public policy categories: "redress for injury" versus "entitlement by color." See Greene, *Affirmative Action*, pp. 1–13.

19. Amy Gutmann, "Responding to Racial Injustice," in K. Anthony Appiah and Amy Gutmann, *Color Conscious: The Political Morality of Race* (Princeton: Princeton University Press, 1996), pp. 135–36.

20. Lucy A. Williams, *Decades of Distortion: The Right's Thirty-Year Assault on Welfare* (Somerville, MA: Political Research Associates, 1997).

21. Nathan Glazer, *Affirmative Discrimination: Ethnic Inequality and Public Policy* (New York: Basic Books, 1975). For an account of Glazer's work and its role within the neoconservative movement, see Peter Steinfels, *The Neoconservatives: The Men Who Are Changing America's Politics* (New York: Simon and Schuster, 1979).

22. Glazer, *Affirmative Discrimination*, p. 44.

23. Ibid., p. 201.

24. Ibid., pp. 68–69.

25. Orlando Patterson, *The Ordeal of Integration: Progress and Resentment in America's "Racial" Crisis* (Washington, DC: Civitas/Counterpoint, 1997), pp. 148–58.

26. Brent Staples, "Quota Bashers Come In From the Cold," *New York Times*, April 12, 1998.

27. See Nathan Glazer, *We Are All Multiculturalists Now* (Cambridge, MA: Harvard University Press, 1997); Glazer's entry in "Is Affirmative Action on the Way Out? Should It Be? A Symposium," *Commentary* 3: 105 (March 1998): 29–31; Nathan Glazer, "In Defense of Preference," *New Republic*, April 6, 1998, pp. 18–25; and James Traub, "Nathan Glazer Changes His Mind Again," *New York Times Magazine*, June 28, 1998, pp. 23–25.

28. Clarence Thomas, "Why Black Americans Should Look to Conservative Policies," *Heritage Lectures* 119 (Washington, DC: Heritage Foundation, June 18, 1987), p. 5.

29. Thomas Sowell, *The Vision of the Anointed* (New York: Basic Books, 1995).

30. Thomas Sowell, *Affirmative Action Reconsidered: Was It Necessary in Academia?* (Washington, DC: American Enterprise Institute for Public Policy Studies, Evaluative Studies 27, December 1975). Sowell argues that factors other than race explain the discrepancy between Black/white and male/female employment patterns in academia. In the case of the male/female ratio, he argues that single women do as well in academia as single men, and it is married women who pay the price with lower salaries and less advancement. He identifies this discrepancy as the result of "social mores," which he argues should be distinguished from gender discrimination.

Sowell makes a similar argument about racial discrimination in academia. Just as Glazer argued that as of 1973 there was no more discrimination in the labor market, Sowell argues that as of 1971, there was no more racial discrimination in academia. He proves this by pointing out that Black professors made salaries equal to those of white professors *when credentials and qualifications are held equal.* He does not mention institutional racism as a reason why so few Black scholars, other scholars of color, and white women *hold* the requisite credentials.

31. Walter E. Williams, "Government Sanctioned Restraints That Reduce Economic Opportunities for Minorities," *Policy Review* 2 (1977): 10–19.

32. Walter E. Williams, *The State against Blacks* (NewYork: McGraw-Hill Book Company, 1982).

33. Founded in 1978 by William Casey, who later became infamous as Director of the CIA in the Reagan Administration, the Manhattan Institute is a publishing operation that funnels money from conservative foundations to right-wing authors.

34. Stephen Carter protests plaintively in *Reflections of an Affirmative Action Baby* (NewYork: Basic Books, 1990) that "what is operating here is plain: the assumption that if a person who is black dissents from the civil rights agenda on the matter of racial preferences, he or she must dissent on lots of other matters too" (p. 150).

35. In a speech before the National Bar Association, the largest association of Black lawyers, Thomas said he has moved to his own destiny. He went on to say that he has "contained his anger" as a Black man to avoid "suffering the fate of Bigger Thomas." Bigger Thomas is a fictional character in African American author Richard Wright's book, *Native Son*, who is consumed by racial animosity and assaulted by racial injustice, all ultimately leading to his death. Curtis Wilde, "Thomas, Confronting Black Critics, Defends His Conservative Views," *Boston Globe*, July 30, 1998, p. A1. When Connerly was asked how his mixed-race children identify themselves racially (Connerly's wife is white), he responded that he "doesn't know," asserting that he has raised his children to be such good Americans that they do not see race. Interview with Mike Wallace, *60 Minutes* (CBS) August 2, 1998.

36. Deborah Toler, "Black Conservatives," *Public Eye* VII: 3 (September 1993) and VII: 4 (December 1993).

37. Cornel West, *Race Matters* (New York: Vintage Books, 1994), p. 98.

38. Glen Omatsu, "The 'Four Prisons' and the Movements of Liberation," in Karin Aguilar-San Juan, ed., *The State of Asian America: Activism and Resistance in the 1990s* (Boston: South End Press, 1994), pp. 19–70.

39. Thomas Sowell, *Civil Rights: Rhetoric or Reality?* (New York: William Morrow and Company, Inc., 1984), p. 118.

40. Shelby Steele, *The Content of Our Character* (New York: St. Martin's Press, 1990), p. 116. Steele's arguments are nicely refuted by Patricia J. Williams in her essay, "White Men Can't Count," in Patricia J. Williams, *The Rooster's Egg: On the Persistence of Prejudice* (Cambridge, MA: Harvard University Press, 1995), pp. 88–108.

41. Shelby Steele, "A Negative Vote on Affirmative Action," in Nicolaus

Mills, ed., *Debating Affirmative Action: Race, Gender, Ethnicity and the Politics of Inclusion* (New York: Bantam Doubleday Dell, 1994), p. 41. Also see Terry Eastland, *Ending Affirmative Action: The Case for Colorblind Justice* (New York: Basic Books, 1996), pp. 9–10.

42. Charles Murray, "Affirmative Racism," in Mills, *Debating Affirmative Action*, p. 207.

43. William G. Bowen and Derek Bok, *The Shape of the River: Long-Term Consequences of Considering Race in College and University Admissions* (Princeton: Princeton University Press, 1998), p. 265 (emphasis in original). Two classes of students at twenty-eight "selective" colleges were studied (184 students in all). The two sampled classes were the class entering college in 1976 and the class entering in 1989. The book includes relatively little data on students of color other than African American students by decision of the authors. Also see Reskin, *Realities of Affirmative Action*, pp. 54–58.

44. Barbara Reskin, in reviewing the literature on the effects of affirmative action programs, found that they have benefited Latino and African American men and women, stating that "the effects of affirmative action have not been limited to skilled or highly educated minority workers." Although skilled African American men benefited most from affirmative action between 1974 and 1980 (after 1980 there was a precipitous drop in OFCCP funding), African American men at all skills levels benefited. Reskin, *Realities of Affirmative Action*, p. 46.

45. Randall Kennedy, "Persuasion and Distrust: The Affirmative Action Debate," in Mills, *Debating Affirmative Action*, pp. 52–55.

46. African American journalist Ellis Cose, when interviewing middle-class Black professionals in the early 1990s, found a very different set of complaints with very different policy implications. Cose found enormous (though sometimes initially denied) rage because of the *racism* his interviewees tolerated on a daily basis in their workplaces. Despite undisputed accomplishments, they found they were subjected to slights and insults that reflected the white supremacism that dominated their work environment. Ellis Cose, *The Rage of a Privileged Class* (New York: HarperCollins Publishers, 1993).

47. William Julius Wilson, *The Declining Significance of Race: Blacks and Changing American Institutions* (Chicago: University of Chicago Press, 1978).

48. William Julius Wilson, *The Truly Disadvantaged: The Inner City, the Underclass, and Public Policy* (Chicago: University of Chicago Press, 1987).

49. Gunnar Myrdal, *The Challenge of Affluence* (New York: Pantheon Books, 1963).

50. Ken Auletta, *The Underclass* (New York: Random House, 1982). For a discussion of the "underclass" in the historical context of institutional racism, see Michael B. Katz, "Reframing the 'Underclass' Debate," in Michael B. Katz, ed., *The "Underclass" Debate: Views from History* (Princeton: Princeton University Press, 1993), pp. 440–77.

51. Wilson and Auletta build on the analysis developed by Daniel Patrick

Moynihan in the 1965 report titled *The Negro Family: The Case for National Action*, which has become known as "The Moynihan Report." The report argues that the Black family is an unhealthy matriarchy that produces underachieving children and an unstable subculture. The report is published in Lee Rainwater and William L. Yancey, *The Moynihan Report and the Politics of Controversy* (Cambridge: MIT Press, 1967), pp. 39–125. The Moynihan analysis was developed further by Edward C. Banfield in his 1970 book, *The Unheavenly City* (Boston: Little, Brown), and by Charles Murray in his 1984 book, *Losing Ground: American Social Policy, 1950–1980* (New York: Basic Books).

52. Edward D. Sargent, "Blacks, Reagan Confer," *Washington Post*, January 17, 1985, p. A14.

53. Robert L. Woodson, "A Legacy of Entrepreneurship" in Robert L. Woodson, ed., *On the Road to Economic Freedom* (Washington, DC: Regnery Gateway, 1987); pp. 1–26; quote on p. 12.

54. Ibid., pp. 19–23.

55. Williams, *Decades of Distortion*, pp. 4–8.

56. George Gilder, *Wealth and Poverty* (New York: Basic Books, 1981).

57. Murray, *Losing Ground*, p. 223. Murray makes much the same arguments about affirmative action in an article published the same year. "Affirmative Racism: How Preferential Treatment Works against Blacks," *New Republic*, December 31, 1984, pp. 18–23.

58. Norman Solomon, "Writers of the Right Unite," *Extra!* 11: 2 (March/April 1998): 14–16.

59. See Greene, *Affirmative Action*, pp. 4–6. Also see Ansell, *New Right, New Racism*, p. 200. Using the rationale that civil rights goals had been reached in the 1960s, the budgets and staff of the EEOC, the Office of Federal Contract Compliance, and the Civil Rights Division of the Justice Department were cut. The Administration appointees, including Clarence Thomas at EEOC, who headed these agencies acquiesced in this scheme.

60. Several writers were intellectually aligned with these political players, including Paul Starr of *The American Prospect*, Black conservative J. A. Parker (mentor of Allen Keyes) of the Lincoln Institute, Peter Brimelow of *Forbes* and the *National Review*, and the best-selling author Dinesh D'Souza.

61. Richard J. Herrnstein and Charles Murray, *The Bell Curve: Intelligence and Class Structure in American Life* (New York: Simon and Schuster, 1994).

62. Margaret Quigley, "The Roots of the IQ Debate," *Public Eye* IX: 1 (March 1995): 2. Galton was the cousin of Charles Darwin, who admired his work.

63. Founded in 1937, the Pioneer Fund is based in New York. It is a tax-exempt foundation created for the purpose of funding research into the problems of "racial betterment," according to the group's certificate of incorporation. See David A. Vise and Thomas B. Edsall, "Battle for CBS Takes on Air of Mudslinging Contest," *Washington Post*, March 31, 1985, p. A16.

64. John Sedgwick, "Inside the Pioneer Fund," in Russell Jacoby and Naomi Glauberman, eds., *The Bell Curve Debate: History, Documents, Opinions* (New York: Random House, 1995), pp. 144–61; quote on p. 146.

65. Stephen Jay Gould, "Mismeasure by Any Measure," in Jacoby and Glauberman, *Bell Curve Debate*, pp. 3–13.

66. See Claude S. Fischer, Michael Hout, Martin Sanchez Jankowski, Samuel R. Lucas, Ann Swidler, and Kim Voss, *Inequality by Design: Cracking the Bell Curve Myth* (Princeton: Princeton University Press, 1996). For a collection of reviews and commentaries on *The Bell Curve*, see Jacoby and Glauberman, *Bell Curve Debate*.

67. Adolph Reed, Jr., "*The Bell Curve*: Intelligence and Class Structure in American Life," *Nation*, November 28, 1994, pp. 654–62. As noted in chapter 6 of this book, right-wing libertarian Murray Rothbard defended *The Bell Curve*. For generally favorable reviews, see Thomas Sowell, "Ethnicity and I.Q.," *American Spectator* (February 1995); Father F. R. Thornton, "Dealing with Our Differences," *New American*, January 9, 1995; and "Bell Curve Symposium," *National Review*, December 5, 1994. For neutral reviews, see Peter Brimelow, "For Whom the Bell Tolls," *Forbes*, October 24, 1994, p. 153; and Malcolm W. Browne, "What Is Intelligence and Who Has It?" *New York Times Book Review*, October 16, 1994, p. 3.

68. Herrnstein and Murray are not the only New Right best-selling authors to support racial hereditarianism. Dinesh D'Souza, wunderkind and editor of the shockingly racist and tasteless student newspaper, the *Dartmouth Review*, was supported, employed, and promoted by right-wing organizations from college to the present. When D'Souza published a book in keeping with *The Bell Curve*'s victim-blaming thesis, titled *The End of Racism*, it was not treated with equal disdain. Dinesh D'Souza, *The End of Racism: Principles for a Multicultural Society* (New York: Free Press, 1995). D'Souza was supported by the American Enterprise Institute when writing the book, received a grant for the book from the John M. Olin Foundation, and *The End of Racism* was published by the rightist editor-in-residence at the Free Press, Adam Bellow.

69. *Changing America: Indicators of Social and Economic Well-Being by Race and Hispanic Origin.* Report published by the Council of Economic Advisors, prepared for the Advisory Board to the President's Initiative on Race (Washington, DC: Council of Economic Advisors, 1998).

70. Bowen and Bok, *Shape of the River*, p. 80.

71. All three judges had been appointed by the Reagan-Bush Administrations. See A. Leon Higginbotham, Jr., "Breaking Thurgood Marshall's Promise," *New York Times Magazine*, January 18, 1998, pp. 28–29.

72. Steven A. Holmes, "G.O.P. Lawmakers Offer a Ban on Federal Affirmative Action," *New York Times*, July 28, 1995, p. A17; Steven A. Holmes, "Political Right's Point Man on Race," *New York Times*, November 16, 1997, p. A24.

73. The term "civil rights" is also used by those who support lesbian, gay, bi-

sexual and transgender rights, as well as others who have suffered discrimination because of a characteristic that can cause their exclusion from jobs and housing. When the right appropriates the term "civil rights" in the case of affirmative action, it is applying civil rights to white people whose only defining characteristic is their race. See Stuart M. Butler, Michel Sanera, and W. Bruce Weinrod, *Mandate for Leadership II: Continuing the Conservative Revolution* (Washington, DC: Heritage Foundation, 1984), p. 155, for the statement: "For twenty years, the most important battle in the civil rights field has been for control of the language. . . . Americans . . . favor 'equality,' 'opportunity,' and 'remedial action.' The secret to victory, whether in court or in congress, has been to control the definition of these terms."

74. The American Civil Rights Institute is Ward Connerly's vehicle for taking California's Proposition 209 to other states by providing financial assistance and strategic advice. The Institute for Justice was founded in 1991 by Chip Mellor and Clint Bolick (former aide to Clarence Thomas at EEOC). See Clint Bolick, *The Affirmative Action Fraud: Can We Restore the American Civil Rights Vision?* (Washington, DC: The Cato Institute, 1996). The Center for Equal Opportunity was founded by Linda Chavez, former director of the U.S. Commission on Civil Rights. See Linda Chavez, *Out of the Barrio: Toward a New Politics of Hispanic Assimilation* (New York: Basic Books, 1991). The Center for Individual Rights' senior counsel is Terence J. Pell, who served as William Bennett's Chief of Staff at the Office of National Drug Control Policy during the Reagan Administration. Its greatest victory was the 1996 *Hopwood v. Texas* case, which overturned affirmative action at the University of Texas Law School. Journalist Laura Flanders argues that, in addition to its aggressive role in attacking affirmative action on college campuses, CIR opposes civil rights protections and has received funding from the racist Pioneer Fund. Laura Flanders, "Affirmative Racism," *Nation*, March 8, 1999, p. 7.

75. In February 1997, Ward Connerly was given the Lincoln Leadership Award for Civic Virtue at a dinner organized by the antifeminist Independent Women's Forum. Mr. Connerly's acceptance speech was described as "an impassioned speech on the wrong-headedness of affirmative action." He used the opportunity to denounce Jesse Jackson and support Justice Clarence Thomas. See "Race and Name-Calling," *Washington Times*, February 19, 1997, p. A14.

76. Trevor W. Coleman, "Affirmative Action Wars," *Emerge* (March 1998): 30–37.

77. Lydia Chavez, *The Color Bind: California's Battle to End Affirmative Action* (Berkeley: University of California Press, 1998), pp. 243–47.

78. Ibid., p. 35.

79. See: Thomas J. McIntyre, *The Fear Brokers* (New York: The Pilgrim Press, 1979). Also see Alan Crawford, *Thunder on the Right: The "New Right" and the Politics of Resentment* (New York: Pantheon, 1980).

80. This argument is made in Skrentny, *Ironies of Affirmative Action*, pp. 36–63.

81. See Amy E. Ansell, "The Color of America's Culture Wars," in Amy E. Ansell, ed., *Unraveling the Right: The New Conservatism in American Thought and Politics* (Boulder, CO: Westview Press, 1998), pp. 173–91; Appiah and Gutmann, *Color Conscious*; Ronald Dworkin, *A Matter of Principle* (Cambridge, MA: Harvard University Press, 1985); Christopher Edley, Jr., *Not All Black and White: Affirmative Action and American Values* (New York: Hill and Wang, 1996); Manning Marable, *Black Liberation in Conservative America* (Boston: South End Press, 1997); Steinberg, *Turning Back*; and West, *Race Matters*. Salim Muwakkil is senior editor at the progressive magazine *In These Times*, where he writes thoughtful articles for the magazine on race and racism.

82. See Derrick A. Bell, *Race, Racism, and American Law* (Boston: Little Brown, 1980); Kimberle Crenshaw, ed., *Critical Race Theory: The Key Writings that Framed the Movement* (New York: W. W. Norton, 1995); Richard Delgado, *The Coming Race War? and Other Apocalyptic Tales of America after Affirmative Action and Welfare* (New York: New York University Press, 1996); Charles Lawrence III and Mari J. Matsuda, *We Won't Go Back: Making the Case for Affirmative Action* (Boston: Houghton Mifflin, 1997); and Patricia Williams, *The Rooster's Egg* (Cambridge, MA: Harvard University Press, 1995).

83. Stephen Steinberg, analyzing a speech by Lyndon Johnson in which Johnson lays out the rationale for affirmative action, concludes that in it, Johnson defines the limits of the rationale, when he specifically steers away from identifying institutional racism as the basis for the need for affirmative action. Instead, Johnson and many liberals who have followed him locate the problems of people of color who do not succeed in society as the result of individual circumstances in their own environment, especially their family and educational opportunities. Steinberg, *Turning Back*. Also see Lyndon Baines Johnson, "To Fulfill These Rights," in Beckwith and Jones, *Affirmative Action*, pp. 56–63.

84. Theda Skocpol, "The Choice," in Mills, *Debating Affirmative Action*, pp. 290–99.

85. Richard Kahlenberg, "Class, Not Race," *New Republic*, April 3, 1995, pp. 21–26. Also see Richard D. Kahlenberg, *The Remedy: Class, Race, and Affirmative Action* (New York: Basic Books, 1996); Richard Cohen, "It's Class, Not Race," *Washington Post*, November 14, 1995, p. A19; and Richard Cohen, "More Important Than Race," *Washington Post*, August 6, 1991, p. A15.

86. Steinberg, *Turning Back*, pp. 179–204.

87. Michael Omi and Howard Winant, *Racial Formation in the United States: From the 1960s to the 1980s* (New York: Routledge and Kegan Paul, 1986); Noel Ignatiev, *How the Irish Became White* (New York: Routledge, 1995); R. Frankenberg, *White Women, Race Matters: The Social Construction of Whiteness* (Minneapolis: University of Minnesota Press, 1993); and David Theo Goldberg, ed., *Anat-*

omy of Racism (Minneapolis: University of Minnesota Press, 1990). Matthew Frye Jacobson, *Whiteness of a Different Color: European Immigrants and the Alchemy of Race* (Cambridge, MA: Harvard University Press, 1998).

88. Gutmann, "Racial Injustice," pp. 110–11.

89. In 1998, the first year that Proposition 209 was in effect in California, admissions of underrepresented minorities dropped 61 percent at the University of California at Berkeley and 36 percent at the University of California at Los Angeles. The system-wide total was a less dramatic drop of 9 percent. The 1999 figures show a drop in the number of Black and Hispanic applicants at the University of California at Berkeley, but a rebound in the number of minority students offered admission to the University of California. Much of the increase in students offered admission is attributed to aggressive recruitment efforts and a "comprehensive application review." "Number of Minority Applicants to Berkeley Drops Sharply," *Chronicle of Higher Education*, January 29, 1999, p. A35; Associated Press, "California Sees Minority Admissions Rebound," *New York Times*, April 4, 1999, p. 18; and James Traub, "The Class of Prop. 209," *New York Times Magazine*, May 2, 1999, pp. 44–51, 76–79.

90. Robert Bruce Slater, "Why Socioeconomic Affirmative Action in College Admissions Works Against African Americans," *Journal of Blacks in Higher Education* (Summer 1995): 57–59.

6. LIBERTARIANISM AND CIVIL SOCIETY:
THE ROMANCE OF FREE-MARKET CAPITALISM

1. For an elegant philosophical defense of the "Nightwatchman" state, see Robert Nozick, *Anarchy, State, and Utopia* (New York: Basic Books, Inc., 1974).

2. Ulrike Heider, *Anarchism: Left, Right, and Green* (San Francisco: City Lights Books, 1994), p. 98. Also see Benjamin R. Tucker, *State Socialism and Anarchism: How Far They Agree and Wherein They Differ* (London: A. C. Fifield, 1911); and Benjamin Tucker, *Individual Liberty* (New York: Vangard Press, 1926).

3. Ibid., p. 95.

4. See Paul Franco, *The Political Philosophy of Michael Oakeshott* (New Haven, CT: Yale University Press, 1990); and Stephen L. Newman, *Liberalism at Wits' End: The Libertarian Revolt Against the Modern State* (Ithaca, NY: Cornell University Press, 1984).

5. Ayn Rand, *The Fountainhead* (Chicago: Signet, 1971).

6. David Boaz, *Libertarianism: A Primer* (New York: Free Press, 1997), pp. 53–54.

7. Joseph Collins and John Lear, *Chile's Free-Market Miracle: A Second Look* (Oakland, CA: Institute for Food and Development Policy, 1995).

8. Alan Crawford, *Thunder on the Right* (New York: Pantheon Books, 1980), p. 97.

9. Llewellyn H. Rockwell, Jr., "Paleoism: Past, Present, and Future,"

Rothbard-Rockwell Report V: 12 (December 1994): 1, 3–9. For a follow-up report on this Congressional class of 1994, see Dana Milbank, "Whatever Happened to the Class of 1994?" *New York Times Magazine*, January 17, 1999, pp. 36–40.

10. Ibid., p. 7.

11. An example of the vitriolic warfare among libertarians is the "debate" that occurred between Richard Cornuelle, who criticizes libertarianism in his article, "The Power and Poverty of Libertarian Thought," published in the *Cato Policy Report* XIV:1 (January/February 1992), and the response to that article by Joe Melton, titled "Left-Libertarianism: The Cato-Cornuelle Connection," published in the *Rothbard-Rockwell Report* III: 4 (April 1992). The nastiness of Melton's attack on Cornuelle, Cato, and Charles Koch is so shrill that the reader can only imagine that there must be enormous stakes at risk when libertarianism is criticized, even by one of its own.

12. Samuel Francis, "Race and Reality," *Rothbard-Rockwell Report* IV: 3 (March 1993): 23–24.

13. Richard J. Herrnstein and Charles Murray, *The Bell Curve: Intelligence and Class Structure in American Life* (New York: Free Press, 1994); Charles Murray, *What It Means to Be a Libertarian* (New York: Broadway Books, 1997).

14. Murray N. Rothbard, "Race! That Murray Book," *Rothbard-Rockwell Report* V: 12 (December 1994): 1.

15. Special Mini-Sampler, *Rothbard-Rockwell Report* (n. d.): 1.

16. David Gordon, "In Search of Buckley's 'Hypersensitivity to Anti-Semitism,'" *Rothbard-Rockwell Report* III: 4 (April 1992): 1, 3–6.

17. Murray N. Rothbard, "Anti-Buchania: A Mini-Encyclopedia," *Rothbard-Rockwell Report*, III: 5 (May 1992): 1.

18. Paul Gottfried, "Why Must Christians Routinely Grovel and Apologize for Crimes against Jews Which They Never Committed?" *Rothbard-Rockwell Report* VI: 5 (June 1995): 2.

19. David Boaz, *Libertarianism: A Primer* (New York: Free Press, 1997), pp. 68–69, 82.

20. For a discussion of contemporary politicians who are libertarian in ideology but unwilling to be open about it for fear of political harm ("closet" libertarians), and libertarians who are equivocal or opportunistic in their commitment to consistent libertarian principles ("pseudo" libertarians), see Jacob Weisberg, "The Coming Republican Crack-Up," *New York*, March 4, 1996, pp. 18–25.

21. David Segal, "At the Cato Institute an Idea Catches On; Think Tank Is Thrust into Social Security Debate," *Washington Post*, January 30, 1999, E1.

22. Michael Lind, *Up from Conservatism: Why the Right Is Wrong for America* (New York: Free Press, 1996), pp. 79–80.

23. Robert W. Poole, Jr., "Introduction," in Robert W. Poole, Jr., and Virginia I. Postrel, eds., *Free Minds and Free Markets: Twenty-Five Years of Reason* (San Francisco: Pacific Research Institute for Public Policy, 1993), p. xiv.

24. Stephen L. Newman, "The Chimeras of 'Libertarianism': What's Be-

hind This Political Movement?" *Dissent* (Summer 1987): 308–16. Newman's conclusions are based on survey data reported in William S. Maddox and Stuart A. Lilie, *Beyond Liberal and Conservative: Reassessing the Political Spectrum* (Washington, DC: Cato Institute, 1984).

25. Richard Dennis, "How a Liberal Becomes a Libertarian." Speech delivered at the 1991 Libertarian Presidential Nominating Convention and Libertarian Education Institute Seminar on Libertarian Philosophy, August 30, 1991.

26. Alexis de Tocqueville, *Democracy in America* (New York: Vintage Books, 1990).

27. Edward H. Crane, "Defending Civil Society," Cato's Letters Series, no. 8 (Washington, DC: The Cato Institute, 1994), p. 4.

28. P.J. O'Rourke, "A Message to Redistributionists." Speech delivered at the Cato Institute's Twentieth Anniversary celebration, May 1, 1997. Published in *Cato Policy Report* XIX: 4 (July/August 1997): 6–7.

29. Steve Forbes, "The Renewal of America." Speech delivered at the Cato Institute's Twentieth Anniversary celebration, May 1, 1997. Published in *Cato Policy Report* XIX: 4 (July/August 1997): 1.

30. For a discussion of "positive" freedom, see Isaiah Berlin, "Two Concepts of Liberty," in Isaiah Berlin, *Four Essays on Liberty* (New York: Oxford University Press, 1969), pp. 118–72.

31. Llewellyn H. Rockwell, "An Anti-Environmentalist Manifesto" (Burlingame, CA: Center for Libertarian Studies, 1990), p. 47.

32. John Lunsford, *Dangerous Territory: The Attack on Citizen Participation and the Environmental Movement* (Portland, OR: Western States Center, 1997); Tarso Ramos, "An Environmental Wedge: The 'Wise Use' Movement and the Insurgent Right Wing," in Eric Ward, ed., *Conspiracies: Real Grievances, Paranoia, and Mass Movements* (Seattle: Northwest Coalition against Malicious Harassment, 1996). Also see William Kevin Burke, "The Wise Use Movement: Right-Wing Anti-Environmentalism," *Public Eye* (June 1993): 1–7.

33. William R. Allen, "Wetlands Policy: Sense and Subversion," *Libertarian Lifeline* 12: 5 (May 1992): 3.

34. Fred Lee Smith, Jr., ed., "Readings in Free Market Environmentalism" (Washington, DC: Competitive Enterprise Institute, n.d.).

35. See Phil Gramm, "Debunking Doomsday," in Poole and Postrel, *Free Minds and Free Markets*, pp. 323–26.

36. Virginia I. Postrel, "Dynamic Tension," *Reason* 24: 6 (November 1992): 4–5. Also see Virginia Postel, *The Future and Its Enemies: The Growing Conflict over Creativity, Enterprise, and Progress* (New York: Free Press, 1998).

37. Fred L. Smith, "Environmental Policy: A Free Market Proposal," *Tulanian* (Summer 1989): 32–37.

38. James S. Robbins, "How Capitalism Saved the Whales," *Freeman* 42: 8 (August 1992): 311–13.

39. Cathy Young, "Victimhood Is Powerful," *Reason* 24: 5 (1992): 18–23.

40. I am indebted to Richard Smith for his helpful comments on this point in written correspondence dated May 7, 1998.

7. WHAT NOW? STRATEGIC THINKING ABOUT THE
PROGRESSIVE MOVEMENT AND THE RIGHT

1. Five general critiques are Michael Tomasky, *Left for Dead: The Life, Death, and Possible Resurrection of Progressive Politics in America* (New York: Free Press, 1996); E. J. Dionne, Jr., *They Only Look Dead: Why Progressives Will Dominate the Next Political Era* (New York: Simon and Schuster, 1996); Michael Lind, *The Next American Nation: The New Nationalism and the Fourth American Revolution* (New York: Simon and Schuster, 1996); Todd Gitlin, *The Twilight of Common Dreams* (New York: Henry Holt and Co., 1995); and Richard Rorty, *Achieving Our Country: Leftist Thought in Twentieth-Century America* (Cambridge, MA: Harvard University Press, 1998). Further contributions have been made by those who are discussing and critiquing the right: Suzanne Pharr, *In the Time of the Right* (Berkeley: Chardon Press, 1996); Chip Berlet, ed., *Eyes Right: Challenging the Right-Wing Backlash* (Boston: South End Press, 1995); and by those who propose a paradigm shift in order to bring the left off its ashes: Loretta Ross, "Practicing Freedom: Human Rights Education," *Sojourner: The Women's Forum* 22: 1 (September 1996): 7; Michael Lerner, *The Politics of Meaning: Restoring Hope and Possibility in an Age of Cynicism* (Reading: Addison-Wesley, 1996); Jim Wallis, *The Soul of Politics: A Practical and Prophetic Vision for Change* (New York: The New Press and Maryknoll: Orbis Books [copublishers], 1994). Some advice is straightforwardly practical: S. M. Miller, "Equality, Morality, and the Health of Democracy," in M. Brinton Lykes et al., eds., *Myths About the Powerless: Contesting Social Inequalities* (Philadelphia: Temple University Press, 1996), pp. 17–33; Daniel Levitas, et al., "Philanthropy, Electoral Advocacy and Citizen Participation: Lessons for the Next Decade," *Network News* (Washington, DC: National Network of Grantmakers; Summer 1995): 1–2, 7–8; Jeff Faux, *The Party's Not Over: A New Vision for the Democrats* (New York: Basic Books, 1996); Robert S. McElvaine, *What's Left? A New Democratic Vision for America* (Holbrook: Adams Media Corporation, 1996). And some is practical but with an inspirational tone: Gary Delgado, *Beyond the Politics of Place* (Oakland, CA: Applied Research Center, January 1994); John J. Sweeney, *America Needs a Raise: Fighting for Economic Security and Social Justice* (Boston: Houghton Mifflin, 1996); Mickey Kauss, *The End of Equality*, 2d ed. (New York: Basic Books, 1995); Jim Wallis, *The Soul of Politics: A Practical and Prophetic Vision for Change* (New York: The New Press and Maryknoll: Orbis Books [copublishers], 1994). Some focus on analysis: Holly Sklar, *Chaos or Community? Seeking Solutions, Not Scapegoats for Bad Economics* (Boston: South End Press, 1995); Manning Marable, "A New American So-

cialism," *Progressive* (February 1995): 20–25; Cornel West, *Race Matters* (New York: Vintage Books, 1994). Other books address the state of particular submovements, such as Christopher Bull and John Gallagher, *Perfect Enemies: The Religious Right, and the Politics of the 1990s* (New York: Crown Publishing, 1996) on the future of the gay movement. Other writers have discussed the progressive movement in the context of identity politics, such as Adolph Reed, Jr., "Token Equality," *Progressive* (February 1997): 8–19; and Salim Muwakkil, "Identity Crisis," *In These Times* (November 27, 1996): 14–17.

2. The most innovative and promising recent conference was the 1998 Black Radical Conference, held in Chicago. See Angela Ards, "The New Black Radicalism," *The Nation*, July 27/August 3, 1998, pp. 19–23.

3. Roberto Unger and Cornel West discuss this approach in their book, *The Future of American Progressivism: An Initiative for Political and Economic Reform* (Boston: Beacon Press, 1998), where they describe a mix of institutional experimentation and independent initiative, as opposed to past progressive models of radical systemic transformation.

4. Tomasky, *Left for Dead*, 36–43.

5. See the large percentage of white women who voted for the anti–affirmative action Proposition 209 in California.

6. Melanie Kaye/Kantrowitz at Jews for Racial and Economic Justice Annual Conference (1996).

7. I feel especially comfortable with the statement titled "A Call to Defend Democracy and Pluralism," written collectively by the Blue Mountain Working Group in 1993 and published in Berlet, *Eyes Right*, pp. 316–24.

8. Tragically, there is an increasing tendency for the crucial distinctions between the ideological bases for the antigovernment positions of the right and progressives to become blurred, leading to antigovernment "collaborations" between left and right. See Chip Berlet, *Right Woos Left: Populist Party, LaRouchian, and Other Neo-Fascist Overtures to Progressives, and Why They Must Be Rejected* (Somerville, MA: Political Research Associates, 1994), a Topical Report; and "The Right Woos the Left: David Barsamian Interviews Chip Berlet," *Z Magazine* 5 (January 1992): 38–43.

9. See Robert H. Weibe, *Self-Rule: A Cultural History of American Democracy* (Chicago: University of Chicago Press, 1995), p. 244. Also see Sheldon Wolin, "Democracy and Counterrevolution," *The Nation*, April 22, 1996, p. 23.

10. The right applies the dismissive term "special interest" to all these single-issue groups.

11. Gitlin, *Twilight of Common Dreams*; Tomasky, *Left for Dead*; and Lind, *Next American Nation*.

12. bell hooks, *Talking Back: thinking feminist, thinking black* (Boston: South End Press, 1989), p. 29.

13. Urvashi Vaid, *Virtual Equality: The Mainstreaming of Gay and Lesbian Liberation* (New York: Anchor Books/Doubleday, 1995), pp. 186–87.

14. Among those within the gay rights movement who "make the connections" and urge other activists to do so are Martin Duberman, a widely known white gay activist and academic; Mandy Carter, an African American lesbian activist who, through the National Black Lesbian and Gay Leadership Forum, opposes the right's incursion into the Black community; Mab Segrest, a white lesbian civil rights activist who has worked tirelessly to oppose the far right; Carmen Vazquez, a Puerto Rican lesbian who is Director of Public Policy at the Lesbian and Gay Community Services Center; Suzanne Pharr, a white lesbian activist and writer from the Women's Project in Little Rock, Arkansas; Barbara Smith, an African American lesbian writer and activist; and Urvashi Vaid, an Indian-born lesbian and Director at the National Gay and Lesbian Task Force's Policy Institute.

15. Two such activists are Loretta Ross, Executive Director of the Center for Human Rights Education, Atlanta, and Charlotte Bunch, Director of the Center for Women's Global Leadership at Rutgers University.

16. See Ross, "Practicing Freedom," p. 7. Also see Marguerite Guzman Bouvard, *Women Reshaping Human Rights: How Extraordinary Activists Are Changing the World* (Wilmington, DE: Scholarly Resources, Inc., 1996).

17. See Gitlin, *Twilight*, pp. 214–15.

18. Chip Berlet and Margaret Quigley, "Theocracy and White Supremacy," in Chip Berlet, ed., *Eyes Right: Challenging the Right-Wing Backlash* (Boston: South End Press, 1995), pp. 15–43.

19. Lerner, *Politics of Meaning*, p. 66.

20. Wallis, *Soul of Politics*.

21. Ibid., p. xvi.

22. Ibid., p. 147.

23. This progressive populist economics should not be confused with the right-wing populism of the armed citizen's militias. Among other things, right-wing populism's use of scapegoats (usually groups thought to be people of color, such as welfare recipients or immigrants) as a substitute for analysis distinguishes it from progressive populism.

24. Sklar, *Chaos or Community*.

25. Ibid., pp. 171–76.

26. Faux, *The Party's Not Over*, p. 173. Also see Sweeney, *America Needs a Raise*; and McElvaine, *What's Left*.

27. Faux, *The Party's Not Over*, p. 208.

28. An important step in the rebuilding process is the Peace Development Fund's multistep effort known as "The Listening Project." See PDF's report, *The Listening Project: A National Dialogue on Progressive Movement-Building* (Amherst, MA: Peace Development Fund, 1999).

29. Urvashi Vaid has emphasized the necessity of coalition work in the progressive movement, arguing against seeing it as simply a tactical device. Instead, she argues, we should see coalitions as a goal of the movement. Urvashi Vaid,

"Coalition as Goal Not Process," *Gay Community News* (Spring 1997): 6–9. Also see Helen Zia, "How NOW?", *Ms.*, July/August 1996, pp. 49–57.

30. Pharr, *Time of the Right*, pp. 96–97.

31. See Stephanie Riger, "What's Wrong with Empowerment?" *American Journal of Community Psychology* 21: 3 (1993): 279–92. Riger discusses the difference between community members feeling more empowered and their actually having more real power within the larger system.

32. Francis Calpotura and Kim Fellner, "Square Pegs Find Their Groove." Available from The Center for Third World Organizing (Oakland, CA) or the National Organizers Alliance (Washington, DC), 1996.

33. Adolph Reed, Jr., "Kiss the Family Good-Bye," *Progressive* (February 1996): 23.

34. See Delgado, *Beyond the Politics of Place*; and Mike Miller, "'Beyond the Politics of Place': A Critical Review." Published by ORGANIZE Training Center, San Francisco, n. d., for an example of two activists in debate over this issue.

35. JoAnn Wypijewski, "A Stirring in the Land," *Nation*, September 8/15, 1997, pp. 17–25; quote on p. 25. Also see Dan Swinney, "Where Do We Go from Here? A 'Co-op Ed,'" *Grassroots Economic Organizing Newsletter* (November/December, 1996): 2; and Mike Howard, "'Where Do We Go from Here?' Another View," *Grassroots Economic Organizing Newsletter* (January/February 1997): 1–2.

36. Howell, *Funding*, pp. 36–37.

37. Jeffrey Goldberg, "Some of Their Best Friends Are Jews," *New York Times Magazine*, March 16, 1997, p. 42.

38. Robert Parry, "The Lord's Work," *In These Times* (November 27, 1995): 14–18.

39. The right's support for Israel has a great deal to do with the belief by Christian apocalyptics that the existence of Israel is essential in order for the Second Coming to occur. During the Cold War, the right also supported Israel as a Middle East bastion against communism. In short, its support for Israel has virtually nothing to do with an independent commitment to the survival of Jews. See Ruth Mouly, *The Religious Right and Israel: The Politics of Armageddon* (Somerville, MA: Political Research Associates, 1985). Another part of the explanation may lie in the conservative nature of the leadership of mainstream Jewish organizations, as opposed to the generally liberal politics of many Jews. See J. J. Goldberg, *Jewish Power: Inside the American Jewish Establishment* (Reading: Addison Wesley, 1996).

40. See Linda Kintz and Julia Lesage, eds., *Media, Culture, and the Religious Right* (Minneapolis: University of Minnesota Press, 1998).

41. See FAIR's newsletter, *Extra!*, available on its Web site, www.fair.org.

42. Two examples of efforts to promote civility are found in Massachusetts. The Institute for Civil Society is a new funding organization and think tank

based in Newton, Massachusetts, and funded by a $35 million grant. According to its mission statement, the institute exists to "research and promote those breakthroughs within civil society which address the most problematic and pressing issues of our day. Our intention is to help build civil society where it has failed to gain a foothold and rebuild its foundations where they have crumbled." The Public Conversations Project based in Watertown, Massachusetts, works to "foster respectful and productive conversation among people who have opposing views on polarized issues of public significance." (Public Conversations Project Mission Statement, 1996).

43. Michael D'Antonio, "I or We," *Mother Jones* (May/June 1994): 20–26. Also see Amitai Etzioni, *Spirit of Community: Rights, Responsibilities and the Communitarian Agenda* (New York: Crown Publishers, 1993).

44. Pharr, *Time of the Right*, pp. 97–98.

45. Benjamin DeMott, "Seduced by Civility," *The Nation*, December 9, 1996, pp. 11–19.

46. Donald Cohen, Paul Milne, and Glen Schneider, *American Progressives at a Crossroads: A Challenge to Lead and Govern the Nation* (San Diego: Institute for Effective Action, 1995).

47. Faux, *The Party's Not Over*.

48. Joel Rogers and Bruce Colburn, "The Promise of Fusion Politics," *The Nation*, November 18, 1996 p. 16.

49. Adolph Reed, Jr., "Token Equality," *Progressive* (February 1997): 19.

50. For a discussion of proportional representation, see Lani Guinier, *Lift Every Voice: Turning a Civil Rights Setback into a New Vision of Social Justice* (New York: Simon and Schuster, 1998), pp. 258–71. Also see Robert Richie and Steven Hill, *Reflecting All of Us: The Case for Proportional Representation* (Boston: Beacon Press, 1999); and Lani Guinier, *The Tyranny of the Majority: Fundamental Fairness in Representative Democracy* (New York: Free Press, 1994).

51. See Michael Lind, "Alice Doesn't Vote Here Any More," *Mother Jones*, March/April 1998, p. 53.

52. See David Donnelly, Janice Fine, and Ellen S. Miller, *Money and Politics: Financing Our Elections Democratically* (Boston, Beacon Press, 1999).

53. See Joel Bleifuss, "Reforming the Beast," *In These Times* (June 24–July 7, 1996): 12–25; and Ronald Dworkin, "The Curse of American Politics," ad run in the *New York Times*, October 28, 1996, p. A9; and "Democracy vs. Dollars: Talking Back to Money in Politics," a Talking Back Advisory (no. 6) published by the Certain Trumpet Program, Washington, DC, July 1, 1996.

54. Sheldon Wolin, "Democracy and Counterrevolution," *The Nation*, April 22, 1996, p. 23.

55. Miller, "Equality, Morality," p. 21.

56. Ironically, the term "political correctness" originated as an internal, self-mocking slang, used by progressives to joke about the complicated process of

changing language and habits to conform to a broad definition of equality that included all marginalized groups.

57. Mark Toney, "Power Concedes Nothing Without a Demand," in John Anner, ed., *Beyond Identity Politics* (Boston: South End Press, 1996), pp. 17–28.

58. See the research of a Washington, D.C.–based organization, the Sentencing Project, available at its Web site www.sentencingproject.org.

59. Evelyn Nieves, "Civil Rights Groups Suing Berkeley Over Admissions Policy," *New York Times*, January 3, 1999, p. A11.

60. In England, where a thoughtful and complex analysis of racism has dominated left politics for several decades, a debate has emerged between those who support multiculturalism and those who promote antiracism. Antiracism, in this context, is the more radical approach to understanding the role of racial prejudice and racial identity. It attempts to go beyond the appreciation of other cultures to address the intractable dominance of white western culture. See Paul Gilroy, "The End of Antiracism," in James Donald and Ali Rattansi, eds., *'Race,' Culture and Difference* (London: Sage Publications Ltd., 1992), pp. 49–61.

61. Every year conferences are held that attempt to bring progressive faculty and social justice activists together to engage in dialog and strategic thinking. This interaction is often tense and sometimes combative, but will only improve if such conferences continue to occur and continue to be funded by progressive foundations.

62. Nikhil Pal Singh has called this model "antiracism universalism," because its goal is to dissolve "race" by shining a light on the attitudes and behaviors associated with racism, and thereby creating a society in which race is not an important concept. See Nikhil Pal Singh, "Toward an Effective Antiracism," in Wendy F. Katkin, Ned Landsman, and Andrea Tyree, eds., *Beyond Pluralism: The Conception of Groups and Group Identities in America* (Chicago: University of Illinois Press, 1998), pp. 221–41.

63. For a discussion of four types of antiracism work, see Becky Thompson, *A Promise and a Way of Life: White Antiracist Activism Across the Decades* (Minneapolis: University of Minnesota Press, forthcoming).

64. John Anner, *Beyond Identity Politics: Emerging Social Justice Movements in Communities of Color* (Boston: South End Press, 1996), p. 1.

65. Christopher Lydon's "Connection" talk show, WBUR-FM, Boston, October 4, 1996.

ACKNOWLEDGMENTS

In the crafting of this book I was fortunate to work at the center of an outstanding group of collaborators and friends. I am especially grateful to Political Research Associates, where I have served as Executive Director for eighteen years. My colleagues there—Chip Berlet, Judith Glaubman, Surina Khan, Peter Snoad, and Pam Chamberlain—withstood my many absences as I wrote the book, and contributed their insights to every chapter. The analysis I present is the result of our collective research and discussion, though the responsibility for it is my own.

My most profound thank you goes to Elly Bulkin, who read and edited every page of the book, sometimes giving me her expert help and guidance through several drafts of a chapter. The members of my writing group—Denise Bergman, Ruth Hubbard, Rosario Morales, and Sunny Robinson—also reviewed every page, always challenging me to make my writing clear and to state my political positions honestly. Betty Furdon provided invaluable research assistance in the Harvard University Library system and other local libraries, often combing several libraries for a book. Erin Miller repeatedly salvaged chapters targeted by a computer virus.

Acknowledgments

I am grateful to Wilma Mankiller for her friendship and for her understanding of what I have tried to accomplish in this book.

Throughout the research process I have drawn on the work of many friends and colleagues, especially Amy Ansell, Chip Berlet, Fred Clarkson, Bill Berkowitz, Jim Danky, Gary Delgado, Sara Diamond, Amy Gluckman, Fred Goff, Ellen Hermann, Aileen Hernandez, Surina Khan, Ellen Leopold, Wes McCune and Gladys Segal, Ellen Messer-Davidow, Suzanne Pharr, the late Margaret Quigley, Rev. Meg Riley, Mab Segrest, Horace Seldon, Holly Sklar, Deborah Toler, Urvashi Vaid, Loretta Williams, and Lucy Williams.

I am grateful to three institutions that provided help and support during the writing of the book: Beacon Press (especially Marya Van't Hul and my editor, Micah Kleit), the Wellesley Centers for Research on Women at Wellesley College, and the Center for Women Policy Studies in Washington, D.C.

A number of friends were particularly present throughout my four years of writing, reinforcing me with their encouragement and their belief in the project. They include Katherine Acey, Rita Arditti, Clarissa Atkinson, Peggy Barrett, Laura Booth, Estelle Disch, Jean Entine, Rayna Green, Ellen Gurzinsky, John Hardisty, Deborah Harris, Robbie Harris, William Harris, Linette Hirschman, Hayat Imam, Marie Kuda, Mary Leno, Blue Lunden, Jean MacRae, the late Jeanmarie Marshall, Nancy Meyer, Maya Miller, Faith Perry, Ann Pitt, Pat Rathbone, Phillida Sawbridge, Peggy Shinner, Faith Smith, Mary Ann Snyder, Ann Tyler, and Leslie Wolfe.

And finally, special thanks to the loyal donors who have made Political Research Associates possible.

Many of the chapters of this book have appeared in print elsewhere. I have considerably revised them for this book. I thank all those who gave me feedback and suggestions on the earlier versions.